THE BEAT OF
MY OWN DRUM

THE BEAT OF MY OWN DRUM

A Memoir

Sheila E.

with WENDY HOLDEN

ATRIA BOOKS

NEW YORK   LONDON   TORONTO   SYDNEY   NEW DELHI

ATRIA BOOKS
A Division of Simon & Schuster, Inc.
1230 Avenue of the Americas
New York, NY 10020

First Atria Books hardcover edition September 2014

ATRIA BOOKS and colophon are trademarks of Simon & Schuster, Inc.

For information about special discounts for bulk purchases,
please contact Simon & Schuster Special Sales at 1-866-506-1949 or
business@simonandschuster.com.

The Simon & Schuster Speakers Bureau can bring authors to your
live event. For more information or to book an event, contact the
Simon & Schuster Speakers Bureau at 1-866-248-3049 or
visit our website at www.simonspeakers.com.

Interior design by Kyoko Watanabe
Jacket design by Anna Dorfman
Jacket photography © Randee St. Nicholas Photography Inc.

Manufactured in the United States of America

10 9 8 7 6 5 4 3 2 1

Library of Congress Control Number: 2013037327

ISBN 978-1-4767-1494-3
ISBN 978-1-4767-1498-1 (ebook)

All insert photographs are courtesy of the author unless otherwise noted.

For Moms and Pops,
who taught me everything I know and gave me the gift of music

To my sister-in-law Dr. Sarah Spinner-Escovedo:
Through the belly-laughs, the tears, the reflection,
and the closure, thank you for helping me to articulate
my story when words sometimes failed me. Your questions
gave me answers. And in your listening, I found my voice.

A special thank you to Wendy Holden for putting my words
into book form. It was an honor to work with you.
To Judith Curr and Sarah Durand, thank you for giving me the
opportunity to share my story. You are Angels.

Rolling river God, little stones are smooth,
only once the water passes through
So I am a stone, rough and grainy still,
trying to reconcile this river's chill

"RIVER GOD"
SHEILA E (WRITTEN BY NICHOLE NORDEMAN)

Contents

Contents

THE BEAT OF
MY OWN DRUM

Author's Note

This memoir is based on my recollection of events spanning more than five decades. As I reflect on the past I acknowledge the fluidity of memories, which often take on different meanings and contexts. My memory of a moment may differ greatly from others' recollections of the same event, since we all see through different lenses. Where conversations cannot be remembered precisely I have re-created them to the best of my ability. Where people need to be protected or to avoid offense, I have altered names. Any mistakes are my own.

Prelude

An introductory piece of music

For a long time, and well into my adult years, I was afraid of the dark. I had to sleep with a light on, and I was drawn toward it like a moth. Some nights, I'd wait until sunrise before going to bed.

Over time, I realized that the blackness was only a reminder of a different kind of gloom—a relentless, debilitating fear that stemmed from some unspeakable memories. Within a blessed childhood, a few isolated incidents had filled me with a secret shame that might have imprisoned me forever had I allowed it to.

With the gifts of music, God, my family, and friends, I learned to readjust the skewed image I saw whenever I looked in the mirror. The girl in my own reflection found a sacred outlet for all her guilt and rage by beating on a drum—just as my father had conquered his childhood demons before me.

Now I'm grown and no longer shackled by my past. I no longer think of myself as ugly. I have rediscovered joy and trust. I am persuaded of my own innocence. The darkness doesn't frighten me anymore. I am not a moth after all.

I am a butterfly. I am filled with color and light. I am soaring free.

1. Crescendo

The loudest point reached in a
gradually increasing sound

You came into my life
In time
That moment I knew
We would share our dreams
And so it seems
That dreams do come true

"NINA"

THE E FAMILY (WRITTEN BY PETE ESCOVEDO)

I could hear the beat as I approached the stage. The connection between the music and me felt like it was in my DNA. The cymbals vibrated through my body and the timbales shook my bones. My father's conga playing touched me somewhere deep within my soul.

"You were kicking in time to the percussion inside your mom's belly!" he'd tell me with a chuckle. "After you were born I took you to clubs in a bassinet and hid you behind the bar!"

It was no wonder that the pounding of his drums felt like the heartbeat of my life.

The preparations for my first live performance that night in 1962 had taken more than an hour at my grandparents' house on Thirty-third and Market Street in West Oakland, California. Some of my older cousins had gathered around to watch, curious, as Moms dressed me up.

I was five years old.

When she helped me into a new white dress with a frilly lace hem, I knew that it had to be a special occasion. I only ever wore dresses for fancy events like birthday parties or going to church on Sundays.

Mama—my Creole grandmother, who was what they called "light skin," with dyed black hair, stockings rolled to the knee, and never without her apron, sat rocking in her chair with a grin as Moms fixed my hair and tied a white ribbon into my almost shoulder-length curls.

The prettier she made me look, the more my cousins complained. "This isn't fair," they whined. "How come Sheila gets to go and we can't?"

My mother told them they weren't old enough to go to a nightclub. They must have been between six and ten years old.

"But she's younger than us!" they protested in unison.

"Yes," Moms countered quickly. "But this is a special night— Sheila's going to go perform with her father."

I looked up into her face, wide-eyed. "I'm gonna play with Daddy?"

She nodded.

I smiled. I didn't feel fazed by the news at all. I played with Pops all the time at home, stepping up to his congas (with the help of a chair) and hammering out a rhythm with my tiny hands.

Even when he wasn't around, I'd create music from anything—beating on pots and pans, a window, a wall, a table, or my chest. Moms and Pops said that each time a Jiffy peanut-butter commercial came on TV, I'd run to the old Zenith set (that looked like something from a spaceship) and tap on the screen in time to the rhythm. The tune had a melody and beat that captured my attention.

Eventually, my persistence wore down the grown-ups. Pops and his friends would laughingly concede and let me join in one of their daily jamming sessions.

"Come and play, Sheila," they'd say. I had no idea that many of them were famous musicians—they were just Pops's friends—and they didn't need to ask me twice. Sitting on the congas opposite my father, I'd mimic his hand movements as if I was looking in a mirror. I'd watch him practice, and I'd practice along with him. I guess he'd decided I was ready to go public.

Moms folded over the ruffled lining of my white socks and slipped me into shiny patent leather shoes with silver buckles. They were uncomfortably new. I arched my feet to test their flexibility and winced a little when they pinched.

"I'll get ready and then we'll go," she told me, stroking my cheek with the back of her hand.

I loved all the attention she was paying me.

I loved that I was going to play with Pops.

I loved that I didn't hurt anymore.

Everything was still very muddled in my head, but that night she was getting me ready can't have been long after the Bad Thing happened.

The thing nobody talked about.

The thing that made me so sick inside.

I didn't realize it at the time, but letting me play with Pops and his Escovedo Brothers Latin Jazz Sextet must have been some kind of reward.

Not that my parents chose to see it that way. "You were a natural real young," they'd say firmly. "We just thought it would be fun for you to show everyone what you could do." Even now, more than fifty years later, they find what happened back then almost impossible to talk about.

No matter what the reason for my first performance that night, it is true that a day never passed in our house without music being played. The words "I want to be a musician" never came from my mouth, though. I didn't even think about it.

In fact, later on, once I'd witnessed the first moon landings (which seemed almost impossible to believe), I had my heart set on becoming an astronaut. I was so excited by the idea; I wanted to know everything about space and the enormity of the universe. I wanted to learn to fly an aircraft. I wanted to fly to the moon. Being my mother's daughter, I didn't want to have to wait to be a grown-up to do it. Oh, no. I didn't want to be the first *woman* to step onto the lunar surface. I wanted to be the first *little girl* on the moon. Later, I switched ambitions and decided I'd win an Olympic gold medal for running track. I had a clear vision in my head of crossing the finish line as the crowd roared, then standing on the podium as the national anthem was played, my medal heavy around my neck.

It never occurred to me that I might not be able to do both, or either.

The one thing that made me truly happy, though, was music. I loved every kind of music, from classical to Motown, and Latin jazz especially touched my heart. But whether I was listening to Pops practicing, tapping away to a Miles Davis record, or watching Karen Carpenter beating her drums, those were the times when I'd close my eyes and lose myself—not realizing that music was going to become my passion and my purpose.

Those times were when I was able to forget.

I don't remember how we traveled to the venue of my first

public performance that warm summer night, though we must have driven. I seem to recall Moms opening the back door of her car for me to get out, and frowning because there was already a crease in my new shoes.

The historic Sweet's Ballroom in Oakland was several miles away from where we lived in an apartment we were soon to be kicked out of for not paying the rent. Not that I minded moving again one little bit—I couldn't wait to get away from *that* house, which I was beginning to think was cursed.

What I do recall about that night at Sweet's—so vividly I can almost smell the cigarette smoke—is holding Moms's hand as we climbed the grand staircase to where the music was playing.

Being only five years old, I was still small, and my arm was fully extended as I gripped my mother's fingers. Moms looked so beautiful in her blouse and pants, with her hair teased up at the top. I felt as if I was in the presence of an angel that night. She seemed so light and luminous that I thought she might float away unless I held on tight.

When we reached the top of the red-carpeted stairs, we turned left and faced an enormous art deco ballroom, complete with a high ceiling and polished hardwood floor.

My eyes wide, I gazed around me in wonder.

There was a balcony upstairs and plush banquette seating to the side. On the dance floor, hundreds of people were swaying to the music being played by a band way up front on a stage. Everyone looked so smartly dressed compared to the adults I usually saw hanging round our apartment wearing tie-dyed shirts and bell-bottom jeans.

The music was very loud—even louder than at home—and the place was packed. The heat from all those bodies made me break out in a sweat as my heart began hammering a beat of its own against my rib cage and butterflies began dancing in my tummy.

When the band stopped playing, there was an enthusiastic round of applause along with some loud whistling. Moms waved at Pops, and he yelled at someone on the stage, "Juanita's here!"

The next part remains frozen in slow motion in my memory.

Pops's voice boomed out of the speakers as he announced, "Hey, ladies and gents, my wife has just arrived and is over by the entrance. My daughter Sheila's with her tonight, and she's going to come up and play for you, so I want you to give her a big Bay Area welcome, okay?"

As if by magic, everybody swiveled around to face us, and there was a thunderous clapping and stamping of feet. They all stepped aside to create a perfect polished pathway to the stage. It was like Moses parting the Red Sea.

Everyone in that big old room seemed to gasp when they caught sight of how little I was. Men and women reached out to touch my head or pat me on the back, cooing "Aaah!" as Moms led me through a forest of legs.

Straight ahead of me, the high stage was bathed in pretty colored lights. I spotted Uncle Coke sitting behind his timbales and my Uncle Phil on bass. Pops stood at the front, beaming down at me. As ever, he was dressed in a suit and tie, and I felt proud to have the smartest dad in the room.

As Moms and I continued what felt like a royal procession, the crowd packed back in around us and shuffled forward too. When I turned to look behind me, I couldn't see the entrance anymore.

Once we reached the stage, Moms scooped me up in her arms and lifted me into the air, my shiny shoes dangling for everyone to see. All eyes were on me as Pops took me from her and held my hand as he led me to where he'd just been playing the congas. The crowd continued to cheer as he lifted me onto the chair so that I was standing on it.

As soon as I was up on that stage, the butterflies in my stomach started to dance again. This was not a familiar setup for me. Although I was with Pops, my uncles, and our friends doing what we always did, I'd never done it in front of an audience before.

Under hot, bright lights I stood behind the congas and waited for my cue. I knew that all I had to do was let them start playing, find a gap, and join in. Like my father, I didn't read music. I just played by the instinct deep in my gut.

I played from my heart.

"Go with what you feel, baby, okay?" was the only instruction Pops gave me that night before signaling to the band. The song began, and after a few beats, so did I. Pops stayed close and I followed his lead. I don't recall what song it was—all my focus was on Pops.

I must have lost myself then, because I don't remember anything else after he counted me in. People tell me that I played—I mean *really* played. With Pops's encouragement, I even launched into my first-ever solo. It was completely ad lib. And the audience went crazy.

Moms stood right up front in the crowd, jumping up and down, clapping and yelling enthusiastically. She put four fingers in her mouth and whistled loudly. Creole by birth and by nature, the woman who'd been born Juanita Marie Gardere had an indomitable spirit. She was the person who taught me that I could do anything, be anything—*survive* anything. Having grown up with seven siblings who were stars at basketball, baseball, and running track, she learned early on how to be strong, stubborn, loud, and competitive.

"A girl can do everything and *anything* a boy can do, and don't you ever forget that!" she'd insist. We teased her that it was the Gardere part of her talking. Whichever genetic line that competitive, stubborn streak came down, Moms taught me that when it came to trying something new, I shouldn't be afraid. I hear her ever-present and always encouraging "Amen!" in my head, even now.

So that night in Oakland was *my* night. It was my chance to shine. That was my moment to feel special. It was a reminder that I was part of something bigger and better than me—or anything that had ever happened to me.

I was blessed to have been born into an amazing family. We might not have been rich and we may occasionally have gone hungry, but we never went unloved. My parents weren't always able to face up to some of life's harsher realities, but on that night, they wanted me to know my talent and own it for the first time.

As I closed my eyes and forgot about everything other than creating music, I blew that room away.

I was no longer a five-year-old girl who'd had something bad happen to her.

I was Sheila Escovedo—one day to be known as Sheila E.

I was a musician.

Years later, I asked Pops what he remembered of that gig. He paused, a twinkle in his eye. "You played great," he said, a smile breaking out and wrinkling the skin around his eyes. "Yep . . . That's what happened. You played loud and you played fast and the audience loved you."

Being up on that stage with him at Sweet's marked the first night of the rest of my life. I didn't know it then, but it was the one that would eventually shape my entire career.

That was when I realized that I'd not only been given the gift of music, but that it was something that would eventually heal my wounds.

Little did I know how powerful that healing would become . . .

2. Rudiments

A basic pattern used by drummers,
such as the paradiddle and the roll

She wants to lead the glamorous life
Without love
It ain't much

"THE GLAMOROUS LIFE"
SHEILA E

As my daddy jokingly likes to remind me, I wasn't always Sheila E, nor did I always lead a glamorous life. After pushing my way eagerly into this world on December 12, 1957, I was born Sheila Cecilia Escovedo to a jobbing musician of a father and a mother who found work wherever she could.

My parents brought me home from Providence Hospital to their downstairs flat on Sixty-first Street and Adeline in North Oakland, bordering on Berkeley. They liked to joke that their front yard was in Oakland and their backyard in Berkeley.

Juanita Gardere and Pedro Escovedo (known as Pete) first met when they were both in junior high school; she was fifteen and he was eighteen months older. He'd had a tough childhood, some spent in Mexico and some in an orphanage in San Rafael, California. Music and art had kept him sane. Poor and hungry as a child, he used to sit outside nightclubs and let the music transport him to another place.

His first proper musical instrument was an old saxophone, but that wasn't to be his calling. Drawn to percussion, he made a set of bongos out of coffee cans and tape. He painted them himself and taught himself how to play. And play he did.

Although he and my mother were at different schools, Pops traveled miles out of his way to visit her. "She was so cute in her skirt, little sweater, and rolled-over bobby socks tucked into buck shoes," he recalled. "Her hair was combed straight down. She was joyful and friendly and seemed to have a skip in her step. I liked that about her."

Initially, though, her family affected him most powerfully. The Garderes couldn't have been more different from his own dysfunctional family, which was scattered across several states and in Mexico. Juanita's siblings were welcoming and warm in comparison to his. But her father, known as Papa Rock, was mean and didn't much like the young musician his daughter brought home to meet him.

Moms's five brothers and two sisters loved, played, fought, and competed against each other all the time. My mother was the second youngest and one of the most competitive. She even had a special "Gardere face"—squinted eyes, scrunched-up eyebrows, and pouting lips. It could appear for any number of reasons, from someone showing disrespect to debating the finer rules of poker. That's when we'd cry: "Hey, Gardere lips! Chill out!"

She'd be the first to laugh. We could tease her about anything and it would bounce right off. I think she had such a strong core and such a deep sense of confidence that she was impossible to embarrass, but, on the flip side, she loved to embarrass us back. For Pops, being among Moms's family was like nothing he'd ever known. He'd never encountered such an open, friendly, and noisy group.

Hailing from New Orleans, the Garderes were also compellingly exotic to him, with their beautiful brown (sometimes light) skin, blond or brown hair, and pale eyes. Being Creole, they acted differently and spoke with gentle southern accents with a touch of French. They said things like, "Y'all come back, bay" (which was short for babe). "What kinda people are these?" the shy teenager thought. Intrigued to learn more, he began walking Juanita home from school every day, even though they lived almost an hour apart.

Moms thought Pops was cute too. She especially loved the way he dressed, even though she noticed that he always wore the same suit and tie. His family may have been poor, but a musician from New York had hipped him to the importance of looking the part.

"If you want to be a musician, you better dress like one," he was told. Heeding this advice, Pops spent all the money he had on a suit, shirt, and tie that he bought from a gentlemen's outfitters on Telegraph in downtown Oakland. There was no money left over for an alternative outfit.

Pops kept that suit of his as clean as a board of health. On a hot day, the jacket would be neatly folded over his left arm, which he'd keep lifted away from his body at a perfect 90-degree angle so as not to create a wrinkle. His fastidiousness about clothes and shoes still makes Moms laugh.

The more time they spent together, the more Pete and Juanita grew to love each other. He affectionately called her Nina or Nit—and still does. On those long walks home they discovered that they had much more in common than they realized. My father had Latin music in his blood, while Moms had acquired her love of music from watching variety shows and vaudeville. She'd studied piano, tap dancing, and singing. She could read sheet music and went for a professional singing audition in San Francisco once but didn't get the part because she tapped her foot too much.

It's always been hard to keep Moms still.

A born ham, she'll tap-dance and sing all day long, or serenade someone at the drop of a hat. She has a beautiful a cappella voice, is a fantastic salsa dancer, and can play a guiro like a pro. She's talented at virtually everything she does, but—much to her chagrin—whenever she gets up on a stage to perform, she freezes.

When my father first sang to her, he melted her heart. From that day on, she knew she wasn't going to let that "cute young boy" out of her sight. Despite my grandparents' fears that the music business wasn't the best profession for a son-in-law, they gave their permission for Moms to marry him, and they did so on October 21, 1956. She was eighteen and he was twenty. She wore a big white dress with a fifteen-foot train, and he rented a tux. Their reception was at a union hall in Piedmont. Their after-party was at the California Hotel in San Francisco, where they danced to mambo music. They couldn't afford a honeymoon.

Sometime after I was born the following year, we moved into a small in-law unit in the back of the Gardere family home, where Moms (who was pregnant again) could rely on her mother for babysitting.

My grandfather, Papa, had a big heart, but he didn't mess around and could silence you with one look. He was a hardworking man who was a janitor for some rental properties. He'd suffered burns and lost the sight in one eye in an accident in his previous job. He smoked cigarettes, and his right thumbnail was stained yellow. His beige coveralls smelled of paint and his breath of sardines from the sandwiches he loved to make, which included the whole fish—bones, tiny faces, and all.

Mama, my grandmother, always seemed to be in the kitchen cooking for her family and any friends who happened to call. The smells I associate with her are all mouthwatering, and I think of her hands as permanently busy—baking, rolling, frying, stirring— sleeves rolled up to her elbows.

The memory of living in that first home behind my grandparents is imprinted like a black-and-white photograph in my mind. It was calm, simple, and quiet. That was where I first came to know the beauty of silence and of being still.

The *quiet* part stands out the most, because after that I can hardly remember any moments of peace in my childhood.

I was a year old when my brother Juan was born in 1959; then Peter Michael came along two years later in 1961. My sister, Zina, followed in 1967, ten years after me. From the day I stopped being an only child, the soundtrack of my childhood was a cacophony of crying babies and screaming toddlers underscored by the rhythms, beats, and melodies of my father's world.

My memories are, for the most part, pretty loud.

Life could not have been easy for my parents and their growing family, especially when a regular income was so hard to come by. Pops tried to get recording work in studios when he wasn't at a gig, but he occasionally had to break the musicians' rule and take a regular job. He worked in a gas station, a clothing store, at Kinney shoes, and the Del Monte cannery—all of which nearly broke his spirit.

My mother found shift work in supermarkets and factories. For a long time she worked in the Carnation ice cream factory, from which she brought us home Popsicles as a treat. If Mama could watch me, then she and Pops would split the child care between them. They couldn't afford babysitters, so they'd also enlist our cousins. If there was no other option, then Pops would me along to rehearsals, jam sessions, and even his gigs. So he'd play two in one night and have to dash across town on a bus carrying his timbales, cowbells, and me.

I can only imagine how hard it was to waltz into a nightclub holding a baby and hoping to get away with it. Back then, Pops was still building a name for himself and didn't have the kind of reputation he has now. Sometimes club owners gave him a hard time, since babies didn't exactly fit their scene. He made it clear, though: "If you want me to play tonight, then my daughter stays."

So while Pops played, I'd be up onstage in a stroller, asleep behind the bar, or tucked into a leatherette booth. Dark, smoky music venues became my second home. Long before I could walk or talk (let alone slap a conga), I knew melodies, rhythms, and arrangements, because my father's music was the very oxygen I breathed.

At home, percussion was everywhere too. It was part of the furniture. Sometimes it *was* the furniture. With little of our own, we'd use a drum as a TV tray or footrest. And sometimes furniture became percussion—tables, chairs, pots, and pans have surprisingly good tone.

There was plenty of real music, too, as Pops played congas, bongos, and timbales as part of his daily routine. He'd wake up, light his pipe, head to the front room, and put on one of his favorite records. Then he'd practice for hours on end, alone or with band members, anything to keep his chops—technical efficiency—up. Being a drummer requires whole body strength, and most drum and percussion players practice every day to maintain their fitness levels and keep on top of their chops. Our home was constantly filled with musicians: old friends, new friends, strangers, and relatives. That was the norm. The Escovedo pad was the place to be. Sometimes they were rehearsing for a show, and sometimes they just came to hang and jam. They were usually led by Pops, who played the music he was most influenced by—a heady mix of salsa, mambo, Latin jazz, Afro-Cuban, and jazz.

For relaxation, he'd put on an old favorite like Frank Sinatra or Nat King Cole and sing along. (Later in life, he was proud to be known as the "Mexican Frank Sinatra.")

I didn't care what the music was; I loved hearing anything with notes, although I especially tuned in whenever Pops was playing. When I was a baby, his music must have been like an invisible mobile above my crib—rhythmic, mesmerizing, and soothing.

Before I had language, I had rhythm. I learned it before I learned my mother tongue.

I wasn't just born into an environment *with* music; I was *of* music.

Music shaped my bones.

Moms danced to it when she was pregnant with me, and then she swayed me in her arms or bounced me on her lap as a baby. As soon as I could coordinate my hand movements I began to copy my father, sitting across from him to imitate his beats on my lap.

Whatever his right hand would do, my left hand would mimic. Whatever his left hand would do, my right hand would follow. Because of this, I continue to play in a way that leads people to assume I'm left-handed, even though I'm not.

What began as a child's imitative play planted the seed for my life's passion.

3. Polyrhythm

Playing two time-signature patterns
over the top of each other

*Of all earthly music, that which reaches farthest into heaven
is the beating of a truly loving heart.*

HENRY WARD BEECHER

The best thing about music when I was growing up is that it was free—which was just as well, because sometimes Moms and Pops really struggled financially.

At best, one of Pops's gigs might earn his band fifty dollars, which they'd split between them. I'd hear my parents whispering late at night and, sure enough, a few days later our latest car would be repossessed—a Mustang or an old white Jag—towed away on a truck while all the neighbors looked on.

If times were really hard, we'd have to move because my parents couldn't make the rent. A notice pinned to the front door would mean it was time to pack our bags again.

Occasionally the lights would go off for a day or two because we couldn't afford the electricity or because in our neighborhood the service was patchy. Whatever the reason, Moms and Pops never gave up on their belief that God would provide, and they turned every setback into an adventure.

"Let's try something new!" they'd cry as we stumbled around in the dark. Out came the flashlights and the candles so they could tell us ghost stories or make shadow puppets on the wall.

We rarely went hungry, although every now and again we'd have to pour water into the milk to make it last. Some nights we only had cereal or sugar on bread for dinner, and Moms would skip a meal. "I'm not hungry," she'd lie, puffing on one of her Salem cigarettes.

Occasionally, my brothers and I would go to a house on the corner where, in return for listening to Bible stories, we were fed peanut-butter sandwiches. Sometimes we stole candy from a store. Moms would have spanked us if she ever found out, but all our friends did it, and sometimes our cravings for something sweet got the better of us.

My favorite candy was an orange flute that you could play and then eat. We also liked Pop Rocks, which fizzed in the mouth, as well as pear-flavored sugar sweets, Twinkies, and 7 Up. There was an orange or red soda we liked called Nehi. We'd drink a little, then pour in half a bag of peanuts to get a combo of sweet and salt. Mostly, though, we just grabbed what we could and ran.

When times were really hard, we went on welfare. I was sent to the corner store, embarrassed, with food stamps. I felt as if the words I AM POOR were stamped across my forehead.

Yet there was at least one toy for each of us under a Christmas tree each year, and our stockings always contained a bag of socks, come what may. Moms was a stellar bargain hunter. We had a gift exchange so that each of us would buy one present only, for a few dollars. I went to the ninety-nine-cent store or made things. One year I took some photographs and framed them. Another Christmas when we had no money at all, my brothers and I made a little house out of the Popsicle sticks Moms brought home. She and Pops acted like it was the greatest gift in the world.

To their eternal credit, our home was always clean, comfortable, and full of joy. None of us ever really knew we were poor because we were so rich in love. Everyone wanted to visit because my parents turned our latest pad into such a welcoming and beautiful space. We had the coolest decoration, too—orange plastic chairs that looked like leather, yellow shag rugs—many of them begged or borrowed from friends or family and then thrown together to look hip. My parents were never afraid of color.

Pops had painted since he was a child, and the artist in him loved vibrancy and contrast. A teacher at his orphanage had been the first to spot his talent and encouraged him as a way of expressing himself. Our walls were adorned with his unique abstracts. He painted oils on canvas, did sketches, and created charcoal drawings. When he couldn't afford materials, he sketched on drumheads, wood, cardboard, plates or boxes—anything he could get his hands on.

When I look back at his art when we were growing up, I'm surprised by how dark a lot of it is. I think he must have felt weighed down by the worry of having to support us all. Not that he ever let on. Our homes may have been small, but they had soul, and, most important, they were full of warmth.

Even during the worst times, Pops never sold or hocked his musical instruments. He refused to give up on his dream as so many musicians are forced to. He and his brothers always kept the faith that one day they'd make it. The tools of his trade may have been all beat-up, but they were cherished, and he took great care of them. He wiped them down after each performance or jam session, then put the drums back into their cases or the cowbells back into their little bag as if they were pure gold.

I don't know how they managed it, but Moms and Pops also

somehow provided for anyone who knocked on our door. Musicians would drop in to eat, drink, and smoke until late. We kids learned to sleep through every kind of noise while they jammed. We'd wake for school the next morning and pick our way through a colorful patchwork of strangers sleeping on the floor.

My parents also found ways to keep us entertained despite their persistent lack of funds. We never had a so-called family vacation, but in the summer they'd drive somewhere like Fresno or King City in Monterey County, where it was especially hot. They'd book us into a cheap motel—all five of us in one room for the night— just so we could enjoy the luxury of swimming in the motel pool. That was us living the glamorous life. We were kings in King City!

To save us having to eat out, Moms would always pack the car full of food, and—now that I think about it—not much has changed. Even when we travel together these days, I can count on her to either knock on my hotel door or call my room each morning to offer me fruit or peanut-butter-and-jelly sandwiches.

"It's okay, I was just going to order room service," I tell her.

"Oh no, Heart!" she insists (using a nickname she sometimes gives me). "Why waste your money when I packed so much?"

Free food has always excited her. I've lost count of the sophisticated venues and pimped-out green rooms I've had to usher her out of once her eyes fall on the buffet. If I can't get her out, I have to convince her not to sneak food into her purse. "Moms," I plead under my breath. "Put that down! You don't need those sandwiches! We just ate and there'll be more food after the show!"

Taking her to an all-you-can-eat buffet is a nightmare. She'll pack five containers in her purse, and I have to tell her, "Moms! They mean all you can eat *here*, not at home as well!" She just laughs and Pops, ever the dignified one, shakes his head (although he still enjoys eating everything she brings home).

Back in the day, drive-in movies were a favorite family destination. There was one near the Oakland Coliseum that we went to, always late at night in an old Buick or Chevy or whatever Pops could afford. As we neared the entrance, he'd pull over and we kids would pile into the trunk, leaving it slightly ajar because it was dark and stank of tires. We'd lie there in our pajamas until we'd been successfully sneaked past the booth without paying more than the one-dollar fee for two adults.

Pops would park somewhere we couldn't be seen, open the trunk, and we'd clamber onto the backseat. We'd snuggle together under blankets or in our coats if it was really cold, eating the popcorn, candy, and other snacks Moms had packed. On summer nights, we'd risk being caught by lying on the roof to watch the movie. Once in a great while Pops would give us some money to buy something from the snack bar, although my mother always resented the expense and complained she could make something for a fraction of the price.

Moms still sneaks food into movie theaters, by the way, even though the hot dogs for senior citizens are only a dollar. In her seventies she looks pregnant because her pockets are so stuffed with popcorn, candy, and soda. If anyone ever asks to check her purse she suddenly pretends that she's forgotten her medicine and rushes back to the car to hide even more food in her coat.

I especially loved going to my grandparents' house as a child, even though my grandmother had a strangely mean streak. As soon as we arrived, we had to stand in line from the back porch and greet her one at a time for an obligatory ritual no one ever seemed to question. She'd be in her rocking chair with a sly grin on her face. One by one we had to peel off our shoes and socks, sit in her lap, and let her pull on our toes until they cracked. It must have been a Creole thing. The more we cried out, the more she laughed. Mama was a tough cookie, and you couldn't tell her no—she was a Gardere, after all.

The upside was that she was the most incredible cook, so going there meant we could eat meat and fish instead of our staple diet of tortillas, rice, and beans. (I swore that when I grew up I'd never eat rice and beans again.) The best days were either when we went to Mama's or on a special Sunday when Pops was paid after working in a big club on a Saturday night. Then we'd get pork chops and applesauce after church—small compensation for being in that drafty old St. Anthony's Church with its boring music that didn't connect with me at all. Old hymns with no melody never touched my heart, but I endured it because going to church meant something to my parents.

One time when I was still very young, I felt deeply honored when my grandmother asked me to help her make her famous gumbo with chicken, shrimp, and crab. That was, until she insisted I drop the crab into a pot of boiling water. I picked it up—not realizing it was still alive until its claws started snapping at my fingers. I began crying and shaking my head, but Mama wouldn't let me—or the crab—off the hook. The more I cried, the more she howled with laughter. When I reluctantly did as I was told, peeling the rubber bands off the creature's claws and carrying out the death sentence as it snapped at me angrily, I could've sworn the poor crab let out a scream.

My other grandmother, whom we called Nanny, was an eccentric, fun character. Having fallen on hard times and given up her children when her husband left her, she kept in touch and was later reunited with them. A hairstylist who had her own shop, she was the woman from whom Pops inherited his beautiful hair. Even when they both went white, there was never a hair out of place. She had a lewd sense of humor, and her house was filled with all sorts of rude items featuring naked men. Her apron had a string you could pull on to reveal an erect penis, and even her light switches were naughty. When I introduced her to Lionel

Richie years later, she reached out and cupped him in her hands, balls and all!

Because my mother came from such a big family, there was always a reason to celebrate, and celebrate we did. Everyone took turns hosting family events, which were accompanied by music and dancing. Best of all, there was always good food—with the exception of the stinky sardine sandwiches provided by Papa, which no one but he ate.

Knowing that every little bit helped in our household, we kids became very enterprising and would try to bring in some extra money to help out. One day we sat around brainstorming how we could surprise our parents and contribute. While they did their best to hide their stresses about lack of finances, we'd pick up on it—especially when we heard them talking through our thin walls late at night.

My brother Juan even went through a phase of eating as little as he could and refusing seconds for three weeks straight. He'd glare at me if I dared ask for more.

After ruling out several ideas (it was too cold for a lemonade stand and we didn't think people would pay to see us dance), we settled on shoe shining. We borrowed Pops's prized shoe-shining kit—which I still have to this day—and walked over to the Safeway market by Lake Merritt.

My brother Peter Michael was the littlest and the cutest, so we used him to lure customers over. He also didn't look as black as Juan and me.

"Please, sir? Do you want your shoes shined?" he'd plead. "We're raising money for charity." Few could say no to his cherubic face.

We stuck at it all day, and then a helpful supermarket employee walked us through our financial options, aisle by aisle. While we were sorely tempted by the ice cream and candy, we were determined to stick to our plan. The sun was setting as we made our way home, proudly carrying milk, eggs, and a loaf of bread.

Our efforts weren't always entirely selfish, either. We raised a lot of money for the Jerry Lewis Muscular Dystrophy Telethon. Jerry was a big deal in our house, so his telethons were especially important to us. I was deeply moved by the cause and consumed with sadness at the thought of all those innocent children in need of aid. My brothers and I sent away for the fund-raising kit, and when it arrived we eagerly examined its contents, which included information about distributing publicity materials, building booths, and organizing games.

One year we threw a carnival for family, friends, and neighbors, charging them twenty-five cents per ticket to see our show, take a ride, or play a game. We excitedly explained to them that this was their chance to have fun while helping "Jerry's kids." Another time, we created a haunted house over the garage of a house we were renting. It was dark in there, and we hung creepy things from the ceiling and had a tape recorder playing screams and other haunted sounds. We jumped out at people who climbed a ladder to get there. We had so much fun!

No one had anything like that in our neighborhood, and it was a big deal. Moms made us a little food to sell, of course, and it felt to me like we raised a lot of money—although it was probably only a few bucks.

Those were my first independent philanthropic endeavors as a kid, and they gave me a glimpse of how fulfilling it could be to use what you had to help others in need, however limited your resources.

Because of the dark days of his childhood when he and his brother Coke had been sent to an institution, Pops made a point of visiting children's homes and detention centers in his spare time. Keen to remind us how lucky we were, he took us along from an early age. He'd load Moms, my brothers, and me into his crazy purple station wagon along with a bunch of drums and some percussion instruments. "The kids we're going to see today," he'd tell us gravely, "are in the system and don't have families of their own. We need to show them a bit of family love, okay?"

In a chilly room in one of those horrid children's homes with bars on the windows, scant facilities, and dormitory beds, we'd help him unload the instruments in silence. After Pops introduced us, he'd share how he came from a large family whose father left home and how his mother couldn't cope with so many children.

"I know what you're going through, because my kid brother Coke and I were sent to an orphanage for a couple of years," he'd tell them, always choking up a little at that point before forcing a smile. "But we overcame the odds. It was in the orphanage that I first discovered art and where I developed my love of music. I've always drawn and painted, but once I started playing music, I knew that would be my life. So we're going to play you some music today and see if you like it."

"What did you say your name was, mister?" one of the children might ask.

"You can call me Pops," he'd say quietly. "Everybody does."

Whenever I heard him say that, I realized what a father figure he was to them and to us all. Pops's heart is huge; he and Moms have more than enough love to go around. It's like the whole world is their family. His childhood always served to remind us that even though we sometimes thought we had it hard, we didn't know what real hardship was.

Inspired by his words, we'd gather around and start jamming for the kids and encouraging them to join in. They were a tough crowd. Despite their initial resistance (and the few who refused to have anything to do with us), we managed to get most playing something. Putting a smile on the faces of those frightened, damaged kids made it all worthwhile.

The worst part was having to pack up and say good-bye. The children, especially the tiny tots and usually the girls, would cling to us—especially Moms, who can't walk by someone without giving them a hug. "Please take us home with you? Can't you adopt us?" they'd beg, their arms wrapped around her legs. That part was heartbreaking, especially for Pops, who used to push the cuter Coke to the front whenever prospective parents came to visit their orphanage. Nobody ever picked the Escovedo brothers.

Tearfully, I'd ask Pops, "Can't we take *one* of them home?"

His eyes moist, he'd shake his head and remind us to smile and wave as we got into the car and left them all behind, with the promise that we'd be back soon. I'll never forget their faces as we pulled around the corner out of view.

It was an image that would stay with me always.

4. Pitch

The quality of a sound governed by the rate of vibrations

All that's left are memories
Of how it used to be
We can't erase the past
We can't change our destiny

"FADED PHOTOGRAPHS"

SHEILA E

My earliest childhood memories reflect an almost pitch-perfect life, complete with caring parents, close siblings, and an abundance of love and laughter to go around. Music was always at the core of it, and whenever the adults stopped jamming because they couldn't play anymore and needed to take a break, we kids would rush to the instruments like it was a game of musical chairs.

Sure, there were times when we'd have liked more meat on the table, shoes that weren't so scuffed, or a real vacation. I remember wanting a Barbie doll so badly but having to wait years until I was given a secondhand one. I also desperately wanted to be a Girl Scout at my school, but my parents couldn't afford the uniform. It took me a long time to understand that they really didn't have the money. Nevertheless, it was hard to see my friends going off in their uniforms, earning their little pins, or talking about the camping trips I couldn't go on.

Then I heard about traffic school, where you learned to walk younger children across the street. It came with a free uniform and even a hat, so I jumped at the chance and ended up being promoted to sergeant. I had to stand to attention and press a button before ferrying the little kids across. It was a job that required a lot of responsibility, and I was so proud to be in charge.

The golden days of my childhood changed for me when we moved to what I think of as *that* house, a duplex on Thirteenth Avenue and East Twenty-third Street. Up until we relocated there, the world seemed safe and harmonious. My life and everything in it was pitched just right. Something went badly out of tune for our family the day we shifted our raggle-taggle belongings into that duplex, though, and the effects of it resonate through my life to this day.

To begin with, we suddenly found ourselves visited frequently by the police—something that hadn't happened much before. First they came to answer noise complaints from our neighbors about the music. We'd had complaints before, but the new and aggressive hammering on our front door was an unwelcome addition to our percussion.

If men in uniforms weren't yelling at us to turn the music down, they'd be banging on a door upstairs, where one of my aunts and my uncle would yell and fight all the time. Once, in the middle of the night, I was startled awake by the sounds of furniture flying in the apartment above ours. Scared, I ran into the front room, where I found my parents looking equally worried.

They ordered me back to bed, but while I was still there my aunt began banging on the door, begging to be allowed in. She then stumbled into our home, covered in blood. Moms and Pops ran to help her, and I almost passed out at the sight of her blood all over Moms's blouse.

After a while, I came to dread the flashing blue lights on the walls and the noise of the sirens, which only added to the cacophony already in my head.

Soon after we moved to *that* house, I went for a walk down the street and came upon a German shepherd tied up with a rope. Assuming he was friendly like all the other dogs I'd ever known, I went to pet him. He shot me a strange look and then suddenly lunged at me. I turned to run but I wasn't fast enough, and the rope was longer than I realized. He sank his teeth into my backside and began shaking me like a rag doll. I screamed and fought him off for what seemed like forever before finally breaking loose.

When I burst into our duplex with blood pouring down my legs, Moms rushed me to the emergency room. The wounds were deep, and I had to have a tetanus shot. It took me a long time to feel comfortable around dogs again.

In a matter of weeks, my kid brother Peter Michael went missing. He was only two years old. Everyone gathered on the street as our neighbors stood watching. Moms and Pops were close to hysterics. For a while the situation seemed hopeless. The police came to take statements, but their presence only made me feel more insecure.

Seeing my mother's tears, I convinced myself that my brother had been kidnapped after accepting candy from a stranger, something we'd repeatedly been warned against. Thankfully, Peter Michael (or Peto, as he was known until the day he announced that he wanted us to call him by his full name) was returned home safely after several hours. Someone had apparently spotted him alone outside and assumed he was lost, so she took him home. Despite the happy ending, my world felt increasingly unsafe, and I continued to harbor a terror of one of us being snatched.

That house seemed forever to be associated with blood in my mind. We were in *that* house when my mother suffered a miscarriage. I don't remember much about it except that she came home late one night and looked wired to me. I asked her what was wrong because I saw blood on her. She said she cut herself and was fine and she told me to go back to bed, but I know she was very sad. Later on Juan hurt himself when the two of us were racing around the backyard. We were weaving in and out of tall weeds when he tripped and landed on a piece of glass, which embedded itself in his knee. I carried him inside as blood dripped down his leg. We spent hours at the emergency room that night.

Juan still has the scar and sometimes points to it affectionately— a symbol of his big sister's heroics.

We were back in the ER a few days later when I had another of my nosebleeds, which had become increasingly frequent since we moved there. One day the bleeding just wouldn't stop, despite Moms's usual remedies like pinching my nose or placing a cold towel on the back of my neck. I drank a glass of water and watched in horror as it turned red. The doctors couldn't stop the bleeding either, and I ended up vomiting up what I couldn't help but swallow, which scared me even more. It seemed like hours before anyone was able to make it stop.

The memory of that incident remains—panic, Moms's helplessness, and my own terror that I'd bleed to death.

I learned of President Kennedy's assassination in *that* house too. Moms and I were sitting on her bed in front of the TV while she folded laundry. Walter Cronkite interrupted whatever we were watching with a report that the president had been shot. Moms gasped and then let out a scream, holding her head in her hands and rocking herself to and fro. I looked up at her and then back at Walter Cronkite and didn't understand. Was it for real? Hearing Moms's cries, I realized that it had to be.

Three days later, I was in front of the TV again when the murder of Lee Harvey Oswald was inadvertently broadcast. There was a shot and screaming and lots of men shouting as I sat open-mouthed and mesmerized. The assassination prompted the news station to air footage of JFK just before he was shot. There was our president on the screen, smiling and alive. I couldn't make sense of it. *Why was he smiling? Wasn't he dead?* It was too much for my five-year-old mind to take in.

It was in *that* house where I witnessed my parents have an argument for the first time, too; the only time I ever saw my father lose his temper. That really frightened me, as he never got angry or yelled or hit us—Moms had all the southern fire that one family needed. I have no idea what it was about—money, probably—but I've never forgotten it.

As if there wasn't enough going on within our four walls, the next thing to happen was that people warned us that our new next-door neighbors were Gypsies. We lived in a mostly black neighborhood, and the newcomers were exotic looking, like Indians, and they didn't send their children to school. At such a young age I didn't know about the Gypsy stereotype, but I detected that it was something not to be envied.

Their arrival all seemed part of the dark power *that* house held over us.

My fears were allayed when one of the dreaded Gypsies turned out to be a friendly nine-year-old boy. It was the 1960s, and everybody's children played openly in the streets or in their yards, moving carefree from one house to another as games or faces changed.

"Go outside and play," Moms or Pops would say, and none of us would be expected home until Moms whistled loudly, which would be our cue to come inside for supper.

One day when I was wearing a dress (so we must have just come back from somewhere special), I ran outside to play in front of the house as usual. Our Gypsy neighbor spotted me and urged me to crawl with him into the gloomy two-foot space underneath his house.

"I have something to show you," he told me with a smile.

Being a natural tomboy, I was all for an adventure and followed him eagerly, completely forgetting about my dress.

Once we got into the cramped, spidery space, though, I wasn't so keen. Then he did something strange and pulled out a tube of glue, unscrewing the top. He squeezed some of the goo into a brown paper bag, which he held up to me in the half light, and said, "Sniff this."

I shook my head. The bag was stinky, the space was dark and dirty, and I told him I wanted to leave.

"Look, it's fine," he said, and shoved his nose into the narrow opening of the bag to inhale. When he lifted his face, he was grinning.

He placed the bag in my hand. "Try it," he urged. "It'll make you feel good."

He made it seem like fun, so I eventually gave in. No sooner had I taken a sniff, though, than I felt unwell. Dropping the bag, I lay back to stop my head spinning. I thought I might be sick.

While I lay there helplessly, the boy reached under my dress and began to touch me. What was he doing? No one ever touched me *there*.

I felt ill.

I didn't feel right in the head.

I knew this wasn't normal, and I told him, "Stop! Please!"

"Don't worry, this'll be fun, too," he soothed.

I squirmed, but he was much older and stronger than me, plus my head was still spinning. As he pinned me down with his leg, I was powerless against him. I remained cognizant enough to know that I didn't like it, and I asked him to stop. But he just carried on groping me.

I felt weird and disoriented. I wanted to get away from him, and I eventually pushed his hands away and wriggled free. "I have to go home," I told him as firmly as a five-year-old can. "My mom'll come looking for me."

Before he let me go, he gripped my arm and told me harshly, "Don't tell anyone what we've done. It's our little secret, okay?" Although he was smiling, he was holding me too tightly, and his words were laden with threat.

I crawled out of there and ran home as fast as my little feet would carry me. I was very confused. What *we've* done? I didn't do anything, did I? I felt suddenly ashamed that I'd let him touch me. Was I to blame?

Moms saw me come in and frowned. "How did you get your dress so dirty?"

I shrugged my shoulders. "I was playing outside."

That was the start of my lying.

"Sheila, you know not to play outside in your good clothes!"

It didn't occur to me to tell my mother what had happened, and in any event I just wanted to forget it. I may have been only five years old, but I made sure to keep well away from the Gypsy boy after that.

I wish he'd been the only one who made me keep secrets, though. I had two older cousins in their teens who, on separate occasions, seemed to find me an easy target. If either of them was babysitting at night, they'd wake me up long after my brothers and I had gone to bed. I'd open my eyes, groggy with tiredness, and wonder what was happening.

"Let's watch some TV," they might say. "There's no one to stop us watching what we like." As soon as we settled down in front of the television, my molestation would begin.

It never took long for me to shake my sleep off and become instantly, terrifyingly alert. What had I done to deserve all this sudden attention? Why did they all want to touch me—*there*? It always felt wrong to me, but it had happened before and I was helpless every time.

Those cousins made me feel as if I had a notice on my forehead that said, IT'S OPEN SEASON. COME MESS WITH ME! I don't know if they were secretly talking to each other or whether, at five, I was just coming to the age when I was getting noticed, but it seemed that everywhere I turned, somebody wanted a feel.

I dreaded seeing them after that; I was always so uncomfortable at family gatherings. I tried to make sure I was never left alone with them, but if they were innocently picked as our babysitters for the night, I'd think to myself, Oh, no, here it comes.

I never said anything to Moms or Pops because I knew family was everything to them. "Family is what we are, and family look out for each other," was the code. "Never stir things up or get anybody into trouble. All we have is family, family, family."

The fear of stirring things up tormented me, along with the relentless questions that spun round and round in my mind, despite my best efforts to make them stop.

Why me?

Why is it always a secret?

Why is it always in the dark?

And then came the darkest night of all. The night the Bad Thing happened. It was a night that changed my world forever.

I was still only five years old.

5. Snare

A length of hide or gut stretched across a drumhead

Let no man pull you low enough to hate him.

MARTIN LUTHER KING JR.

I was fast asleep. Moms and Pops were out at a gig, and my brothers and I had gone to bed in the room we shared, just like always. Juan was three years old and Peter Michael was still a baby. They were in bunk beds while I had a single bed all to myself.

A teenager who was a distant relative was babysitting us for the first time in that duplex. When my parents had asked if he'd mind keeping an eye on us for a few hours that night, he smiled and said he'd be happy to.

In what felt like the middle of the night, I awoke to find myself being taken into the next room. It was the dining room that Moms and Pops had made into their bedroom by placing a mattress on the floor. I looked up into my babysitter's face, but he wouldn't return my gaze.

Why is he bringing me here? I thought sleepily, not suspecting a thing. I hoped I hadn't wet the bed again—something I'd done a few times lately.

He sat me on the mattress in the half light that shone in from the hallway, and then he told me we were going to have a good time.

I rubbed my eyes with my fists and yawned.

"I've got something special to show you," he said. Then he unbuttoned his pants and took out something I'd never seen before.

The boy with the glue under the house and the cousins who crept into my room had only ever touched me, never themselves.

As my whole body stiffened with tension, the babysitter unscrewed a jar of my mother's Vaseline, covered his hand in it, and then spread the sticky goop over *my* right hand. I've never been able to smell Vaseline again without my stomach turning.

I turned my head away when he placed my hand on his penis and clamped his fingers around mine. We sat there together like that for a bit, but I had my eyes closed, and all I wanted was for it to stop. He made a moaning sound, and I was frightened by it and by the effect of my hand.

Rigid with fear, I was still frozen to the spot when he lifted my nightgown—my favorite one with a pretty flower pattern. He laid me on my back and then he lowered himself on top of me. His body was heavy and his breathing ragged in my ear. He forced my legs apart with his hands, and the next thing I remember was searing, burning pain.

I cried out and pleaded with him to stop, but he kept going, pushing, thrusting. I screamed out loud, and he pressed his hand so hard against my mouth that I tasted my own blood. His hand was so big it covered my nose, too, and I thought I would suffocate.

"Be quiet!" he hissed. "No one can hear you! You'll be in even more trouble if you make another sound!"

I tried to stop crying, but the pain only got worse and worse. It left me breathless and, in the end, voiceless. He removed his hand, and my mouth opened and closed in a gasping, silent scream.

The next thing I knew I blacked out, or at least my mind shut down.

When I eventually became aware again, he was lifting himself off me. I heard a noise and realized it was coming from my mouth, which was fighting for breath with rasping sobs of pain and fear.

I lay there, exposed, shivering and crying.

"Go to the bathroom and clean yourself up!" he snapped.

I couldn't move.

He went away and fetched some paper towels. I wondered why. Then he started frantically wiping something off my parents' dark sheets before wiping himself.

Feeling sick, I rolled away from him onto my side. The pain made me cry out once more.

"Shut up!" He gripped my wrist and yanked me roughly to my feet as I almost blacked out.

I could barely stand. Everything was wet and sticky between my legs.

Shaking all over, I stood watching as he grabbed a wet rag and continued scrubbing at the sheets.

"Go clean up!" he commanded.

I shuffled to the bathroom with baby steps and switched on the light. I looked down and almost fainted, clutching the basin as my knees buckled. There was blood everywhere—running down my thighs and soaking into my nightgown. I think I must have blacked out again, and I don't know to this day what happened to my favorite flowery nightie.

The next thing I remember, my attacker was with me in the bathroom. He looked as frightened as I felt. He must have seen all the blood. I stood in front of him shivering so much that my teeth were chattering.

Somehow I'd been changed into clean pajamas, and through the screaming in my head I could distantly hear him telling me to go back to my room and go to sleep.

"Forget about this and don't tell a soul—or else . . . " he said, his eyes boring into me.

I shuffled painfully to bed and fell facedown onto my pillow. Afraid of waking my little brothers, I used it to stifle my cries.

Whenever I try to remember more details of that night, it comes to me in jagged pieces like fragments of broken glass. As an adult, I know that I must have disassociated myself from what was happening as my only method of dealing with it. Even today, when the memories occasionally creep back into my dreams, they appear as shards, but they always bring fear, pain, and shame—feelings I'm still unable to fully articulate.

Or perhaps the experience of a five-year-old girl being raped simply defies language.

The pain woke me the next morning. I didn't know exactly where it was coming from, but I ached all over, and my tummy really hurt. I hobbled to the bathroom and tried to urinate, but I couldn't—it stung too much. I wiped myself and cried out when I saw blood on the paper. Once again, I couldn't understand its source. Having seen so much blood the night before, this fresh bleeding only intensified my fear.

Was I dying? What if I had to tell Moms what I'd done?

I sat on the toilet rocking back and forth, cradling myself with my arms and trembling all over.

It must have been summertime, as I can't have gone to school that day and I have no idea how I spent the next few hours, apart from worrying how much my tummy hurt.

I couldn't pee or poop, and I was so afraid of Moms finding out. I didn't eat or drink anything, and when she asked me what was wrong I merely mumbled that I wasn't feeling well.

Instead of showing Moms the blood, I tried to figure out how to tell her what had happened. I kept waiting for the right moment, but there never seemed to be one. It wasn't until much later the following night that I finally broke down and told them that a Bad Thing had happened.

"What do you mean?" Moms asked.

"He hurt me," I blurted, saying it as quickly as I could to get the words out and away from me. As I said them, big, fat, oily tears began to roll down my cheeks. Catching my breath, I looked out the window and noticed that it was dark already. Night was coming, and I didn't think I could face another one with all that pain and fear.

"Who hurt you?"

"The babysitter."

"The babysitter? How?" my mother pressed.

I shook my head. I knew from her expression that he was going to get into trouble for what I'd said, and then he'd be really mad at me. If he was mad at me, he might come back and hurt me again. I believed that I'd be in trouble for making trouble. Too afraid to say another word, I shut down once more.

So that was as detailed as my allegation got. At such a tender age, I lacked the vocabulary to explain what had happened, and my fear of stirring things up prevented me from saying more.

The ensuing hours and days have remained so confusing and distressing to me and to my family that we are rarely able to discuss them—even after all these years. I do know that after my parents gave up trying to pry more information out of me, there was suddenly a lot of movement in the house. I remember how upset and angry they were. That's when I knew I really was in trouble.

They confronted the babysitter about what I'd said, but he laughed and flatly denied everything. Then they came home and continued to question me, asking, "Are you sure, Heart?"

They wanted more details.

"You have to tell us what happened—exactly."

"Are you sure you didn't just have a bad dream?"

It had never occurred to me until that moment that they didn't believe me or that I couldn't tell them the truth.

"This is serious, Sheila. Talk to us!"

I began to panic.

They didn't know what to think.

"Maybe you had a nightmare?" Moms pleaded again.

I half nodded, afraid to say any more. I couldn't speak the words I wanted to say, and she wasn't able to hear them. I'm sure her mind blanked them out, as the truth was simply too painful to face—for all of us.

The more she asked, the more I clammed up, until the silence seemed for the best.

Not long afterward, my attacker cornered me in the hallway, pulling me to one side. His fingers pinched my arms, and his eyes glinted as he lowered his voice to a growl. "I'll be back," he told me between gritted teeth. "Shut your mouth, or next time I'll hurt you even more."

His threats worked, because I decided never to say anything about it again.

Incredible as it may seem now, because of my silence nothing was ever done about it. The young man who raped a five-year-old girl in what should have been her safe haven got away scot-free. He remained part of the family and was even an occasional guest at reunions and celebrations.

That's the part that kills my parents to this day.

That's what my mother especially still holds on to.

She feels that she let me down.

The truth is, I couldn't talk about it then, and I wasn't able to speak about it properly for more than thirty years. It was my dirty little secret, and I locked it away in the dark where no one else could see it.

My ordeal might have ended there but for the fact that I developed a morbid dread of going to the bathroom. In my child's-eye view, everything distilled down to the blood—the blood between my legs. My blood on him. The blood he'd wiped from my parents' sheets.

Blood had come to symbolize the intense and unhappy time we had in *that* house. I'd had terrible nosebleeds there. My aunt upstairs had blood all over her hands. I'd bled after the dog bit me. Moms had lost a baby there and bled. Juan had spurted blood after falling onto the glass. The president and his assassin had all been covered in blood on our TV screen.

Blood stained everything there.

I bled for a few more days, and every time I saw it, I felt even more afraid and ashamed and dirty and bad. Those feelings poisoned both my mind and my body. For the next few nights I waited until daylight to go to sleep because I was convinced the babysitter would come back.

I went from being a carefree little girl from a happy, loving home to someone who felt scared and anxious all the time.

Our bathroom became the center of my universe. Part of me wanted to lock myself away in there, but the other part was frightened to, in case I saw blood on the toilet paper again.

Whenever I did enter that scary place, everything around me seemed to come into much sharper focus. That little space became all I knew, and I saw every detail with dazzling clarity—the tiled white floor, the sink on the right, the toilet to the side of that, the shower to the left. There was opaque glass in the window so you could see people walking by, or—worse—standing outside waiting.

And all the time I was sitting and rocking and holding everything in, hyperventilating with the pain.

I was still so sore, it was uncomfortable even to sit. I couldn't allow myself to strain in any way. I couldn't do anything. I couldn't function. I stopped eating and drinking so that I wouldn't have to go. After a while my stomach began to bloat and I became feverish and sick.

When I wasn't in the bathroom, I shuffled around with my head lowered. My entire focus was down—down to where it all happened. Moment to moment, I was just trying to exist and breathe through my fear.

What am I going to do?

How can I not go to the toilet?

What if I can never go again?

Everything hurt. It was getting worse. I lived in secret horror for weeks.

My parents were both busy working and Pops was out every night, but they kept asking me what was wrong. I merely repeated that I didn't feel good. I wouldn't explain why, and their growing frustration with me was evident.

All my life they'd been supportive and protective, but they couldn't help me, and I couldn't ask them for the comfort I needed—comfort they'd have lovingly provided if only they'd known the truth.

I had never felt so alone in my life.

After weeks of being unable to use the toilet, I became so sick that my mother had no choice but to take me to the hospital. My stomach was badly distended. The doctors at the community Highland Hospital checked me over and took my temperature and drew off some blood.

When they got the results, they told Moms it was a good thing she'd brought me in when she did. "Your daughter is so full of toxins that if you'd waited any longer, her life could have been in danger," they told her gravely.

To my enormous embarrassment, they put me in a diaper. I was humiliated and begged them to take it off. "I'm too old!" I cried. Then they said that they'd give me some suppositories. I didn't know what they meant, but when I learned that a stranger planned to put something inside me I became hysterical, screaming, "I don't want anyone to touch me! Moms, please don't let them touch me!"

The doctors tried to reassure me that suppositories would release my blockage, but I wouldn't let them near me. My mother persuaded them to let her administer them at home, which she did while I cried. Then she took me to my grandmother's house.

All the while, she kept asking me over and over why I didn't tell her something was wrong. "Why did you feel like that?" she asked. My grandmother quizzed me too.

I couldn't tell either of them; I was clammed up so tight. I wasn't letting anyone else in.

What seemed like hours later, Moms found me standing awkwardly in the hallway outside the bathroom. The suppositories were finally taking effect, and my stomach was cramping painfully.

"I'm scared," I told her as she knelt down beside me. I was still convinced I was going to die. Eventually, and despite my best efforts to contain myself, I began filling my diaper, and the shame of that forced me to the bathroom.

I sat on my grandmother's toilet and finally let go. I didn't want to hold on anymore. I purged. Outside, I overheard my cousins asking Moms what was wrong. "Sheila's just a little sick," Moms told them.

I was "just a little sick" for a very long time. I felt damaged. Violated. I didn't know the word *rape*. I just knew that I felt different; that I *was* different. A part of me was gone forever.

I became so terrified of the dark and of going to bed that I asked for a night-light. My parents also had to keep my bedroom door open so that the light from the hallway shone into the room.

My innocence had been stolen, without warning or apology.

The Bad Thing that happened *that* night in *that* house scarred me forever.

I suppose I must have recovered my senses eventually, because that same year my parents took me to Sweet's for my first live performance with Pops. Nobody can recall now if it was designed to cheer me up, but—whatever the reason—it worked.

It felt so wonderful to be up on that stage in the spotlight that night and to lose myself to the music. I was happy again. I didn't so much play those congas—those congas played me.

That night was the moment the dark direction my life had taken began to turn back toward a brighter path.

Not long afterward, we moved away from that evil house and all its horrid memories, which was a huge relief for me. I tried to put what happened there behind me.

It was never discussed again.

Many years passed before I could finally begin to acknowledge the profound sense of loss that accompanied those events and to start to believe in myself again. I locked my secret deep away inside me for so long, never realizing what damage it was doing.

In my thirties, after decades of venting my emotions through hitting a drum, I rediscovered that sweet little girl inside me. I now know in my heart that she was never to blame.

Music helped me to move beyond the events of that night and to no longer allow them to define who I am.

6. Rest

An interval of silence of a specified duration

Sometimes raging wild
Sometimes swollen high
Never once I've known this river dry

"RIVER GOD"

SHEILA E (WRITTEN BY NICHOLE NORDEMAN)

After a short stay in our next home, which we always refer to as the White House (and which we left after Juan and Peter Michael started a fire in the bedroom that burned half of it down), we moved to my favorite home—a house on East Twenty-first Street in East Oakland.

Our new address was right across the street from my uncle Coke, who was a loving and fun presence in our lives. Coke's real name was Thomas, but he was given the nickname after a winning horse called Coco Mo Joe for some reason no one can recall. Later, when he became a party animal and known for his love of alcohol and recreational drugs, his name suited him more and more. Everybody loved Coke—he was a sweetheart and, although he ended up a substance abuser, we always think of him fondly.

Although I was still haunted by the Bad Thing and scared of the dark, I longed to put the memories behind me and start afresh. All I needed to heal was right there within our four new walls, and it felt to me like a place where I could learn to smile again.

Pops was always looking for work and we weren't much better off financially, but we did have some of our happiest times there. We'd belly-laugh together at our favorite TV shows, we played with the neighborhood kids, and we devoured Moms's special-recipe meals, including her famous chili beans and rice, potato salad, or tortilla creations dressed with mayonnaise.

As soon as anyone walked in the door, Moms would ask, "Are you hungry?" We never knew how she whipped up a full meal in ten minutes when there never seemed to be enough in the fridge. And, of course, there was always music, which continued to provide a constant source of pleasure and—for me—salvation.

Just as before, our home was rarely empty, and the door stayed open, especially in the summer. Almost every night there were parties and jam sessions whenever friends and family dropped in to eat, drink, and play.

Pops's fellow band musicians continued to rehearse with him in our tiny front room, but his bands grew bigger and bigger as more people wanted to join. One night they had timbales, congas, bongos, singers, dancers, horn players, guitar, bass, and piano all squeezed into one room.

My brothers and I would peek out from our bedroom door to watch them play, or—if it was especially good—we'd wander out in our pajamas.

"Why aren't you in bed?" the adults would ask.

"Can't sleep." (What child could when there was a live band in the front room?)

Giving in to our pleading, the grown-ups would often let us stay. There wasn't exactly a lot of structure in our house—even on school nights—although we must have got used to late-night jamming as lullabies or we'd never have slept.

On the rare occasions that we had the place to ourselves, Juan, Peter Michael, and I would put on our favorite records. The very first 45 single I bought was Edwin Starr's "25 Miles" from the little record store on East Twenty-first Street. Sometimes we even played our own discs when Pops was home, so at any one time there might be his Latin music blaring in the front room while my brothers and I were in our room trying to drown him out with the Temptations or James Brown.

We must have driven the neighbors crazy with the sounds of overlapping musical genres—a strong mix of clave and congas and a hearty bass line blasting out of the open windows. In other words, cha-cha with a distinctive Motown flavor.

All of this music continued to envelop me, blend within me, and become even more of who I was. The boundary between music and me became increasingly blurred.

Without even realizing it, whenever Pops had his friends over, my brothers and I were soaking up the sounds of some of the most talented musicians of their era, sitting right there in our front room. These were mostly people from the Bay Area of Oakland, San Francisco, and Berkeley, but many had traveled there to work with like-minded musicians.

Slouching around on any given day might be the legendary Cuban jazz percussionist Mongo Santamaria, the Puerto Rican pianist Eddie Palmieri, or the Latin jazz and salsa composer Tito Puente.

Even though we were "family," it was still a bit more of a deal when Tito came to the house; it was a bit like Frank Sinatra dropping by. He had an entourage that included security guards and a bunch of guys who reminded me of what I'd seen of the Mafia on TV. At home my father wore mostly flared slacks and brightly colored hippie shirts, so by comparison Tito was extremely well dressed in a smart jacket, pants, shirt, and tie.

The community loved Tito—he did so much for kids and schools—and Pops really looked up to him, too. He later became famous with a younger crowd when he wrote "Oye Como Va" for Carlos Santana, yet he always seemed so reachable and humble. Tito wasn't directly related to me, but I felt like he was my uncle, and I never knew what to call him. When I was about seven I settled on Grandpa, but he complained that made him feel old (he was forty). We agreed that he'd be my "godfather" instead.

He and Pops had been friends since the fifties and had become two of the world's most famous *timbaleros*, or master players of the timbales. Tito had played on many of the records we owned in the house, but that didn't mean that much to us kids back then, surrounded as we were by numerous musicians with record deals. So Tito Puente jamming with our father was just a normal event in the Escovedo household as far as we were concerned.

We might not have been wealthy, but musically we sure were rich.

Lou Rawls was another guest, a chilled-out R&B singer and a really nice guy who was always smiling. He was Mr. Smooth, with a deep voice like Barry White, and he talked real slow and casual. Other visitors might include Bill Summers, Ray Obiedo, Willie Bobo, Cal Tjader, Neal Schon (later of Journey), or members of Con Funk Shun. The Whisperers were another group who hung around a lot, too. Their drummer, James Levi, was especially close to my brothers and me and would take us to the YMCA or a community facility to play basketball.

Pops's band, the Escovedo Brothers, was doing well and playing at venues like the Jazz Workshop, the Matador, and the Basin

Street West. They were gathering quite a following, which meant even more visitors. This eventually prompted Pops to buy more furniture—something he'd been waiting for more money to do—as the house lacked what most people would consider standard items such as comfortable chairs.

"I had to do something," he explained. "I couldn't have all those cats hanging out on the floor."

We had to sit on the hard plastic chairs or the yellow shag rug whenever we huddled around our Zenith TV to watch our favorite shows. That funky old set didn't work very well, and he always had to get it fixed, but as soon as the picture warmed up we'd be transported inside the box to the music shows and the fantastically glamorous lives that seemed a million miles away from ours.

Moms and Pops loved old black-and-white movies like *It's a Wonderful Life*, *The Philadelphia Story*, *Bringing Up Baby*, and *Mr. Smith Goes to Washington*. They were also crazy about Ginger Rogers and Fred Astaire. I watched *Top Hat* so often I knew almost every line. I loved *The Wizard of Oz* and *West Side Story*. We all watched Goldie Hawn and the gang on *Laugh-In* along with Johnny Carson, Ed Sullivan, and Carol Burnett.

We kids were especially gripped by programs such as *Gilligan's Island*, *Leave It to Beaver*, and *Lost in Space*. There was *The Mod Squad* and *The Flip Wilson Show*. We loved *American Bandstand* and *The Andy Williams Show*. Family acts struck a real chord in my household, needless to say. I watched five-year-old Donny Osmond perform *You Are My Sunshine* for Andy Williams and thought to myself, "He's almost the same age as me and yet he's on TV. Why aren't I?"

Lucille Ball remains one of my all-time favorite entertainers. I knew every story line of the *I Love Lucy* shows by heart. I especially liked that she was married in real life to her TV husband, Ricky, played by Desi Arnaz. The show's dynamics reflected those of my own family, and not just because Ricky was a musician. We still call Moms Lucy, because she'd always yearned to be in show business and couldn't help but try to get in on the act—just like Lucy always did. You'd understand if you saw how Pops shakes his head with a grin and a Ricky-like expression that says, "What am I gonna do with her?"

Meanwhile, Moms still stands behind me patting my head when I play even now, or jumps in to slap her hand on a conga drum while Juan keeps time, or grabs the mic when Peter Michael's singing vocals. Mostly she'll freeze up in the end, but for a short while she *is* Lucille Ball.

As kids, what we saw and heard on TV and the radio influenced us massively. Every night was showtime as my brothers and I worked on mimicking our favorite acts and tried to replicate their dance moves—even their outfits. We constantly refined our impressions. We regarded bands like the Osmonds and the Jackson 5 as equals; the only difference was that we had no record or TV show.

We practiced our "One Bad Apple" routine for hours on end, integrating our impressions of their dance routines while singing our hearts out: *"One bad apple don't spoil the whole bunch, girl . . ."*

Yes, we little brown kids from Oakland got down with some Osmonds music. Those Osmonds have serious *soul*!

And when we pretended we were the Jackson 5, we practiced their harmonies and steps over and over. As far as we were concerned, the Escovedo 3 could still give the Jackson 5 a run for their money.

One day Pops brought home another new record and put it on the turntable. It was Sammy Davis Jr.'s *The Sounds of '66*. As it began to play, I walked slowly over to the speakers as if in a trance and sat down. The voice, the instrumentation, the musical dynamics—Sammy sounded ultracool, and Buddy Rich played the drums brilliantly. He was phenomenal. The recording had been done live at the famous Sands Hotel in Las Vegas. The overall concept of it was so great—the arrangement and the composition and the horns. I was in awe.

I listened to that album a hundred times over, sometimes with Pops, sometimes with my brothers. Often by myself. While songs like "Come Back to Me," "What Kind of Fool Am I?" or "Please Don't Talk About Me When I'm Gone" played, I'd stare at the album cover and admire its classy minimalism—that black background with a kind of halfway silhouette in blue. Tapping my feet or my hands on the sofa, I'd let my imagination drift into a musical wonderland where Sammy was performing and I was in his band, singing with him.

Within a week, I knew each part of every song, from the vocals to the horns to the drums. I even learned the minute-long introduction word for word. My mother thought this was great, and at any family gatherings she'd put the record on and say, "Okay, Sheila—showtime!"

As everyone watched, the drumroll would begin, and I'd lip-sync Sammy introducing himself and the band to the audience: *"For you folks at home who might listen to this record eventually, I would like to say that this is a very special night for me."*

I did the whole thing in perfect time. I even wore a hat, a trench coat, and dark glasses. I tried to half close my eye to look like his fake one. Crazy! It was the start of a lifelong love affair with Mr. Sammy Davis Jr., such a consummate performer who could do everything—sing, tap-dance, play the organ and the drums, do impersonations, and even act. His versatility astounded and inspired me.

I wanted to be just like Sammy!

Probably the most remarkable aspect of my childhood is that in spite of what had happened to me and the insecurity that plagued me at a much deeper level, I was raised to have such belief in my own abilities that whenever I heard or saw someone doing something I liked, I immediately pictured myself doing the same.

"I can do that!" was a common cry in our household, thanks to our parents.

I remember seeing Karen Carpenter on television once and telling Pops, "I can sing and play drums! Why aren't I on TV?"

Pops smiled and told me knowingly, "You will be."

The Beatles were another big deal in our household. I was six when the Fab Four first arrived in America. My family gathered around the black-and-white screen to watch them descend the steps from their plane, smiling and waving to their screaming fans. We all thought their performance on *The Ed Sullivan Show* was the best thing that we'd ever seen. Their music was so cool and different.

I sat there in my bunny-printed flannel pajamas, wide-eyed and speechless. I had a crush on all of them. Paul McCartney reminded me of my brother Peter Michael, but I thought George Harrison especially cute. The drummer, Ringo Starr, was—to use an expression of the time—groovy. Watching them all arrive in my country, I fell in love. When they sang "I Want to Hold Your Hand," I was even more smitten.

I want to hold your hands too!

My brothers and I were fascinated and full of questions: "Who are they? Where's England? When can we play with them?"

It never once occurred to us that we couldn't.

I was in second grade when I first got my hands on James Brown's single "Papa's Got a Brand New Bag." Man, my brothers and I wore that record out. We'd lie on the floor between the speakers that were raised on bricks and soak up every note. Later we'd practice James's famous dance moves, such as the skate and the splits, in the living room or on our "stage" (outside) until we had them down solid.

We worked out line formations, dance steps, and harmonies to dozens of songs, including Marvin Gaye's "I Heard it Through the Grapevine," "Respect" by Aretha Franklin, the Isley Brothers number "It's Your Thing," "ABC" by the Jackson 5, and "It's a Shame" by the Spinners.

Our stage was wherever we felt like dancing, complete with a transistor radio. In preparation for our next "show," we'd rehearse for hours and argue over every detail. Then, whenever one of our favorite artists would come on the radio, we'd immediately assume our positions and sing our hearts out to passing cars.

I'm sure Moms encouraged our practicing because it was a far healthier way for us to play together than some of our other more daring adventures. Whenever she heard us perfecting our routines, she knew we were safe and could breathe a sigh of relief that we weren't flying down the streets without stop signs in stolen shopping carts; exploring creeks and then tramping muddy shoes all over her carpet; or being chased by Juan as he hurled his nunchuks during his *Kung Fu* phase.

If we weren't rehearsing, we'd probably have been distracting Moms with some elaborate story so she wouldn't notice the other two trying to tape up the window, which had been cracked by a foul ball, or sneaking into her purse to find some change. If ever she caught us, we'd be in *big* trouble, and she was not averse to using a belt or her hand to slap us every now and again.

Both my parents smoked. Pops smoked pipes, and mostly when he painted, but Moms smoked cigarettes until she was forty. When I was seven years old, I stole one of her cigarettes and showed my brothers how to smoke. We were standing by the back bedroom window. Both Juan and Peto started coughing, and I looked up to see Moms standing at the window giving us that Gardere look. We were in big trouble.

We got spanked with a belt big-time. She folded us over her

knee as we yelped in pain, and we weren't allowed out of our room. Sometimes she'd catch the back of our legs with her hand while we were walking past. I'm sure we deserved it most of the time, because we were bad—lying and stealing and taking money to buy soda or bubble gum. If we weren't doing that, then we were yelling and fighting and getting into some other kind of trouble.

Pops was never a disciplinarian. Having suffered violence as a child, he could never raise a hand to us, which would have hurt him more than it hurt us. He couldn't even kill a spider or a fly, and he usually cried about things more than we did. He didn't want to be mad at anyone, hurt anything, or be hurt. Listening to us singing and dancing and laughing together was what really made him happy. That was all he'd ever hoped for when he was a boy, imagining a family of his own one day.

So we focused our energy on music and dance instead and couldn't wait to show off our routines to him and Moms, who were always proud to introduce us at the next family gathering. Both parents got a kick out of our musical collaborations, but it was Moms who mostly encouraged us to perform for others, even if those "others" were our grandparents, aunts, uncles, and cousins— not exactly paying customers.

Not yet, at least.

"Okay, everybody, gather round!" she'd cry, clapping her hands. "The kids are going to do their latest number for you!" Guests at every party—at least once a week—knew they were going to get some entertainment from the Escovedo family, whether it was us kids, Pops jamming, or Moms tap-dancing, singing, or being goofy. It was a given that they'd be in for a treat.

None of us knew it at the time, but our childish song-and-dance impressions were setting the stage for our future careers. The way we learned to work, dance, and play together back then in the sixties taught us invaluable lessons about being in a band that would serve us well for many decades.

In spite of her boundless enthusiasm for what we were doing, Moms was no stage mother and had little interest in our entering an industry she'd witnessed Pops struggle in. He, too, actively discouraged us from thinking of a career in music and constantly warned us how tough it was to live without a guaranteed income.

He sometimes went so far as to lock his instruments away when he left the house so that we wouldn't be tempted to jam with them. It wasn't hard to pick the lock, and Juan definitely had the knack. So when Pops left, we'd run to the closet, pull out his instruments, play our hearts out, then quickly return them the second we heard his car pull up. As he walked in, we'd exchange triumphant smiles, the beats still reverberating in our ears.

There was unlimited access to live music beyond our walls too. In Oakland back in the day, it was as if the streets had their own soundtrack. As a second grader, I became obsessed with a band that rehearsed in an apartment on the corner of the next block. Rather than play with dolls or try on my mother's makeup—the preferred activities of most little girls my age—all I wanted to do was listen to that band rehearse. Whenever I heard the distant bass of their kick drum as they started riffing on a James Brown number, I was like a kid in a candy store and would race over to where they were.

The band rehearsed on the top floor of a house halfway up a hill. When I got there I'd listen for a while, and as soon as there was a break in the numbers, I'd yell: "Hey! Can I come up and listen?" or "Won't you let me play?"

One of them would put his head out of the window and laugh at me, the skinny little kid on the corner. "You're too young. Go home!"

He'd try to shoo me away repeatedly, but I couldn't be deterred. The same way my father used to sit outside nightclubs as a child, I'd sit on the curb and listen to the band playing whatever covers they were working on at the time. There was something about their drumbeat that really got to me.

Sometimes I sat there for hours, absorbing their incredible sound and tapping away in time on my legs. Listening to them made me so happy for a whole year, until they unexpectedly moved away. I never even saw the whole band. I only ever saw that one guy's head out the window. They were so good, but to this day I have no idea who they were.

While we found all kinds of ways to enjoy ourselves, music was always at the heart of it. I learned to play a little guitar, but only James Brown barre chords. I could also play a bit of bass and some keyboard, too, and I did both later on. It was percussion that attracted me most, since that's what surrounded me, but Pops saw my interest and became concerned that my focus would be too narrow.

"If you're really serious about music, Sheila, then you must learn to play a classical instrument," he told me. And so, in third grade, my violin lessons began. To my father's mind, the violin was a more sophisticated instrument that would offer me greater opportunities, like playing in orchestras and symphonies or maybe scoring music for film.

I enjoyed the violin, but it never connected with me in the same way as playing the congas. Nor was it exactly cool, and I'd get teased for it at school or on the street, where bullies were beginning to dominate my life. The mean kids already had me singled out for the color of my skin or the state of my clothes. I wore my white shoes until I couldn't wear them anymore. I used to polish them every night to try to get them whiter, but they were so worn and cracked that the polish wouldn't take. I hated wearing those shoes and I was also embarrassed by my old dresses. Having a violin case was just another reason to be singled out.

The bullies would push me around and ask, "Why are you carrying that stupid case around all the time?" Or they'd try to grab it from me and say, "You think you're special because you play some fancy violin?"

I tried to ignore them, but their words hurt, and I began to lose my enthusiasm for the instrument. Because I had a good ear and could easily mimic what I heard, I stopped learning how to read sheet music and got away with faking reading. I only needed to hear a piece one time and I had it—a trick I'd learned from copying my father.

I played pretty well in spite of that. Within a short space of time, I made it to the top of my class and became first violin in the school orchestra. I even received a scholarship offer from an elite summer music program.

Then one day my teacher asked me to start at bar eighty-three and play a certain line. Instead, I just started playing where I felt like. "No," she said firmly. "I want you to read the music and play it as it is written."

I hesitated. "Can you hum it for me?"

"No, Sheila. I want you to read the music and play it as it is written."

I shook my head, and her mouth dropped open as she called me to the front of the class.

"Don't you know how to read music, Sheila?"

"No, but my mom does."

"That's impossible! You're my best student. How can you have got this far without reading music?"

"I do what I've always done. I listen to it and then I hear it playing back in my head."

Learning to read music had always felt like a waste of time, but I knew I could never survive in a scholarship program without that skill, so I quit. My parents were very disappointed, but I told them

I was giving it up because it was too "square." They tried to persuade me to stick with it, but by then they had to pick their battles.

Putting away my violin for good was the first indication of the defiance yet to come. The classical instrument they'd picked for me didn't go with the hip, tough-girl image I was aggressively cultivating in order to defend myself against bullies, so I went back to banging the heck out of percussion instruments.

Mostly, I didn't want anyone telling me what to do.

Too late, I'd discovered the word *no*, and I liked the power it carried. My love for it stemmed from those nights when no wouldn't have worked anyway. I started to say no to my mother, my teachers, and anyone who tried to make me do something I didn't want to do. My father was out on tour a lot and was rarely confrontational anyway, so Moms bore the brunt of it.

Never being able to bring up what had happened to me when I was five only made me madder. Full of anger—conscious and subconscious—I began to test the stormy waters of rebellion.

My poor parents.

Little did they know how much of a handful I was yet to become.

7. Tremolo

Quick repetition of the same note or a
rapid alternation between two notes

I take it back—all of those crazy things that I did to you
I take it back—the way I took your heart and broke it in two
I take it back—the things I said that just cut like a knife

"I TAKE IT BACK"
THE E FAMILY

What secretly set the stage for my teenage revolt was that moving away from the evil house hadn't provided the escape I'd hoped for after all. Even though I was happier and we had music and laughter all around, my secret sexual abuse continued.

Because I'd never told my parents that my cousins had groped me as a child, they were still invited over and continued to wake me up after Moms and Pops had left for the night. Mostly I would just lie there in disbelief and let them grope me. In the dirty little world they dragged me into, the one that almost always happened in the dark, I veered from one horrible experience to the next.

With hindsight, I think I blocked out much of what happened as I was growing up. I know I shut down each time. Who was I going to tell? Everything had led me to the point where I felt that nobody would believe me, not even my parents.

I was on my own.

Having already been raped, I was petrified that one day my cousins' sexual molestation would lead there too. There seemed to be a helpless inevitability about it, almost as if that was my chosen path.

With hindsight I can see that I was still trying to protect the five-year-old girl within me. I didn't realize that—deep down—I was still blaming myself. I was also inadvertently protecting my abusers whenever I asked myself, "What is it about me that made them do this?" I was convinced that I had to be at least partially responsible. And so the abuse continued, and I was repeatedly warned that it would be "real bad" for me if I ever told anyone. Not knowing what else I could do, I had no choice but to comply.

I have no clear recollection of how many years the abuse went on for, or how often, but I vividly remember the night I started to put an end to it. The same cousin had woken me and was doing something that I didn't like when I pushed him away and cried, "Stop! Please stop!"

He looked shocked. "But I thought you liked it!" he said, which shocked me.

"No, I don't!" I cried, disgusted. "Now leave me alone."

I ran from the room, and that particular cousin never touched me again.

Then a few months later, we were at the home of a relative when one of my cousins who had never molested me before woke me up, grabbed me, and pulled me into a room. Then he locked the door. As I watched, dumbfounded, he unzipped his pants, spat on both my hands, and made me touch him *there*.

Smiling, he instructed me to give him a blow job.

I must have been eleven or twelve years old.

I didn't know what a blow job was, so he explained.

When I eventually took in what he was asking me to do, I recoiled in horror, snapping my hands back to my sides. A familiar feeling of fear came upon me, because I thought this was done and over with. He grabbed my hair and yanked my head down toward him.

Pushing him off me, I shouted, "No!"

I listened to the word crackle through the air like electricity, and I liked the sound of it.

"Do it, Sheila!" he repeated under his breath.

"No!" I repeated. "This isn't right." Then, more pleadingly, I asked, "Why are you asking me to do this?"

He told me to be quiet before grabbing me and pulling me toward him once more. My fear turned to anger, and by then I knew how to fight back. I'd been bullied for playing the violin. I'd been picked on at school for being too dark or too athletic. I shoved him harder than I'd ever shoved anyone in my life and watched as the force of it sent him crashing back against a daybed.

"No!" I cried. "I'm not doing this!" Then I raced to the door. Unlocking it, I turned and told him firmly, "And don't you dare ask me again."

He never did.

The sexual abuse had finally stopped.

Unfortunately, the physical and emotional torment at school and on the streets was only getting worse. It was sometimes so bad that my entire neighborhood felt to me like a battleground.

Fortunately, I had a best friend by then. Her name was Connie, and she lived just down the street. She was Mexican with two sisters and two brothers. Her father was a professional boxing coach who trained a famous fighter by the name of Yaqui Lopez.

We went to see him fight a couple of times, and I was seriously impressed. I longed to learn how to knock someone out with my clenched fist!

Connie and I didn't go to the same school and we didn't become friends right away, but I ran home past her house every day (often pursued by a gang), and we ended up friends for life. The running-home part started in the fourth grade when two girls from my school, who were two years older than me, constantly picked on me. They'd taunt me on an almost daily basis, pushing and shoving. They progressed to proper beating, punching me in the stomach and knocking the wind out of me, or slapping me across the face really hard.

Another time they told me to tie up one of my friends so that she'd be beaten. I didn't want to, but I was afraid, so I did. She was such a nice girl and would never have done the same to me, but she understood how it worked. Still, I must have disappointed her. I know I disappointed myself.

One day, during recess, I was playing tetherball with another friend named Rebecca when I spotted my tormentors approaching. I could see they were ready to pounce, scowling at me with their fists already clenched.

Oh, no. Here they come again, I thought. It was just like with my cousins—that same sense of helplessness and inevitability. But this time I couldn't face another beating or public humiliation and I panicked, so determined was I not to be touched by anyone I didn't want to touch me.

As they closed in, a thought suddenly occurred to me. If I picked a fight with Rebecca, they might back away. Without saying a word, I shoved my friend, hard. She regained her balance and looked back at me, shocked.

"What did you do that for?" she asked. I can still see her hurt expression and the confusion that flashed across her face.

"Cuz!" I yelled, knowing my would-be assailants were watching. Then, out of the blue, I threw a punch that Yaqui Lopez would have been proud of, making direct and painful contact with Rebecca's jaw. She fell back and began to cry.

I saw her glare up at me in tears, and I was filled with shame. I didn't know who I was anymore. My guilt was immediate and consuming. Before I could apologize, though, I realized that my strategy had worked.

"You crazy, bitch!" one of the bullies cried, laughing. "You just hit your best friend! We ain't gonna mess with *you* no mo." They walked on by.

Later, when I tried to explain and apologize, Rebecca claimed she understood, but our friendship was never the same, and I was devastated that she never forgave me. Who could blame her? I couldn't forgive myself, either. I was disgusted that I had chosen to lash out at her just to avoid being hit myself.

Despite my success in fending off those particular bullies, my insecurity on the playground remained. Other kids continued to provoke and tease me. Sometimes they'd claim it was because I was too skinny or too much of a tomboy or too ethnically unidentifiable. Mostly there'd be no reason at all.

My growing talent in sports provided me with a welcome distraction. It gave me immediate goals, positive attention, and a means of releasing the emotional tension that was rising in me like sap. I especially loved running track. Like Moms, I was good at it and relished the challenge of beating boys.

Then, quite unexpectedly, a boy became a new distraction in my life. His name was Luis, and he was Brazilian. We were eleven years old and crazy about each other. To my surprise, I went through yet another radical personal transformation—from thinking that I never wanted to be anywhere near a boy again to wanting to be with Luis all the time.

Our "dates" were mostly over the phone, while we both watched the same television show. Whenever *Love, American Style* came on, he'd call. Moms would hand me the phone and, already excited, I'd say "Hi, Luis!" Then, together, we'd watch the whole episode, giggling at the jokes, analyzing the plot, and deepening our bond. With him and yet alone: that was as close as I could allow myself to get.

Luis was so sweet, but we were too young to have a relationship. Besides, I had developed very old-fashioned ideas about getting married and having kids. Based on Moms and Pops's marriage, I'd formulated an idealistic model of how a relationship should go before it eventually led to a church.

Or maybe I just wanted to be careful. I'd seen and experienced too much.

I allowed Luis to kiss me several times, little pecks on the lips, but that was it. He was my first kiss. I liked him; he made me laugh. It was fun to have an official "boyfriend," and while I enjoyed being near him, I had a wall up when it came to physical affection.

I never told him about my history. I never mentioned what had happened to me.

Poor Luis, he never even got within a mile of first base, let alone past it. Neither did my next boyfriend, Monty, who lived nearby and had the greenest eyes. He looked as if he could have been in the Jackson 5.

Fond as I was of both boys, I wasn't ready for anything physical. That would have felt too strange. It was too soon and I was way too young.

Even in junior high, when it seemed everyone was doing a lot more than kissing, I was hesitant. I could be quite the flirt, but I didn't want to get too close to anyone. I wanted to wait for the right relationship, and I told myself that I should be in love when I gave it up to the right boy.

I didn't plan on falling in love anytime soon.

Instead I threw my energies into running and—increasingly—fighting for my freedom to walk the streets. I was attending so many track meets that my skin went really dark in the sun. The consequence of that was that I was then beaten up for my color.

Sometimes the girls would get mad at me for having what they called "good hair." Because of my mixed background, if I blow-dried my hair it went straight and not in an Afro like theirs. That alone could trigger a whole new wave of bullying and teasing.

Often there was no reason at all. I'd get attacked out of nowhere. It was always stressful, humiliating, and scary.

I was at the end of my rope, desperate to avoid being hurt anymore. No matter how tough I tried to be or how quick my defensive moves, I couldn't win a fight if I was outnumbered. That was when my survival instinct kicked in. I decided to get even better at outrunning my tormenters. If I could run faster and farther than they could, I could escape.

This served me well in my neighborhood, too, where the threat of violence was also lurking around every corner. I was especially afraid of the East Twenty-first Street Gang, who hung around looking for victims. Moms often sent me to get bread or milk at the corner store, so I had to plan my trips carefully. I'd take the money she gave me, then peek out the front door to check that the coast was clear before running to and from the store as fast as I could, on a self-preservation kick she had no idea about.

Sometimes the gang would catch me and pull my hair until I cried or hurt me so I bruised, and I'd have no choice but to tell Moms and Pops. Whenever I did, they'd confront the bullies and their parents, though both would deny any wrongdoing.

And while the adults talked, one of the bullies would punch a fist into his palm to show me that I'd pay for being a tattletale.

Yet again, I was on my own.

I wasn't the only target; my brothers and other kids were

grabbed and beaten or tied to telephone poles to be slapped or punched. My friend Connie was among them, and we'd often share our miserable stories in the sanctuary of her room. The corner store and my house were the only safe zones; everywhere else, we were fair game.

As I grew into my teens, I began to wear my growing anger and frustration like a suit of armor. I was hormonal and frustrated. I felt victimized, stigmatized, and ignored. Mostly I'd argue with friends, my family, or my teachers just for the sake of it. If they told me the sky was blue, I'd tell them it was red. I'd argue the time of day just to push up against anyone in authority.

Increasingly, I began to direct my anger toward sociocultural issues. We may have lived in the liberal Bay Area, where the law had banned segregation, but society still allowed it.

Our community especially was becoming more and more violent, or perhaps it was my awareness of violence that was growing. We heard frequent reports of fights, stabbings, and race riots. Once in a bleak while there'd be a shooting in our neighborhood, and sirens became a familiar background noise again. Squad cars constantly drove by, and it always seemed like someone was getting arrested on every other street corner.

Despite the police presence, our community felt unsafe, and it was the question of race that seemed to be at the epicenter. The Black Panther Party, founded in Oakland in 1966 when I was a child, was extremely active, and its influence was growing. I became fascinated by it, along with the wider civil rights movement. I longed to stand up in public and raise my fist in the Black Power salute.

Hungry for more information, I read everything I could about Rosa Parks and Harriet Tubman—two women who inspired me with their courage and conviction. I saw them as models for my own emerging aspirations.

Secretly, I reveled in the idea of creating revolution. It made me feel stronger as a young girl on the brink of womanhood.

I was fighting for my right to be heard.

I longed to make some noise.

I wanted a voice.

My biggest problem was that I had a hard time knowing exactly where I was placed within the community. People couldn't easily tell what race I was by looking at me, so I didn't "belong" to anyone.

I knew Pops was born to Mexican parents and Moms was Creole, but in school and on the streets, I was pressed to come up with an answer to the question "Are you black or are you white?" There was no gray. No in-between. "Mixed" wasn't an option—another reason for my persistent discomfort.

I was just me.

I knew I wasn't white, but I wasn't brown, either. I considered myself black, even though many of my relatives looked white or brown.

Faced with such a stark choice, I picked black, because that's where I felt most comfortable. I not only grew up in a largely black community, but my family spoke the slang of the "hood."

I wasn't the only one who was confused in our family. Moms's parents' birth certificates categorized them as "Negro," yet they had fair skin. On my birth certificate, it says "white." My brother Peter Michael came home from school one day and Juan teased him by saying, "Hey, do you know Moms is black?"

Peto replied, "Don't you say Mommy is black, 'cause she's not!" Then he started crying and yelling.

It wasn't until I was in my midteens that I even realized I was Hispanic. Up until then I honestly considered my family African-American—one of those that had a little light and a little dark. The day it hit me that I was something else was the day one of my father's relatives invited me to play soccer on a team named Guadalajara. He took me to a rough part of Oakland for a practice game, and when we got there I couldn't believe how many Mexicans were in the park. I'd never seen so many in one place at the same time. Had they been bused in specially across the border?

"Where did they all come from?" I asked incredulously.

Before he could respond, the team crowded around to meet me and all started talking at once with strong Latino accents. Incredibly, they seemed to know who my father was.

"Oh, your dad is Pedro Escovedo!" they told me. I rarely heard him called Pedro at home and was surprised that they'd heard of him.

When I nodded and smiled and replied in English, they laughed and said, "Speak Spanish!"

"But I'm not Spanish!" I said apologetically.

They looked shocked and said, "Yes you are!"

"I don't think so!" I replied, blushing, but then it dawned on me that I kind of was.

Up until that point I'd attributed being Latino to having an accent and being part of an entirely different culture. My father grew up speaking Spanish because, before the orphanage, he lived with his grandmother in Mexico, and she only spoke Spanish. She made him sleep on the kitchen floor and she kicked him around a lot. He never spoke Spanish after that.

I don't know why I was in denial about being Hispanic. I think I was ashamed of being Mexican because I'd heard that they were the lowest of the Latin race. I'd had to dress in satin to go to a quinceañera (when a cousin turned fifteen), and I went to soccer dances where all the men wore cowboy boots, hats, and jeans and were short in height. But despite that, I liked tall, bowlegged men with Afro haircuts who looked *fine*. I made fun of the Hispanics with my friends until the day it dawned on me that I was Mexican.

Caught in an agony of indecision and still constantly picked on by black girls, I realized that they thought I was white. I couldn't win. I knew the rules of the game, and I also understood that it would only get worse the longer it went on. I tried to run at first, and I also tried to fight back, but I always seemed to be outnumbered.

It got so bad that I took to carrying a screwdriver or a set of keys to defend myself if I had to. Occasionally, I even carried a switchblade knife to wave or point at someone if anything happened, although I'm relieved to say I never used it.

There is an expression that goes, "If you can't beat 'em, join 'em."

Worn down by fear, I reluctantly decided that if I couldn't defend myself, then I might as well try to befriend them. Some kids join gangs because there's no love at home: the gang becomes their family, and they'll die for that family—and often do. Some join because it's the easier option and they like feeling in a position of power.

I joined a gang in order to survive.

My only protection would be to try to outwit them.

One afternoon I was cornered on my way to the store and pinned down—something I hated even more than the beating. The toughest girl in the gang loomed over me and leered, "If you think you're such a good runner, let's see you beat my sister—she's a track star."

I had no choice but to accept the challenge, unless I wanted another beating.

The gang leader appointed someone to stand at one end of the street—the designated finish line—while the rest stood by my rival and me (she was five years older). My heart was pounding before I'd even started the race.

"On your mark, get set, go!" a voice yelled.

We set off, and it was close from the start, but I ran for my life that day. Those few minutes are another slow-motion memory for me: my arms and legs pumping, my hair bouncing, the other end of the street looming in the distance. She was behind me all the way, but in my mind I was running for Olympic gold.

And I won!

From that day on, the gang members didn't bother me nearly as much, and I even won their respect. I didn't know it at the time, but that was my initiation into the East Twenty-first Street Gang.

8. Batter Head

The side of the drum that you hit

Everybody is a star
I can feel it when you shine on me
I love you for who you are
Not the one you feel you need to be

"EVERYBODY IS A STAR"

SLY AND THE FAMILY STONE

The pressure to decide whether I was black or white only intensified when I switched to a new school in the eighth grade. My parents were concerned that the junior high school in our neighborhood was becoming too violent and decided to send me somewhere else.

Under the new equal rights regulations, inner-city children (mostly black) were bused to (better) white schools to fill a government-set racial quota. So I took a bus each morning to Montera Junior High in Oakland Hills, a school formerly consisting of mostly middle- to upper-middle-class white students. I used my cousin's address as my own so that I could qualify.

Being bused every day from home to school, I would sit in the back with the black kids and play beats on the windows of the bus. With so many kids crammed inside, the windows steamed up, so to pass the time I'd write things in the condensation that people could read from the outside. I might write PEACE, LOVE, or SEE YOU LATER. It became so natural for me to write backwards that I could do it with any word I wanted. It was as if I'd always been able to.

At my new school I was always hanging out and skipping class. Moms suspected I was doing this, and while checking up on me one day she caught me smoking openly in front of my school. She was so mad, and she told me she couldn't understand my attitude. All of a sudden she looked sad and asked, "What are you doing with your life?"

"I don't want to be at school!" I told her angrily. "I don't care about class. If I'm going to learn, I want to learn something new every day, not once a week."

She already knew that the only classes I cared about were science and art. I did some drawing and silk-screening, but the subjects were always about freedom and escape. My only other interest was in running track. In my heart I was still determined to make it to the Olympics one day. Life for me during those tricky teenage years was all about competing and staking a claim.

It didn't help that being part of the black contingent bused in to junior high created an acute divide on campus. There were a couple of other races there, as well as some "mixed" like me, but for some reason everyone assumed there were only two. I was frequently asked, "What are you, Sheila? Are you black or are you white? You choose."

Under the black faction's mean tutelage, I vowed that I was black, and my perspective on color became increasingly narrow. Anyone lighter than me deserved to be bullied—that was the rule. My fair-skinned cousin went to the same school, but we hardly ever spoke, because she'd chosen white. Luckily for her, she stayed out of our way.

As I reflect back now on my hateful ignorance, I know that I was really just externalizing my unacknowledged rage. It was easier to turn it against others than to deal with it myself. A militant, I felt the need to take back control, and I did. Control was something I'd not had in years.

Unfortunately, I received support and encouragement from my fellow gang members. Being part of their group gave me a false sense of confidence, and I soon became one of the leaders. They looked up to me, and we fed each other's misguided righteousness.

When we found out that Martin Luther King Jr.'s birthday wasn't an official school holiday, we decided to plan a mass walk-out. We regarded it as our own personal protest against racism, completely failing to appreciate that Dr. King never would have approved of our actions.

Somebody snitched on us, and the school principal announced to the entire school that any student who walked out that day would go directly to juvenile hall. Our little gang was indignant. Defiantly, we tried to sneak out the back through the woods, but the principal had kept his word and arranged for police cars and paddy wagons to surround the school.

Outraged, we rallied together to decide what to do next. Our plans ranged from beating up the girls who'd tattled on us to spray-painting the walls. In the end we decided to initiate a food fight in the cafeteria. When we got there, though, we remembered that several black women worked there, and we didn't want to mess up their workplace.

For some reason, I decided that we should collect rocks and create as much damage to the school building as we could, which is pretty much what happened. Windows were broken, glass cas-ings destroyed, and the people trapped inside were understandably scared. The police moved in to stop us and, before long, a full-fledged riot ensued.

Needless to say, I was in trouble.

With a capital T.

Being summarily kicked out of that school meant I never officially graduated from junior high. Moms and Pops already suspected I was becoming a hothead, but they were shocked to learn that I'd taken it so far. They were furious and, more than that, they were bitterly disappointed.

As ever, Moms took the lead. She negotiated a place for me in a better school in San Leandro for a year, and then she gave me a stark choice. I could either live near the school with my aunt Love, or wake up every day at five A.M. to catch a bus across town.

I adored my aunt Love—she was always such fun to be with. She would lock the doors of her house and not let us leave until we sang her a marching song she especially liked or chimed in with her, *Now is the hour (when we must say good-bye).*

It was Love who took us to Tahoe skiing once and into the country for a hayride. It was Love who took us camping in the valley where Roy Rogers lived. She'd tried to show us the big wide world beyond our funky rental duplexes in the city, but we were freaked out by such wide-open spaces.

By the time Moms gave me her ultimatum, I wasn't getting along with her at all, so Aunt Love seemed like a far preferable option. I also didn't want to wake up that early. So I packed a bag and transferred to my aunt's house and into the ninth grade at San Leandro High.

"This is a clean slate for you, Sheila," Moms warned me the night before I left. "Don't mess it up."

I was in for a major shock.

For the first time in my life I went from being surrounded by people and noise to being by myself at my aunt's house. My two cousins weren't around much, and when they were, they did their own thing. It felt incredibly strange, being in this silent home without parties or music or streams of visitors.

I ran with a pack—hell, I'd been its leader—but suddenly I was packless. I had nobody around to lead. It was such unfamiliar territory, and I was overwhelmed with strange and scary feelings.

I asked myself, *Am I alone?* Yes.

Am I lonely? I don't know.

I wasn't sure of the difference. I just knew I felt friendless and miserable. I didn't even have Connie to talk to anymore.

The student population of San Leandro High was all white, so on my first day I walked into the cafeteria and felt like there was a spotlight on me. Everyone was staring. I felt strange, ugly, and totally out of place. I immediately realized that this is how I'd made all the white kids at my last school feel. Only now I was the new girl, the brown girl—the one being judged.

I'd never felt so alone.

The next morning I packed my own lunch and rode my bike to school. From then on—and for the rest of that school year—I'd ride off campus every lunch break and eat by myself on a park bench or under a tree.

Was I alone? Was I lonely?

Both. Definitely both.

By removing myself from school for the break, I at least felt as if I was in control of my aloneness. I told myself that this was solitude of my own choosing. Needless to say, I had a lot of time to reflect—too much.

I began to wonder what it was like for the other colored students at San Leandro. There was a Latina girl in the twelfth grade, and younger black twins who were constantly picked on. Whenever I saw them being bullied, I felt utterly ashamed of the way I'd behaved at Montera.

It was like looking in a mirror and seeing what it was like on the other side of the glass. With no one around me, I had few distractions. I'd always been so busy telling everybody what to do, but suddenly it was just me and my thoughts. Drowning in remorse, I asked myself the same questions over and over again:

Who am I? Why am I so mad all the time?

Why am I so mean?

I was carrying things around inside that had turned me into someone I didn't like at all. I'd become incredibly angry, and I didn't want to be angry anymore. Secretly I was still ashamed that everything that had happened to me was my fault. It wasn't, but I didn't know that yet.

I was growing tired of my relentless self-analysis, and time spent alone with myself became something to dread. I had music—I'd always had that, although there wasn't music at my new school—but I needed another outlet.

Running provided the only respite for me, since it was the one thing that made me feel truly confident. Physical activity also kept me out of my own head. By focusing on my athletic goals, my mind didn't have the luxury of wandering, as it did during my lonely lunches.

I'd always been good at running, but at San Leandro I took up gymnastics as well, which I quickly grew to love. The school offered great facilities, and I excelled on the balance beam and uneven bars. I also continued to shine at track, breaking records in the 50-yard dash and the 220 and 440 relays, which began to bring me a little respect. I still didn't have any friends, but during that time of awkward adolescence and self-doubt, being a winner made me feel a little more socially comfortable.

For the first time, I enjoyed acknowledgment from my coaches and my peers. Doing well made me feel special. I was different, sure, but I had a talent. This only fueled my commitment even more. I rekindled my childhood ambition to be an Olympian and made the firm decision that one day I would run in the Olympics.

I was shocked to discover that first I'd need a sponsor in order even to train officially. I knew my parents couldn't afford anything like that. So I just kept running in the hope that someone might magically offer me sponsorship. They never did.

It reminded me, too, of the time when I was nine years old and wrote to Yamaha in Japan asking them to endorse me as an artist and provide me with a free drum set. They never did, but my father kept a copy of that letter because it always made him smile, especially my postscript: "P.S. I'm a girl."

Every time I ran, in my mind I was going for gold—the only goal that kept me motivated. I was in it to win it, even if no one else knew that yet.

Soccer had become another outlet and a source of much-needed recognition for me. When I was younger I'd been invited to play as a forward for an all-girl team that wasn't affiliated with my school. They'd heard I was a good runner and were delighted when I picked up the sport so quickly. Once I got the ball and knew how to control it, I adapted well. No one could catch me.

What I loved even more about playing was winning, which was everything to the team. My competitive spirit really kicked in then, and soon nobody could beat us. Helping them achieve that gave me the greatest satisfaction.

Over time and taking life day by day, with the help of my love of sports and my own intense reflections, I came to a new understanding of how I should try to get along in this world, and how I should treat not only others but myself. During this period of searing self-examination, I became more and more willing to look at myself and what motivated me. But it wasn't until I received some generous words from an older Latina girl at school that I tried to make reparations for my sins.

I had admired her from afar. She looked a bit like me and could have been one of my relatives. Out of the blue she approached me in the hall one day and said, "I know how it is. If anyone bothers you, let me know and I'll handle it. I've got your back. We have to stick together; there are only two of us."

That made me think about the twins, so I sought them out and repeated, "I know how it is. If you need anything, let me know. I've got your back."

A few days later I spotted some boys teasing them about their hair, so I stepped in and told them to cut it out. "How would you feel if you looked different from everyone else?" I asked them. "Stop being so mean! What did they ever do to you?" I was so hurt and offended on the girls' behalf that my conviction must have made an impact. The boys backed off.

I'd been so mad at my mother for sending me away to San Leandro, but I had to accept eventually that she'd been right. As much as I'd hated having to leave my gang, my friends, and my school, moving there was a gift, because it turned my life around. Being on my own sparked a transformation in me. I realized for the first time that I had a choice about how I could behave.

A lot of kids stay in gangs or keep committing crimes because their friends do. Being away from all that gave me a different perspective. I had a chance to move forward and move on. I didn't just have to accept that this was how my life was going to be.

I grew wings.

Flying high, I learned to face my demons, challenge their power over me, and start to put them behind me. Accepting that began the long process of bringing me back to the values of love and tolerance that Moms and Pops had modeled for me all along.

9. Resonance

The quality of a sound being
deep and reverberating

Music has no color, has no lines
It's a language that reaches all nations
We bring this gift of love for everyone to share
Just take some time to show someone you care

"PEACE AND JOY"

THE E FAMILY

Music remained my lifeline, and its umbilical pull on me only intensified during the months that I was away from home. Surrounded by silence, I realized how much I missed noise.

I also came to appreciate that playing music and being around my crazy family made me happier than anything else. From the day I first tapped along in time to Pops on my lap to the night I stood on the stage with him at Sweet's, music was what brought me back to a place of serenity and safety.

Whenever music filled my ears, I could lose myself in the rhythms and the beats that reconnected me with the vibrations that had shaped me in my mother's womb.

Living at my aunt's house I found music in everything around me, just as when I'd played with Moms's pots and pans. I found comfort in slapping out a rhythm with my hairbrush on the wall of my room or beating a rhythm on a trash can. I also had more conventional access to music, of course, and played records and listened to the radio. And I didn't much care about what kind of music I listened to—my tastes were expanding.

I loved Chicago and Creedence Clearwater Revival, the Jacksons and the Beach Boys. I was still crazy about Motown and discovered the musical genius of Stevie Wonder. When I found out he was blind it seemed so incredible to me, until I realized that I often closed my eyes when I played.

James Brown never lost his impact on me—and his 1968 number "Say It Loud—I'm Black and I'm Proud" really resonated. I thought of him as a modern-day Sammy Davis Jr.—the way he could sing and dance, he had so much soul. Plus he had two drummers who had to watch, call cues, and make signs to each other. I thought, How do they do that?

Feeling homesick for the crowded, noisy spaces I'd grown up with, I decided one day that it was time to go home. My lesson had been learned. I thanked Aunt Love and packed my few belongings.

I was still attending the San Leandro school, so when I moved back home I had to get up at five A.M. every day to catch the bus. But it was worth it just to be back in the bosom of my family. Moms and Pops, Juan, Peter Michael, and little Zina welcomed me with open arms and open hearts.

The best part about being back home was being around live music on a daily basis. That truly fed my soul. Things seemed to be much better financially, too. My uncle Coke and my father were still in the Escovedo Brothers band, but in 1971 they'd also joined a hot local band called Santana, which cleverly blended Latin jazz, rock, and jazz.

A charismatic Mexican called Carlos Santana, who often came around our house to hang out and jam, fronted it. He was ten years older than me, and the first person I really came to think of as "famous." Carlos and his band had played "Soul Sacrifice" at the 1969 Woodstock music festival, which was filmed by a documentary team that went on to win an Oscar and made the Californian band instantly recognizable around the world.

Woodstock was such a big deal in Oakland—everyone talked about it for years afterward; we all wished we'd been there. And it was doubly cool to have a local band do so well on such a global stage. Scores of other bands started up to mimic their sound or play Santana covers.

Carlos had been born in Mexico and was inspired by his father, a mariachi violinist. Until he became successful he'd worked in a series of local bands just like everyone else and sometimes washed dishes in a restaurant. He'd been especially influenced by my "godfather," Tito Puente, and by our friend Eddie Palmieri, which is how he came to meet my uncle Coke and Pops.

I thought Carlos was so handsome, with his big brown eyes and curly dark hair. He spoke softly, and I remember feeling a little shy around him. When he asked Pops and Uncle Coke to join him on tour and in the recording studio, that was a big deal, and we all felt the consequences.

Riding high, my father and uncle ended up working with Santana on and off for the next three years. Pops was grateful and honored, but he still had his own dreams to follow, so eventually he and Coke left Santana to form their own band, Azteca.

My little brothers and I were blissfully unaware of the machinations of the music industry, with all its politics and ego clashes.

All we knew was that we loved jamming with friends. Still inspired by the Osmonds and the Jacksons, along with the Temptations and the Supremes, we worked out a whole new bunch of songs and dance routines. Buying the latest hit records continued to be our passion, and we sometimes pooled the allowances we earned doing chores to buy what we wanted.

To do our musical heroes justice, we knew we needed matching outfits, so we threw together what we had or asked a neighbor to make up some color-coordinated clothes for us.

I look back at some of the photos of us from that time and laugh out loud. What were we thinking? For one gig we wore the strangest combination. My friend Anna Marie worked at the Kaiser Hospital as an intern nurse, and she managed to find us three sets of green scrubs. For some unknown reason, we accessorized them with boots and belts, cowboy boots (with a Cuban heel), or platforms. We thought we were so cool.

Another time I wore flowing white dress pants with a swooping-neckline top that draped at the sides. It was sleeveless, because I'd discovered early on that I couldn't bear to have my arms covered too closely when I played congas. The fabric brushed against my skin when I was moving my hands so fast and became a distraction, so my arms had to be free.

To complement my look, Juan and Peter Michael wore white bell-bottoms and shirts with thin black ties.

That white dress was probably the classiest outfit I ever had back then, and it made me feel feminine for the first time. Suddenly I was aware of my own sexuality and comfortable with it. I wasn't just a skinny fourteen-year-old with no idea what to do with her own body.

I can't remember the name of the first band we formed, but I do recall we only played Mexican music. We also jammed in a few local garage bands. My brothers worked hard to keep on top of their game, but I was lazy and never rehearsed—I just got up and played.

Juan, especially, had to work harder to be a musician than Peter Michael or me. He just didn't seem to have the same feel for it in those early years (although he's sure made up for that now!). There was a hit song at the time called "One" by Three Dog Night, which had the line, "One is the loneliest number that you'll ever know." Apart from the fact that it sounded like they were singing "Juan," the words of that song always reminded me of my brother, the first boy in our family, and made me sad.

Growing up, Juan was accident-prone and often got hurt. He became partially blind from a rare disease, so he missed a lot of school because he was always in the hospital, which made him a little insecure. He always seemed to be by himself, and I knew how lonely that could be.

After I was sent away to Aunt Love's, he took up with the East Twenty-first Street Gang. He gave up the sports he'd always loved and started getting into fights instead. By the time I returned home, he and Moms were clashing frequently, and she was tough on him because she was so scared of where he was heading. All that he had left to save him was music.

I decided to be a better big sister to him, so I persuaded him to come to the pool hall with me, where we'd try to beat my uncles for money. We spent much of our teens in those halls and both became mean players, but our uncles were professional gamblers and unbeatable. We didn't have a hope in hell of beating them.

Peter Michael had started off being the cute one, and that's how he remained. He did well in hurdles and the high jump at school, and everyone loved him. He probably got into as much trouble as Juan and me, but he was slick about it because he always cried if he

THE BEAT OF MY OWN DRUM

was caught, and—as the baby—he got away with everything. He was definitely the favorite for a long time, and no one could argue with that when he looked so adorable.

As a matter of fact, he is still Moms's favorite, although she won't admit to it!

Like Juan and me, though, music was to become Peter Michael's one true love, and he went on to be an Emmy-nominated music director, composer, and musician.

My sister, Zina, was still very young at the time, so she tended to be home with Moms. She never seemed to share our passion for playing music and was always destined to follow her own very different path. While she has a beautiful singing voice (she sings the bridge on some of our later songs) and dynamite dancing abilities (you can spot her in a few of my videos, some of which she choreographed), she didn't choose to become a professional entertainer like the rest of us.

Pops likes to say, "That's because she's the only one with any sense!"

Ask Zina why she didn't become a musician and she'll tell you it wasn't her calling. She loves music as much as we all do, but I suspect she simply wanted to get away from all the noise, not make more of it!

It can't have been easy for her to be born into a house filled with so much sound.

Not only were most of our friends musicians, but there were other musical families we hung out with, too, like the Guzmans, Floreses, and Godinezes. It seemed like everyone we knew had a band. We all played together, exchanged licks, and created temporary bands with a fluid membership that often depended more on our abilities to recruit than our musical talent.

If someone had equipment or a place to rehearse, they were in. No audition required. After a few months of playing around, though, we decided to up our game and try to get ourselves into a proper band.

We'd heard from one of our friends, Tony Flores, about a group that was looking for a percussion section, so we hopped on a bus across town to audition. The band was headed by a girl named Martha, and it primarily played the Mexican music known as cumbia, which we weren't crazy about. But it was a *real* band, and that was good enough for us.

For the audition, Juan was on bongos, Peter Michael was on congas, and Tony was on guitar. I played the band's own set of drums (which I wasn't so well versed in, but I did it so that we'd stand a better chance). By the end of our audition, the band said they wanted us to join them, but they already had a guitar player, a bass player, and a conga player.

"No problem," said Tony. "I'll switch to timbales."

That left Peter Michael out on a limb, so the band decided not to take him. We felt kind of bad, but he said he understood, and we all hoped we might get him in later on. When we returned home and told our folks what had happened, though, they weren't having any of it.

They were perfectly clear: "Either you're all in or none of you are in!"

Our faces fell. Juan and I begged them to understand. "But they already have a conga player. If we tell them that, we'll all get turned down."

"Too bad," Moms and Pops said firmly. "You guys stick together. You're family."

Even though we were worried that sticking up for our kid brother might ruin our chance, we reluctantly agreed that joining the band without him would be wrong. We'd grown up knowing that family came first; we looked out for each other, we resolved things within the family, and we tried to honor each other.

So back we went with our tails between our legs to explain that we were a package deal. The band must have respected our decision, because they just shrugged their shoulders and said, "Okay. I guess we'll have two conga players, then."

Shortly afterward, we were booked for our first gig—a quinceañera. The night went well, and when we were paid ten dollars each we felt immensely, stupidly rich.

The band was doing okay, but it wasn't really playing the music I liked, so I was excited when I got a phone call from a guitarist named Joe Cano, who led a local band called Grito (which means "yell").

"We heard your dad plays with Santana."

"Yes, he does," I replied proudly.

"We have a piano player, a guitarist, a bass player, and two percussionists," Joe told me. "But we need a drummer." Grito also wanted to perfect a Santana sound, so—with Pops and Coke's connections—I was a valuable commodity.

"Come for an audition tomorrow afternoon and bring your drums," Joe added.

Taking a cue from my mother, I agreed without hesitation. Her attitude to life had rubbed off on me so much that if anybody had asked me, "Do you know how to pole-vault?" my answer would be, "Sure! Show me how and I'll try it. Let's go!"

I'd said yes to Joe even though I had no idea where I'd find a drum set on such short notice. The only sets I had access to were owned by musicians who came to our house, but they were all working and needed them.

Thinking quickly, I asked another of my cousins, Maurice, if I could borrow his. He was bemused. "I've been playing for two years. You're fourteen years old and you've barely touched the drums, but you're the one with the audition?"

"I guess I'm just lucky!" I replied.

He laughed. "How are you going to audition as a drummer when you don't even know how to set them up on your own?"

"Can you show me how to do it so that I look like I know what I'm doing?" I replied.

He said yes, and when I arrived for my audition I took special pride in my effortless drum setup, having practiced it to perfection with Maurice. I was hoping they'd notice how quickly and comfortably I arranged every piece, just like a pro.

Once I was settled on my stool, the band asked me to join them in a Santana number.

"Sure. No problem."

Luckily I knew all of Santana's songs because Pops rehearsed so regularly with Carlos at our house. Once the rest of the band started playing, I just listened and felt my way and played what I thought sounded right.

Whatever I did must have worked, because the guys kept nodding and looking at each other with broad grins. By the end of the first song, I'd been offered the job.

I said yes, again not thinking about what that might mean. The challenge excited me. I couldn't wait to test my skills, which had barely been warmed up playing in the little Mexican band.

I guess I just knew that if I wanted something bad enough, I'd be able to do it.

No problem.

Through music, sports, and my family, I'd developed a tough inner drive. I was prepared to step through any door that opened to me and make decisions that gave me control over my own outcomes.

Nobody else would ever control me again.

I think of this overwhelming confidence as the blessing that came from a curse.

10. Quarter Note

A note played for one-fourth the length of a full note

We will go to the moon. We will go to the moon and do other things. Not because they are easy, but because they are hard.

JOHN F. KENNEDY

Joining Grito was a major step up from my first band, but it didn't have its own PA system (a hot commodity), which was a disadvantage. When a new drummer arrived in town with his own system, Joe suggested we ask him to join us, as we'd get more gigs.

Without flinching, I made the switch to playing percussion alongside the other conga player, an original band member whose name was Tam.

The interesting difference for me by then was that when I sat down to play the congas I realized that, as a young woman (and not a kid standing on a stool), I had to sit sideways or wear pants to keep my dignity. I also found it hard to play in high heels, but I adapted my posture to accommodate them rather than kick them off.

All of my chosen instruments were extremely demanding physically. I played with all four limbs, and I often sang at the same time. With the congas you have to use your legs to hold the drums in place, and when I play my arms and hands are in constant motion.

I used to look down at them and think they moved as fast as a hummingbird's wings.

Playing congas involves passion and power. You're the time-keeper of the band, and you can't let sore hands or an aching back slow you down.

Although I was young and still at school, I started playing clubs with Grito two or three nights a week. We were managed by one of my mother's brothers, Uncle Harold, who owned a nightclub called Garderes International with two other uncles, Kookababy and Lulu. These men were all professional gamblers and pool players who worked in a meat market too—a sideline that permanently infused their clothes with the smell of bacon.

Legally, I was too young to be allowed into clubs (except Garderes, where nobody minded how old I was). Uncle Harold would persuade the owners to let me sit in a back room or at the side of the stage until it was time for me to play.

"My father's been taking me to places like this since I was a baby!" I protested, but I still had to do as Uncle Harold said.

As Grito got more exposure, we were booked for several parties in the East Bay area, as well as gigs at venues like the Eagles hall on Thirty-fifth Avenue.

Aside from the hassle I sometimes got from the club owners, I also began to attract a different kind of attention for being the only female in the band. I didn't want to overshadow any of my fellow musicians, but Grito was definitely getting a buzz, and a lot of it was because of me. Knowing that made me proud and secretly brought back the exhilarating feeling I'd enjoyed beating boys at track meets.

Not only was I doing what any male musician could do, but I was doing it as well—or even better.

Grito entered several battle-of-the-bands contests, where instead of trophies the winners earned bragging rights. The great Latin bands around inspired a lot of the local bands at the time, such as Malo or Sapo. Sometimes our band won, and other times bands like Secate won. Being highly competitive, we kept tabs on who we felt were the best musicians and constantly tried to learn from them, hoping one day we could reach their caliber.

There is a Bay Area expression—*hecka* or *hella*, which is another way of saying "really" or "extremely." We'd say of a great musician, "That brotha is hecka bad!" or "He's hecka fine!" It became a kind of band slang, and we used it all the time.

My brothers liked what we were doing in Grito, but they favored the percussive chops of bands whose members included Dale Villavicencio, from a sizzling Latin salsa band, or Arthur Wong—a funky Asian drummer—who was in a Tower of Power knockoff band. Scott Roberts was another hecka good player and was in the hottest band around, Salsa de Berkeley.

In the mid-1970s, there was a real divide in terms of sound between bands from Berkeley and Oakland, despite the fact that the geographical distance was minimal. To us it seemed like the Berkeley bands, which grew from jam sessions on the UC Berkeley campus, were more influenced by the hippie scene. They used a lot of African percussion, steel drums, and *shekeres*, whereas Oakland music had more of an R&B feel, with a focus on bass and drums.

Whatever the difference, Oakland definitely had something in the water. In the seventies alone there must have been at least a hundred bands that originated from the Bay Area. We would excitedly talk about the Grateful Dead, the Pointer Sisters, Graham Central Station, Tower of Power, Cold Blood, and, of course, Santana, as well as Jefferson Starship, Journey, the Sons of Champlin,

Creedence Clearwater Revival, Sylvester, and Sly and the Family Stone.

I was determined to see as many of these great new artists as I could so that I could absorb their individual sounds. I couldn't afford tickets, and I was underage for the clubs anyway, but I wasn't my mother's daughter if I was going to let that stand in my way.

Sneaking into a venue was easy. I learned early on to just act the part. If I avoided eye contact with security and strutted my stuff like I was *somebody* and knew where I was going, then I was rarely questioned. If anyone quizzed my age or my right to be there, I'd lie and tell them I was on the guest list or flash them my fake ID.

"I'm Sheila Escovedo . . . what do you mean my name's not there? You guys forgot to put it down again? Well, that's your problem." If that didn't work, I'd deliver my trump card: "I'm Pete Escovedo's daughter. You know who he is, don't you? He plays with Santana!"

I sure was bold, but a Gardere gets what a Gardere wants.

Once allowed in, I'd saunter over to the side of the stage—and by that I mean the curtained-off area of floor in the middle of the room. If I could, I'd get right on the side of the stage, or better still, onstage.

There I'd stand proudly with my Afro (I'd long since stopped straightening my hair, because everyone had a 'fro), my face dusted with a little blush, and my lips coated in my favorite gloss—baby oil. I'd wear bell-bottoms, platform shoes, and a halter top—no bra. I modeled myself after my mother, who never wore a bra, either. It wasn't in homage to the women's-lib burn-the-bra movement—it was just what we did. My image was influenced by a mix of pop fashion, seventies music, and counterculture. I must have looked such a product of the times: soul sister, hippie, *conguera*, and Bay Area fashionista.

Sometimes when the band started playing I'd stick a platformed boot a few inches past the curtained boundary. That way I felt like I was actually on the stage, even if nobody else knew it. In my mind, my foot (and therefore the rest of me) was performing with some musical greats. I longed to get all of me onto that forum, preferably behind the congas.

I'd stare, wide-eyed, at one of the musicians, telepathically urging him to turn and recognize me as Pete Escovedo's daughter and invite me to join them. Sometimes I was less subtle. I'd wave to one of the guys I knew and plead, "Hey! Let me on! I could play the cowbell! How about the congas? Just one solo, guys?" But they rarely let me join them.

If I was lucky I might see Raul Rekow, one of the baddest *congueros* at the time and a man who really inspired me to play in a particular way. When he sat down to play the congas I especially took note, because he used his belt from his pants to hold the drum in place. He sat high and slanted the drum toward the audience, which allowed him to use his wrist to play fast—a method that called to me. He's the reason I play that way. It gives me a much better grip, which allows my wrists to have more power and speed. Since I was small in stature, this also helped me to pick up the drum with my legs to get a different tone, in the way that a lot of musicians from New York did.

One day I heard the news that Larry Graham (from Sly and the Family Stone) and his Graham Central Station band were rehearsing somewhere in the Fifty-first Street neighborhood, so I took a bus to try to find them. I wandered around several blocks, listening hard, until I heard some great music coming out of one of the buildings. It had to be them—it was all bass and drums and sounded funky.

I banged on the door and tried to get inside so I could see them rehearse up close, but they weren't allowing visitors. Undeterred,

I bought some chips and soda from the corner store, sat on the sidewalk, and let the music in—a rapt audience of one.

Crystals of a dream were forming.

I was still enjoying playing in Grito and being part of a team. There was an added attraction, too—Tam, whom I'd started dating and who was my first love. He was a year younger than me, with long beautiful hair, and he played congas better than me. My parents knew and liked him, which only made me love him more.

I am thankful to this day that the first boy I loved after my horrible childhood experiences was kind, gracious, and gentle. He could really have messed me up even more, but he didn't.

Bless you for that, Tam.

Music was instilled in everything Tam and I did together—rehearsing, jamming, playing, hanging out, listening to records, and sharing our musical experiences. I was always jumping up to join in. I listened closely to what and how everyone else played and tried to add something a little different each time. As my passion increased, I began experimenting with new rhythms I didn't even realize I knew.

Tam had much more experience than me, so he'd tell me what to do. I'd begin just as he suggested, but would always work something cool into it. Afterward, he'd say, "Hey, I didn't teach you that! Where did you learn that?"

I'd shrug and shake my head. "Pops, I guess."

In all those years of watching my father play, I'd been like a little sponge soaking up his rhythms. Now that I was expressing myself freely whenever I lost myself to the music, all those different sounds and techniques began to seep out of me. After a while, I started looking at our band differently. I realized that I was moving forward musically, but they were standing still. It was weird—they even started sounding a little immature to me.

A big part of the problem was that everyone was getting high all the time, which was never my scene. I did try weed and cigarettes, but both made me cough, and that scared me. I'd grown up in a musicians' house in the 1960s, so I was familiar with pot, but I also knew I didn't care for it. I didn't like the smell, I didn't like the taste, and it only ever made me paranoid. A lot of my friends embraced it wholeheartedly, though, and were often in such a funk that they couldn't play a note, which only made me increasingly frustrated. Once they started smoking weed, we could forget about how we were supposed to sound. They thought we were just like Santana, but that was the dope talking.

I, on the other hand, wanted to get up and do something.

"Let's learn some new songs or shoot some pool!" I'd encourage, but they'd lie around red-eyed and giggling. They never knew I was faking taking hits off a joint; I never wanted to let them know how much I hated getting high. Frustrated and feeling peer pressure, I'd tell them, "Hey, this is our time, guys. We're crazy if we miss out on it!"

Around that time my father was out on the road a lot with Uncle Coke in either Santana or Azteca, which had grown into an eighteen-piece band and included several Santana musicians. I missed being able to talk to him about how I felt, and I began to feel lonely musically, as if I wasn't in the right place.

I didn't know how to broach my restlessness with Tam; all I knew was that I was ready for a change. I had no idea how that might happen—I just wanted more. Tam didn't sense my unease until I was wooed by a couple of other bands and accepted some offers for session work.

"You and I need to stick together," he insisted.

I said okay, but I remember thinking: "No, that's not right. Nobody else is gonna want two conga players." Plus I knew it was time for me to leave. There was no space for me to grow.

A few more bands approached me, asking me to "enhance"

their sound. What they didn't say was that they also wanted my marketability. "Sheila's really starting to make a name for herself," people kept telling Pops and Uncle Harold. "It's so rare to see a young woman play percussion and do it so well."

It surprised me that people were surprised. Once I looked into it, I discovered that in ancient cultures most of the drummers were women, as proved by archaeologists working in Egypt and the Mediterranean. It was a tradition passed from mother to daughter—they were handing on the spiritual heartbeat of life. But that ritual died out over the centuries, and men took over.

By the time I started slapping my hands on the skin of a drum as a little girl in the 1960s, female drummers were few and far between. The ones who were around were often derided and struggled to be taken seriously, including the wholesome Karen Carpenter and a lady named Moe Tucker from the Velvet Underground, who played standing up.

In my family I'd never experienced any of the prejudices of being in a "man's world" playing a "man's instrument." It was only when people started commenting that I realized there could even be a gender attached to any musical instrument. What makes drums more male than a piano or a guitar, for example? I didn't understand the logic. In my house the instruments were for everyone to play—boys, girls, children, parents, great-grandparents, men, women. Nobody cared as long as you could keep time (or have a good time).

Once I discovered that I was considered unusual, though, I became even more committed to the instrument I'd chosen as a teenager. I'd never set out to be a pioneer, but the indomitable Gardere spirit kicked in the minute I realized I was doing something out of the ordinary.

I suffered such agonies over what to do about Grito, though. I dearly wanted to remain loyal to my band and was anxious that they'd think badly of me if I abandoned them after they'd given me such a great start. I was also worried about what leaving might do to my relationship with Tam, whom I really cared for, but music was eclipsing the affection I had for him.

Deep down, I knew I had to honor my burning desire to go further, do better, and expand my horizons. My path to the future was set.

I didn't fully understand it back then, but music was to become the one true love of my life.

11. Shuffle

A rhythmic motif based on
a shuffle dance step

If you feel it moving
Deep inside your soul
Don't stop that rhythm
It's gonna make you dance

"IT'S GONNA MAKE YOU DANCE"

THE E FAMILY

The opportunity to move on came far sooner than I expected. Azteca was doing very well and had been opening for Stevie Wonder, the Temptations, and Earth, Wind & Fire. The new lineup had also been signed by Columbia/CBS Records and was touring to promote its debut album, *Azteca*, which was released in 1972.

As part of that world tour, they were booked to perform at San Francisco's Civic Center at a huge rally, but a few days before the gig Azteca's conga player, Victor Pantoja, fell sick and had to drop out.

Pops was freaking out. Azteca had been the first band of its kind to blend different genres of music in an orchestral setting with a strong undertone of Latin music. In what became known as "brown sound," it had some of the best Latin jazz, rock, and soul musicians from the Bay Area, including drummers, vocalists, guitarists, horn players, keyboard players, and percussionists. There was Paul Jackson on bass and Lenny White on drums, Uncle Coke, of course, and Santana guitarist Neal Schon, along with many other gifted musicians.

Even if Pops could have found a replacement player on such short notice, he wouldn't know the music.

I, however, did.

I'd heard that band rehearse so often at home and had jammed with them almost every time. I knew every one of their songs by heart.

"Let me sit in for Victor." I pleaded, but Pops laughed at me.

"This is a really important gig," he told me, shaking his head. "Besides, you're just a kid."

"I'm fifteen!" I protested. (I look at my nieces and nephews now who are the same age and I think I must have been crazy).

Pops laughed again. "You're fifteen years old and you don't know anything!"

"I know all the songs!"

"There'll be three thousand people in the audience."

That made me even more determined.

"Great," I said with a grin. "I can do it."

No matter how much I begged, Pops insisted that I was too young and inexperienced. Realizing he wasn't going to change his mind, I went to work on Moms. "You always taught me that I can do anything I want," I reminded her. "Well, I really want this and you know I can do it. Please talk to Pops?"

I nagged and nagged until I wore her down. My father didn't

stand a chance once Moms was on my side. She and I sat Pops down, and together we convinced him to give me a shot. Since he couldn't see any other options, he allowed me to audition for him in our living room. He'd seen a few of my gigs, but none lately, so he wasn't really aware of how much I had grown musically.

Whatever I played that day for my father must have done the trick. "Okay, okay," he said, a little less testily. "You've got the gig."

I'd always been nervous about playing, but that night I suddenly felt butterflies dancing around in my stomach for the first time since Sweet's. It was almost a comfort, because butterflies had long been an important symbol to me. Whenever I saw one, I felt a little bit happier. They struck me as such extraordinary creatures, bringing otherworldly magic to the most ordinary of days.

Maybe it was their remarkable transformation that resonated so profoundly with me.

My butterflies would become a frequent, and welcome, part of my life.

Although I'd yearned to be on a big stage, I'd never imagined playing in front of three thousand people as part of a grown-up band that had just signed a major record deal. I desperately wanted to make Pops proud and show him that he'd made the right decision. Despite my crippling nerves, I was also exhilarated, because I somehow knew that things were about to change for me, forever.

The show started, and we were midway through the first song before I was finally comfortable enough to look out into the audience and soak up the experience. People liked us! They were swaying and dancing and clapping in time. The band sounded amazing live with speakers, and its brilliant musicianship elevated my conga playing exponentially, forcing me to stretch my talent and rise to the occasion.

I could hardly believe that I was sharing a stage again with my father and his band. My memories of being at Sweet's when I was five were foggy. At the Civic Center, in front of all those people, I was determined to remain fully present to the moment and take it all in.

Musically, I wanted not only to blend in but also to enhance what was already something wonderful. I remained in the pocket but added a lick here and there, which seemed to sound okay. It was all going great until Pops suddenly turned to me and yelled, "Take a solo!"

I froze.

What did he mean?

How long? How fast?

I wasn't ready for all eyes to be on me.

I shot him a panicked look that said, "What, me? Now?"

He placed the palm of his hand on his chest as if to say, "Play from your heart."

I understood then, and I nodded.

This was it.

I closed my eyes and began to rhythmically slap the congas with palms that were already glowing.

When you get behind a big band like that, the power of it takes over. I'd only ever played with seven or eight musicians before, but with Azteca there were almost twenty of us on the stage. In their talented company I was exposed to something truly creative that had never happened to me before. The power and musicianship of that band was overwhelming.

I took off playing and was quickly transported to a different zone. I played completely spontaneously as I felt the moment and the emotion and the spirituality connect deeply with the music in my heart.

In the next few minutes I had what I can only describe as an out-of-body experience. I felt like I was looking down on myself from about twenty feet up. When I finally opened my eyes toward the end of my solo, I didn't even know I was on a stage until I suddenly realized that thousands of eyes were watching my every move.

I'd been somewhere else entirely.

I looked out to the audience and saw them jumping in time to the beat. My hands were on fire, and I was playing in a way I'd never known I could. My hands were in charge, as if they were telling me what to do. They were moving so fast I couldn't even follow them with my eyes.

I looked across at Pops and could see he was holding back tears. Mine started to prick the backs of my eyes. I remember thinking, *This is what heaven is supposed to feel like.*

I wanted to feel like that every day of my life.

As I finished my solo, I looked around me in a daze, as if to say, "What just happened?"

The audience went wild. The sounds of their screams and stomps, cheers and whistles gave me the chills right down to my nail beds. From my head to my toes I was shaking. I couldn't speak. I could barely breathe.

My father stood at his timbales equally stunned. He couldn't believe what he had just witnessed.

I don't remember much of the rest of the concert, but by the time we eventually made it backstage, Pops was beaming with pride. For a while we were both without words, hugging and crying. Finally he said: "You have it, baby! I had no idea you had that in you!"

I laughed and cried at the same time. I didn't know what to feel; there were so many emotions racing through me simultaneously.

The rest of the band congratulated me one by one. I was so happy and excited all at once. God had given me a glimpse of paradise, and I finally knew that this was to be my true calling—my gift.

I had wanted to be an astronaut ever since I watched a man walk on the moon, but now I'd found a different way to go into space.

The moon was mine for the taking.

No matter how many other dreams or goals I'd had before, *this* was what I was supposed to do.

12. Paradiddle

Four even strokes played in order

Fly me to the moon
And let me play among the stars
Let me see what spring is like
On Jupiter and Mars

"FLY ME TO THE MOON"
BART HOWARD

I couldn't wait to share my life-changing decision with Moms and Pops. As soon as we got home after my first-ever concert, I blurted: "I'm quitting school to join Pops's band!"

They both looked at me like I was crazy.

"You're in the tenth grade—you have to graduate!" Moms cried.

Pops was distraught. I was never meant to be a percussionist like him. It was such a hard life and one he hadn't wished on any of his children. He knew it would be even tougher for a girl.

"What can we do to keep you interested in school?" he asked hopefully. "Hey, you love to draw! I'll buy you some new art supplies. We'll pay for extra classes!"

I shook my head. My mind was made up, and a shiny set of colored pencils couldn't change that.

I reminded them that the only job I'd ever held down was helping a friend fold clothes in her store at Christmas. "I'm not cut out for a regular job, and I've never been happy at school."

I didn't tell them that for most of my childhood, I'd never even wanted to be called on or asked questions I didn't know the answers to. I was scared to be wrong, and the classroom setting made me feel like I was drowning in a pool of unknowns.

Reading aloud was also challenging for me because I was so insecure about my comprehension (something that lingered into my late twenties). I hid my report cards, hoping my parents would forget to ask about them.

Some subjects held my attention, but for the most part I didn't feel confident in any academic setting. Aside from sports, art and fashion were the only subjects I cared about, and even they were directly related to my love of music. Moms and Pops always dressed up for gigs, and from an early age I'd noticed every detail of their clothing—the cut, the fabric, the pattern, the fit. They wore a lot of leather and suede and accessorized them with funky fabrics.

They dressed us up a lot, too—I had some pretty dresses for special occasions, and Moms thought it was cute to put Juan and Peter Michael in matching outfits when they were younger so that they looked like twins. It was probably the cheapest option.

In fifth grade, I snuck into my mother's closet one morning and put on her black jumpsuit with elephant pants, pinning them up to fit me. I walked around school that day like a fashion model. But my moment on the "catwalk" ended abruptly when Moms caught me sneaking in after school and was none too pleased.

Music influenced my fashion choices, too. My brothers and I loved platform shoes and bell-bottoms and would take the bus to

Berkeley to find hip clothing. Even in the thrift stores I was always on the lookout for something that would make me look sexy from the waist up.

As a percussion player I couldn't wear skirts or dresses, so I'd try to come up with a look that integrated the coolest pants or shorts. At one point I wore a special creation designed out of a pair of denims cut at the knees, with the hems tucked into my socks.

The academic side of my schooling didn't interest me nearly as much. The lower my grades fell, the worse school became for me. Along with the other losers, I'd been relegated to the "portables"— pseudo-buildings at the far end of the campus for students who struggled academically.

I'd passed too many miserable hours in there to ever want to return.

Some of my teachers did take an interest and frequently reminded me I didn't have long before graduation. They fought hard to keep me in, and—sensing my unease—they even gave me special assignments that let me write about the "real world."

I went through the motions and, to please them (and at the insistence of my parents), I didn't leave school immediately—even if mentally I was on my way out. My attendance was patchy, but I did go to art class, especially silk-screening, because it allowed me to design T-shirts. I even made a silk-screen print of Sammy Davis Jr., which was one of the only things I left school with that I was proud of.

Ironically, I was a lot more socially comfortable among my classmates once I knew I was leaving. Being in a band meant that I was suddenly regarded as "cool." I felt in control of my life for the first time, holding my own with professional musicians and being propelled into my future by a newfound sense of purpose. I half-heartedly finished the last of my assignments, which allowed me to pass from tenth to eleventh grade, then I left and I never went back.

Many years later I was offered an honorary GED from Oakland High School. I thanked them for the thought but turned them down flat. I felt it would be a disservice to those who'd stayed, studied, and made the grade. I wanted to earn my GED authentically or not at all.

I truly regret not graduating. I missed out on graduation from junior high school because I left Montera after the riot, and I didn't graduate from high school, either. It wasn't until much later when I saw my nephews and nieces graduating that I realized what I'd lost out on. I sincerely wish I'd stuck it out so that I could have earned my high school diploma and fully experienced the ceremony itself with its prom party—a significant rite of passage in any teenager's life.

Earning my GED is on my bucket list of things to do—and I'm going to do it, if only to make Moms and Pops proud of me. I might even throw a party and turn it into a real high school graduation ceremony. What was to eventually become my glamorous life may have given me a unique "real world" education, but I wish I'd realized at fifteen years old that the real world could have waited and that I'd forever regret denying myself a complete education.

Thankfully, Pops finally accepted my decision, because he'd also quit school at fifteen to follow his musical heart. Once he'd seen me perform, he recognized the passion in me and he honored it because he'd felt the same way. True to his word, he allowed me to take Victor's place in the band and go on tour with Azteca.

I no longer had to dip my toe over the line of the stage.

I was on it!

When Azteca was booked to play some shows in Colombia, I thought I might faint from excitement. I'd never even left California before, and I couldn't wait for my first chance to step over a very different kind of border.

Flying to Bogotá proved to be one of the scariest experiences of my life, however. I'd never been on a plane before and wasn't used to the terrifying sensations. When I went to the bathroom midflight, I didn't think to lock the door behind me, and so I was embarrassed when a huge man walked in as I was sitting on the toilet. Then when the landing gear dropped, I thought something was wrong with the plane. I was scared out of my wits, but I didn't want anyone to think I wasn't a seasoned traveler, so I resisted the urge to cling to Pops, screaming "We're all going to die!"

Colombia was even more of a culture shock. From the moment we arrived, it felt like we were in the middle of Mardi Gras. It was an amazing experience for someone who hadn't yet turned sixteen. Fortunately, I had plenty of people around me to keep me from harm. Apart from the musicians and crew in our own band, we must have had twenty others in our entourage—mostly for protection.

Cocaine was on offer everywhere. As soon as we got to our hotel, we were mobbed by dealers selling giant rocks of coke—which would have cost a thousand dollars in America—for five and ten bucks. Needless to say, some of the guys were lining up.

My mother hadn't been overly worried about me going to such a place, but she should have been. Even the coffee had coke in it, and after a few sips I was wired. The night we arrived, the partying began. Pops took me into a room and locked the door. As I watched in amazement, he prepared two lines of cocaine and told me, "Have you ever had this before?"

I shook my head.

"I want you to try this right now in front of me. Everybody will be doing this, so I want you to be careful and tell me every time you do this, okay?"

All my childhood in the sixties, I'd grown up around musicians who smoked pot and took other drugs pretty much every day. It was just part of the Californian musical scene. Alcohol was too. There was no way my parents could hide it from us children when our homes were makeshift studios, but they always tried to instill caution in us, along with a sense of moderation. It worked—for me, at least. I have never been one for drugs and am not that much of a drinker.

Although I was surprised that Pops was complicit in my trying cocaine, I knew that he was doing it that way so that I wouldn't be tempted to try it without his supervision.

I did try blow a few times in Bogotá, but it was way too strong for me. I was running around the hallways bouncing off the walls. My eyelids felt like they were stuck open and my heart raced, which scared me. I needed to take something to calm me down.

Instead, Pops bought a bottle of Hennessy cognac most nights and let me have a little, too, and it became our drink. He called it "spider leg."

We were in Colombia for nearly two weeks, and the promoters had made the mistake of promising to take care of food and incidentals. What they didn't realize was that there would be so many of us or that people would take advantage. Cart after cart came rolling along the corridor until the bill got so high that on the second day the promoters stopped paying.

"We're cutting you off!" they said.

I'd always taken it for granted that I could walk freely down the street, but in Colombia I couldn't. Men carried machine guns, and the whole place felt extremely dangerous. Whenever we did venture outside, and always with bodyguards, a few people shouted, "Go home!" which I couldn't fathom. Pops never let me out of his sight. We did manage to go shopping one day—to a place with the best platform shoes ever, complete with huge square heels. We emptied that store. I couldn't wait to get home and show Moms.

Our first gig was to be played in the middle of the Santamaría bullring—the largest in the country. The event was humongous. The stadium was built in the 1930s and could hold up to fifteen thousand people. Our stage was set up midfield, which meant we had to walk to it from the outer ring, stepping over pools of blood where they'd just slaughtered a bull. That place was nuts.

The first night I was so excited that my butterflies were doing a tango. Ever since my crazy solo at the Civic Center they'd been fluttering inside for each performance, keeping me company as I prepared to do what I love most.

My heart raced. My body felt electric. My breathing was shallow. I never felt more alive, wrapped inside the moment, than I did as I waited to play for a live audience. It was the purest form of self-expression I had, giving of myself through music. Since that warm Colombian night, I realized that the day the butterflies are gone is the day I'll stop playing.

The butterflies are what keep me alive.

Feeling them prancing in Bogotá, I checked myself out in a mirror once more and made sure I looked like a rock star. Then someone suddenly shouted, "Okay! Let's go!" and we ran into that bullring to tumultuous applause.

My school friends back home were sitting in one of those dreary portable classrooms studying algebra, and there I was in a bullring in Bogotá with my Afro, in a funky top and pants, ready to perform with some monster musicians for a massive Latino crowd.

I could hardly believe what was happening.

Geographically, I was more than nine thousand miles away from those portables. Psychologically, I was on another planet.

Pops took his place behind the timbales and—on his cue—the band began to play. The crowd went ballistic. I couldn't believe how much our music was appreciated by people who were willing to embrace whatever we played for them. That night I gained a newfound understanding of the power of music to bridge cultural divides.

I sat waiting behind my instruments, my mouth dry with nerves. Then, after a few minutes, Pops gestured to me to go ahead.

Okay, Sheila, I told myself. *It's time to fly to the moon . . .*

Two years old and cute as a button.

Looking pensive, age nine.

On East Twenty-first Street,
Oakland, age thirteen.

Wearing my hair in braids for the
George Duke show as a teenager.

Playing with Pops at the Greek in Berkeley, California.

Happy with Carlos Santana.

The group all together. Sheila E & Con Funk Shun, 1977. © *Connie Guzman*

Michael Jackson, sister Zina, and me in Oakland, 1979, at an in-store signing of *Off the Wall*.

The George Duke band backstage in Europe, 1977. *From left:* Josie James, George Duke, Sheila E, Lynn Davis. © *Terry Lott*

Having a blast on Lionel Richie's *Can't Slow Down* tour. *From left:* Sheila E, George and Corine Duke, and Lionel Richie.

At the *Happy Together* album cover shoot, glamorous with Pops. © *Bruce W. Talamon*

The Escovedo family all together. *From left:* Peter Michael, Sheila E, Pops, Moms, Juan, and Zina Escovedo. © *Jack White*

Ray Charles, me, and the rest of the group at the "We Are the World" recording session, 1986.

Hanging out in Las Vegas at a fund-raiser for the Andre Agassi Foundation. *From left:* Sheila E, Peter Michael Escovedo, Andre Agassi, David Foster, Lionel Richie.

Taking some time in the spotlight. Me and Ringo Starr & the All-Starr Band.
© *Lynn Mabry*

Rocking out with Ringo Starr & his All-Starr Band in 2001. © *Lynn Mabry*

Live at *The Magic Hour* TV show with Magic Johnson, 1998.
© *20th Century Fox*

Nicole Richie hanging out with
her auntie Sheila in 2005.

Prince and I together again at
the 2007 Alma awards.

Me, Pops, and our timbales. © *Rob Shanahan*

The modern-day E family
still performing together.

This is how I see the world from behind my drum set. © *Rob Shanahan*

The Obama family jamming with the E family, Washington, DC, 2012.

Life is good! From pain to purpose. © *Rob Shanahan*

13. Roll

A prolonged and reverberating sound

Pride and the passion
Laugh all night, cry all day
If true love is old-fashioned
Should we pass or should we play?

"PRIDE AND THE PASSION"

SHEILA E

Visiting Colombia had been such an amazing experience that I was sorry when it was time to leave. That feeling quickly changed, though.

While entering Colombia had been an almost seamless process, leaving was nothing short of traumatic. The customs officials there pulled all our bags at the airport and searched everyone for drugs. There was a frightening and aggressive energy to the guards, and I began to feel uneasy.

Pops was talking to them in Spanish, but I couldn't understand him or what anyone was saying. I kept saying, "I'm only fifteen! I don't do drugs!"

Then, while Pops was being questioned, a female guard asked me to accompany her. I argued with her for a couple of minutes until she pulled out a gun and waved it in my face, repeating, "You come with me!" I looked across at Pops in terror. He asked them where they were taking me, and they showed him a room and he told me, "It's okay, Sheila. Do as they ask." I followed the guard and her female companion into the room, and they shut the door and informed me in broken English that they would be giving me a full-body search.

I exploded with rage and fear. The tough little kid from Oakland fought back, yelling at them, "Oh, no, you're not! I don't have any drugs on me!"

That's when one of the guards pulled out a gun again and pointed it at my heart. There I was, separated from Pops, in a faraway country for the first time in my life, secluded in a room with strangers and a gun at my chest. As I watched in horror, the female guard stretched a surgical glove onto her right hand and informed me she was about to begin the search.

Shaking violently all over, I began to sob. My legs buckled, and I begged her, "Please believe me! There are no drugs! Please don't search me! Please!"

I must have convinced her that I was telling the truth, because she looked at the other guard, spoke Spanish very quickly, and then pulled off the glove.

Thank you, Jesus!

She released me to join the rest of the band, who were all undergoing interrogation. I ran to Pops and refused to leave his side. I wouldn't even use the bathroom and held it all in.

The officials kept us for hours. They riffled through all our possessions and ripped the heels off all the treasured platform shoes we'd bought, searching for hidden rocks of cocaine. They didn't find anything, thankfully, but they still declared that we couldn't leave the country. They kept our equipment and told Pops he'd have to meet with a government official the next day to "negotiate" our release. Scared and confused, we went back to our hotel.

Pops and I got up early the next morning and went to the government office as advised, but the officials refused to meet with us. They ignored us the next day too. Finally, late on the third day, they let us in and informed us that we'd have to pay ten thousand dollars to leave. Pops didn't object and handed over most of the profit from the tour, eager to do whatever was required to get us home.

I don't think any of us exhaled until that plane lifted its wheels off Colombian soil. The Colombian officials kept our equipment for months before shipping it back to us, so not only did we not make any money on the tour, nobody had their instruments to play. The entire experience ruined my first big tour, and it took me a long while to get comfortable with international travel. As soon as the tools of our trade were returned to us, however, we went straight back on the road to earn the money we'd lost. And work we did. That next year flew by in a blur of gigs, but I can honestly say I loved every minute.

What I didn't love was having to split up with Tam when I officially left Grito to tour full-time. I really liked him, but he wasn't the one for me and, musically, I needed to fly.

Being in Azteca, surrounded by so many men and the vocalist Wendy Haas, was an unusual experience. Everyone was so much older than me, although I was very comfortable around them, having grown up right before their eyes.

What was much more of a challenge was witnessing the many infidelities, especially as I knew that many of them had wives or girlfriends at home. There was a lot of drug abuse backstage, too, which had always made me uncomfortable, but I tried to ignore the negatives and focus on the positives.

Besides, I was still so excited to be a part of the group, and I cared for them all deeply. Despite my lack of interest in joining some of their recreational activities, I still loved being with them and learning from them. I especially loved hearing their stories from the road or legendary recording sessions. I wanted to hear about the challenges and triumphs they'd faced in the industry.

I may not have been learning anything academically, but my street-smarts IQ was shooting through the roof. In any event, the lessons I learned on the road were far more valuable than anything I could have learned in high school.

Traveling with Pops over the next few years, we played big venues and little ones. Later on, Pops started playing tiny dive bars around the Bay Area like the Shell on Grand Lake, which had dark smoky rooms that smelled of stale cigarettes and beer. Aptly named, it was just a shell of a club.

On any given night, there might have been three people sitting at the bar, all of them permanent fixtures. Two others might have been sitting at a table in the corner, hardly noticing our band setting up right in front of them. The place held only about twenty people and—counting the band and the bartender—there would be about ten of us in all.

Those were the leaner years. Fame, financial security, and the validation of critics never came overnight. There were many, many gigs like that one—a far cry from the sold-out arenas that I'd had a taste of and that would come again much later.

We made so little money that we barely had enough to eat at a fast-food joint after the gig. Our forty- or fifty-dollar fee was just enough to pay for a burger and fries or maybe some fried shrimp or chicken for each member of the band. Sometimes Pops and I wouldn't even do that because we felt bad not going home with something for Moms, Juan, Peter Michael, and Zina. We couldn't even afford drinks at the bar and would go to a liquor store to buy our own Hennessy.

I didn't understand the significance of money yet, and the low pay never bothered me. I was so in love with playing that for a while I even found it a little distasteful to be paid. "Work" to me meant something that people got paid to do because they wouldn't do it otherwise. Playing with my father wasn't work to me!

He quickly set me straight.

One night when we returned from a gig at the Shell, the whole family was at home. Moms greeted us at the door, happy to see us and to hear how the night went. My little sister, Zina, six years old at the time, ran up to give us hugs—adorable in her colorful pajamas. Juan and Peter Michael were there too, hanging out in the living room.

As Pops and I unloaded our instruments in the garage, I casually mentioned that I didn't care about not getting paid much that night. "Why would I accept money to do something I love?"

Pops said nothing, but he took my hand, led me into the kitchen, and opened the refrigerator door to show me shelves that were half-empty.

"That is why we get paid. If you are serious about choosing music as your career, you deserve to get paid, and you *need* to get paid. Never feel ashamed of being paid for doing something you love."

I got it.

I was still a child in so many ways, living under my parents' roof. And while our home was rich in joy, laughter, and love, that wasn't enough to fill our bellies. We lived from paycheck to paycheck much of the time and still occasionally relied on welfare and food stamps.

That night, I realized that playing music was more than a way to express my creativity and vent my frustration with the cruelties of this world. It was a means of survival. The responsibility was sobering. But in a way it also opened another door in my head.

Suddenly I felt incredibly lucky , because I understood—unlike so many people—that my work would forever be my play too. That was a true blessing, and after that I never begrudged receiving or paying back one cent.

Pops's beloved Azteca didn't go the distance, sadly, despite having released a second album, *Pyramid of the Moon*. The band had originally been Uncle Coke's vision, but it grew too big—sixteen members at least, augmented by others—and there was never enough money to go round. Debts began to mount and musicians jumped ship. Columbia Records dropped the band, and then Uncle Coke left to pursue a solo career and to work with Herbie Hancock and Stevie Wonder.

In a little over ten years, dear old Coke would be dead at age forty-five from cirrhosis of the liver. He was still much loved, but he had become someone who was very unhappy and for whom drinking and drugs had become a crutch. One time he had asked to borrow my father's precious timbales for a gig one day, and then he sold them to buy what he needed. My father was devastated, but—kindhearted as he always was—he forgave his little brother who'd been in the orphanage with him all those years earlier.

As Pops said, "We grew up in an era of doing some crazy things. Some of us were smart enough to get out of it, and some were not. Coke was one of the ones who couldn't get out of it. Eventually it was his downfall."

He died in 1986, on Pops's fifty-first birthday.

Azteca eventually disbanded in 1974, and Pops's dream of making it big sank with the ship. Not that he had any intention of going down with it. He'd struggled all those years to make it that far, and he wasn't giving up so easily. So he reassembled a smaller version of his Pete Escovedo Band to make ends meet. There was a bassist, a lead guitarist, me, Pops, and sometimes a drummer or vibe player.

We were doing a gig at the Reunion Club on Union Street in San Francisco one night in 1975 when Billy Cobham walked in. I thought Billy was the greatest drummer in the world. A master of jazz fusion, he'd played with Miles Davis, James Brown, the Fania All-Stars, and all the other greats. At that time he was touring with his Mahavishnu Orchestra, and he played balls-to-the-wall drums.

The minute Billy walked into the Reunion Club, we knew exactly who he was. He sat down, bought a drink, and listened to us play. There was me, Pops, Roger Glenn, a bass player, and Ray Obiedo. I'm not sure which drummer we used that night—the band members often changed depending on who was available.

I was still under twenty-one and wasn't allowed to be in the club legally, but they made an exception for me at that spot because they loved Pops's music and we always drew the crowds. At other clubs, like Biff's on Broadway and Twenty-ninth, the management went through that old routine of making me wait in the back during breaks.

It was so boring back there that I wore the manager down until he finally cracked and let me stay in the main room, but with a stern warning that I was to plant myself in a chair against the back wall and wasn't to get up unless I had to use the bathroom.

My plan worked.

I positioned the chair to the right of the pay phone, where I could call my best friend, Connie, and chat for most of the night. I may have been a professional musician, but I was still a teenager whose top priority was talking on the phone.

What did we talk about? Girl stuff, probably—which guys we hoped might be at a party later that night, what we'd wear, or how we'd do our hair.

Ray Obiedo has a cassette recording of a rehearsal we did

where he and the other guys were constantly trying to get me off the phone so they could rehearse. Connie kept calling and I kept putting down my drumsticks so I could answer and chatter away, which obviously frustrated those who were trying to get through the song. Ray said that on that thirty or so minutes of tape I did way more gossiping and giggling than drumming.

I sure was drumming for my life at the Reunion Club, though. I have to admit to feeling extremely nervous as Billy Cobham's eyes followed my every lick. As soon as we took a break, he came over to see us.

"I've never seen a father and daughter play together like this!" he told us. "You were both terrific!"

I couldn't believe that Billy Cobham, *the* master drummer and percussionist, was excited by *us*!

He was super nice, really cool, and we got on so well that he surprised everyone by sitting in and jamming with us during our second set. It was such a privilege to share the stage with one of the baddest musicians around.

After the show he asked for Pops's phone number. He said he was going on tour but wanted to produce a record of Pops and me when he got back in September. I still remember that part like it was yesterday, the way he said "September" in that mellifluous voice of his.

"Wow!" I cried, and clapped my hands with excitement. I could hardly contain myself. Pops smiled and shook Billy's hand and told him that would be cool.

After Billy left, Pops and I headed to the bar and toasted the handshake deal. "Cool, Pops?" I said, smiling. "That would be fricking amazing!"

While driving home with him, I continued to talk about the new record as Pops kept his eyes on the road and showed no emotion. Eventually, he told me, "People say things in this business,

Sheila. I've lost count of those who've said they'll help me make it or produce an album, but they never follow up. You must learn not to get your hopes up. Let's just wait and see."

Sure enough, weeks passed and we didn't hear a thing. My heart sank a little with each new day. When two months had gone by, I'd almost forgotten about it. But then, come late September, Billy contacted us and repeated his offer. I couldn't believe he'd kept his word. He asked us to meet him at the legendary Fantasy Records studio in Berkeley.

I'd already been to Fantasy a few times for demos, and I'd made my recording debut there a few months earlier playing congas and percussion on Alphonso Johnson's *Yesterday's Dreams*.

This was something else, though—this would be an album with my name next to my father's on the cover. It would be *our* record. That was almost too good to be true. Better still, Billy Cobham was to be the producer, writing or cowriting many of the songs. Man, that was like having Sammy Davis Jr. produce us!

Billy helped us put a band together, and Pops assembled an awesome crew that included Ray Obiedo on guitar and vocals, Bill Summers on percussion and vocals, trumpet player Tom Harrell, and Mel Martin on woodwinds. Mark Soskin was on piano and keyboards, while Pops and I were to play congas and timbales and a lot of hand percussion. Billy would play the drums.

Fantasy had been going for thirty years and was the studio where Chet Baker and Dave Brubeck had recorded albums, along with Creedence Clearwater Revival and so many other of my musical heroes. Once we got set up and put on our headphones, all we had to do was wait for everyone else to get ready.

I had never really practiced, studied music, or learned how to warm up before playing. Yet to be a drummer or percussion player you need whole body strength, and most players practice every day to keep their chops up. I never did. I was still young and in good shape. I barely warmed up to run track, so I didn't see the point of warming up just to play a few rhythms.

Fascinated by how Billy would prepare, though, I watched him closely. He stood in front of a snare drum with his back against the wall and his elbows pressing against it so they couldn't move.

Then, while still carrying on a conversation with someone, he did unbelievable rudiments. I was amazed by his control. He'd alter the distance of the strokes, but the velocity, intensity, and volume of each stroke never varied, whether the sticks lifted between his waist and his ribs or between his waist and his shoulders.

Then he moved on to pressed rolls. *Rrrrrrrrrrrrrrrrrrr*. Most of my rolls were single-stroke rolls, but he'd warm up with singles, doubles, triples, quadruples, quintuples, sextuples, and hextuples. And he still casually chatted away to someone the entire time.

I'd never seen anything like it.

Billy's skill and precision truly inspired me.

I was in the presence of greatness.

I started to hyperventilate.

He had so many toms on his drum set, why did he even need me? Where would I fit in on a song? How could I avoid getting in his way?

I thought I was going to be sick.

I was more nervous in that cramped, soundproofed space with my father by my side than I had ever been on a stage. The butterflies morphed into elephants that were trampling around my insides. I became unreasonably obsessed about the red light coming on, which meant that we would be officially recording. That red light was so scary, and I tensed every time it lit up.

Pops had his own anxieties to deal with, I'm sure. Besides, I didn't want to let on how freaked out I was. The only person I could think of to reassure me was Connie, so I left the room and used the studio phone.

"You can do this, Sheila," she told me encouragingly. "No sweat!"

She calmed me down enough to put the phone down and get into position when instructed. As Pops and I prepared to record *Solo Two*, I pretended to be calm, cool, and collected, but I was far from it.

Back then you didn't overdub your solo. The band was all in one room and we played our solos live, right then and there. Me on congas, Pops on timbales, and Billy on drums. Wow, this was crazy!

When Billy said, "Okay, ready? Let's record!" the red light went on, indicating that recording had begun. That light remained so intimidating in my mind. I sat in front of my big red conga drums, stared at the red light, and tried to slow down my breathing.

On cue, I began my solo, giving it my best and desperately hoping I wouldn't be the one to mess up, because then everyone would have to start over. I made a mistake every now and again, but so did everyone else, so I didn't feel so bad. My hands hurt after each day of recording because I played so hard.

Despite all my misgivings, Billy seemed very happy with what I did. Later on, some of my favorite percussionists, including Giovanni Hidalgo, Karl Perazzo, and Armando Peraza, would tell me how much they enjoyed my playing on that album. I'm always a little surprised to hear compliments about that record because of my nerves at the time, but with Billy's encouragement, I guess I just played raw from my gut and eventually let go to see what happened. To this day, Pops says that was the best conga solo I have ever done and the one of which he is most proud.

Fear can be good for you sometimes.

Solo Two by Pete and Sheila Escovedo was released with a cover featuring me standing behind Pops with my hands on his shoulders. The cover notes said: "Special thanks to Juanita, Juan, Peto, and Zina for their love and understanding; to Billy Cobham, for his creative help and direction . . . *Gracias también* to everyone who kept faith in us and our music."

It felt like only yesterday that I'd been fighting in gangs and miserable at school. All of a sudden I had my own record with a picture of me on the cover and was garnering some serious respect in the very community I was in awe of. I could hardly get my head around it.

What on earth would happen next?

14. Stick Grip

The style in which a drummer
holds the drumstick

*I have learned over the years that when one's mind is made
up, this diminishes fear; knowing what must be done does
away with fear.*

ROSA PARKS

Before I even had time to consider the answer, along came
George Duke, another legend in the world of jazz fusion and
a man who'd worked with Frank Zappa, among others. George
and Billy had a band together called the Duke Cobham Project—
later known as the Billy Cobham/George Duke Band—and when
George heard me playing congas with Pops, he decided that he
wanted me to go out on tour with them.

When he asked me, I was thrilled, but then my heart sank. I was
playing pretty much full-time with the Pete Escovedo Band by then.
My father and I had a record out, and things were good. Going
on tour with George would mean walking away from all that for a
while, and I'd be abandoning Pops the way I'd left Grito for Azteca.

I knew I'd have to prepare myself for that conversation with my father before I went on tour with George, and I felt bad. In the end, I lost courage and asked George to speak to Pops for me.

The two of them had a man-to-man chat, and George promised that he'd take good care of me. (He talks about his conversation with my father to this day.) Pops knew I could take care of myself, and said he was fine about letting me go.

"This is a great opportunity for you, honey," he told me, but I felt like his smile didn't quite reach his eyes.

He was so much a part of me and my career that I was heartbroken at the thought of leaving him. It took me years to shake off my guilt about "abandoning" Pops to work with other musicians. He had given me the gift of music and he'd taught me everything I knew. Thanks to him I'd been able to play and start to make a name for myself. It felt like a betrayal to move on without him.

Pops was right, though—the George Duke tour would really open doors for me and expand my musical horizons well beyond the Bay Area. We took off almost immediately for Europe before coming back to do shows across the US. I couldn't believe that I was a real professional musician, touring the world in my teens, playing percussion and singing backing vocals.

I flew home every now and again to make a second record with Pops and Billy at Fantasy, which was entitled *Happy Together*. It was eventually released in 1978, when I was just twenty years old. Pops and I also went on to play on a few more of Billy Cobham's albums, *Magic* and *Inner Conflicts*. I was offered other opportunities as a studio musician, too, recording on Con Funk Shun's *Secrets* and their later *Loveshine*.

The George Duke tour consisted of back-to-back gigs; one day melted into the next. We'd play and get on a bus, or play and crash at a hotel, then set off again early the next day. I didn't know which city or even country we were in much of the time because of the time-zone changes and strange hours. I'd send postcards to my family, telling them how much I missed them or about the crazy new world I was in with its different food, music, and cultures.

The physicality of playing every night took its toll on me, too. One morning, I woke up to discover that I could hardly move. My hands were bleeding after every show. At night I'd have to soak the open sores on my palms and fingers in Epsom salts. And the next day, to warm up, I'd have to slap them against the wall until they went numb. I'd welcome new calluses, because they at least provided a little protection.

It was a lot to take sometimes—along with the drugs and the infidelity all around me. In a couple of towns I actually tried to keep the groupies away from the guys. I'd shut the dressing room door and try to keep out the women who wanted to come backstage and hang out with all the guys. "We need some privacy in here!" I'd say, hoping that the men would take the hint and at least not betray their wives (most of whom I knew) in front of me. I never succeeded, and I hated knowing how these musicians behaved away from home—yet another dirty little secret I was expected to keep. In what was then Communist Yugoslavia, I developed strep throat and felt wretchedly homesick. I had a fever, and my throat was so sore I couldn't even swallow my own saliva. I lay sweating in a skinny little twin bed in a tiny hotel room with bars on the windows. In my feverish hallucinations I dreamt Dracula came through the window to feed on me. Byron Miller, the bass player, stayed with me until the doctor arrived with a needle as long as my arm.

"Shoot me, doc," I told him, knowing that if I didn't get better I'd have to fly home. That was one of the most painful shots I've ever had, but by the morning I felt so much better. Rain or shine, strep or fever, the show must go on.

In Germany I turned heads, but not in a good way. I wore my

hair in braids by then, with beads jangling. Strangers stared at me in the street, pointing and wanting to touch my hair as if I was a circus freak. They were laughing and saying things I didn't understand. I'd never experienced anything like that; it was as if they had never seen a woman of color before. Moments like those made me long for Oakland, where my color wasn't unusual and my braids were considered cool.

George Duke, who was only eleven years older than me but seemed like a father figure, kept his promise to Pops and protected me from physical harm. He couldn't do much about the men who kept hitting on me, though. Every day I found myself navigating the choppy waters of inappropriate assumptions and attitudes.

It usually went like this: a musician might initially be rude to me and doubt my ability to hang with the group musically. Then, as he realized I was talented and worthy of playing with them, he'd become more comfortable with me, even friendly. And then he'd get a little too comfortable, so to speak. He wouldn't see me as a musical equal or a buddy but as a possible one-night stand.

I wasn't down with that.

I learned fast to set my boundaries and walk the fine line of a female musician in a male-dominated environment. I was surrounded by lots of amped-up, lusty guys who thought it was just a matter of time before I accepted their advances and slept with them. They couldn't have been more wrong.

George was always supportive if I needed him. "I had to keep the hounds away," he reported to my parents later, laughing. He'd promised that he'd keep me safe and comfortable, and he did. But I didn't like relying on George or anyone else to fight my battles, so I learned quickly how to project strength and self-protection. Soon enough I had built an invisible wall that was so impenetrable, guys just stopped trying.

Part of that self-defense mechanism had undoubtedly been

forged in my childhood, allowing me to create the necessary arm's length between me and anyone whom I sensed could pose some sort of threat—sexual or otherwise. Another part of that wall's strength had to do with the influence of my family. I grew up with a deeply ingrained sense of my gender and the feeling that I had the right to hang with the guys as much as anyone else.

Out on the road in an all-male band, I realized once again that some people saw the drums as something only a man should play. The Gardere in me immediately bristled. I wanted to tell them, "Let me play my music and make the rest of you sound better. Your beliefs and assumptions about why I'm here or how I compare to a man don't interest me. Nor do I want to sleep with you afterward!"

Fortunately, the guys had all seen how hard I beat the drums. They knew I was fit and physically very strong; I was probably at the peak of my physical health back then.

The signal I put out was: "Don't mess with me. I may be sexy, but I have a powerful right hook."

That's not to say they didn't try to get away with things, but I wasn't interested.

Music was my date.

It consumed me, as did the humbling certainty that I still had so much to learn. I'd never really played fusion music like that before, which had different time signatures. I had to listen very closely and learn fast, because everybody read sheet music except me.

I felt like I'd enrolled in music school, but everybody was collaborative and encouraging, offering up ideas and giving me the chance to suggest a melody that someone would write down or pen some lyrics to. I learned a great deal working with George and later cowrote a song on his *Master of the Game* record.

Due to his versatility, I had the opportunity to play all kinds of music. His shows and records integrated a little bit of everything— funk, R&B, jazz. I really appreciated his approach to Brazilian music, which I'd never played before, and I grew to love its intense and distinct chords and voicings. They were so sensual and passionate, completely different from all that I'd known.

When George's R&B song "Reach for It" became a crossover hit, he picked up a whole new following. We were asked to play at a lot of festivals where I came across even more great musicians like George Benson, Teddy Pendergrass, and the O'Jays—to name just a few.

I also met a successful husband-and-wife singer-songwriter team named Ashford and Simpson. I grew up listening to their music and had so many of their records, including "Ain't No Mountain High Enough," "Reach Out and Touch (Somebody's Hand)," and "Ain't Nothing Like the Real Thing." They listened to me play and said, "Hell, girl, where did you come from?" I was delighted, and it seemed I was getting a whole new audience.

Testing the waters musically taught me so much about different styles and tastes. I discovered that there was intense rivalry between the East and West Coast bands, especially when it came to salsa or Latin music. The New York musicians played more traditional Afro-Cuban style, which is based on the clave rhythm pattern commonly used in rumba, congo mambo, and salsa, to name a few. Bay Area musicians didn't always apply the clave to their music. I also discovered that some of the East Coast musicians looked down on us because Pops didn't play traditional salsa but rather Latin jazz, which was freer and more spontaneous and not locked into the clave. Our view was that there were no rules, and Pops taught us to express ourselves in that way.

In keeping with that spirit, I just loved playing, whether the venues were big or small. People kept telling me that I'd get my "big break" any day and "make it," but I didn't know what they meant. As far as I was concerned, I had made it! I was completely fulfilled and would have been content to continue playing in bands like that for the rest of my life. I never dreamed I'd be the leader of my own band one day, or have any sort of name in the industry.

To my delight, the George Duke Band was invited to *Don Kirshner's Rock Concert* and, later, to Wolfman Jack's *Midnight Special* on NBC—the definitive Friday-night pop-rock variety show. That show featured all kinds of artists, from music to comedy, including a young Chevy Chase and Steve Martin. It was like *American Bandstand, The Ed Sullivan Show, Soul Train*, and *Saturday Night Live* all rolled into one.

When we arrived at the studio in Burbank to tape in front of a live audience, I was nervous but excited. I'd played on television twice before—on a local Bay Area program on KQED with Grito, and then with a band I'd set up briefly called Cho Cho San (with my brother Peter Michael, Cat Grey, and Wayne Wallace), but these national television specials were something else and would bring me to a whole new level of attention.

The famous DJ Wolfman Jack announced us, and when it was our turn to go on I played percussion and then switched to drums when Ndugu Chancler, the drummer, went up front to rap. I knew Moms and Peter Michael and Zina were all watching us back home on the old Zenith TV set, along with the extended Gardere and Escovedo families in their various Bay Area homes.

Playing and singing along, on congas and then on drums, I looked at the giant television camera pointed at me and I grinned right into the lens. I wasn't even a woman yet, but I'd already achieved one of my childhood dreams.

I was playing music *inside* the box, just as I'd always wanted, not outside looking in.

It had been twelve years since I first saw Karen Carpenter playing the drums on TV and asked Pops why I couldn't be on TV too.

"You will be," he'd told me knowingly back then, and he was right.

15. Butterfly

A tenor crossover or sweep lick that
produces a butterfly arm motion

Why we hide our feelings when we're older
Is a movie I don't want to see
Truth is all that matters in a month of Saturdays
When you're seventeen

"TOY BOX"

SHEILA E

One of my family nicknames is Cho, short for Cho Cho San. It was given to me by Carlos Santana.

"It means 'Madame Butterfly' in Japanese," he told me, flashing his soulful brown eyes. Since I always loved butterflies and I really liked Carlos, I was flattered.

When I was younger and buying his records, my girlfriends and I would sit around and giggle about which of our favorite musicians we would marry. "He's *soooooo* cute," I'd always say when I was talking about Carlos.

Once he got to know Pops, he'd come with him sometimes

to watch me play in a couple of my teen soccer games, which was pretty cool. I mean, Carlos Santana standing on the sidelines and cheering me on? I like to think I played really well those days.

I loved his music, that Bay Area sound incorporating multiple percussionists into a Latin rock movement. And I always had a thing for a guy who could play a guitar. I mean *really* play a guitar. There's something about guitar melodies that touches me in a unique way.

I'm intrigued by melodic expression, because rhythmic expression is a whole different world. It's not that drums don't sing—we drummers can absolutely make them sing—but I'm a frustrated guitar and bass player myself, always dreaming of translating my rhythms into melodic notes the way a good player like Carlos does.

I had just turned eighteen when I began my relationship with him. He was twenty-eight, tall and thin, with a gentle but powerful presence. I can't remember how our relationship started. My family had known Carlos for years. Even before his band Santana, he'd come to see the Escovedo Brothers perform. Uncle Coke started playing with him around the time of Woodstock, and Pops began playing with him in the early seventies.

Once our romantic relationship blossomed, we'd date like any normal couple, seeing movies together or going out to eat, catching other artists' shows, taking a picnic on Mt. Tamalpais, or enjoying beautiful road trips along the Pacific Coast Highway.

We had such happy times together. Every moment with him was beautiful. We'd talk about music, love, and life. He taught me about vegetarianism, meditation, and the peace of mind that comes with appreciating nature.

The first time he took me to his house in Marin County I felt like a queen—I couldn't believe how clean and white that house was. I'd never been inside such a beautiful mansion my whole life.

Having grown up sharing a bedroom with my brothers and living in cramped and noisy homes, I couldn't get over how much space and silence he had at his disposal.

I fell for that handsome, loving man, and I fell hard. I'd never felt that way about anybody in my life. I thought music was going to be my only love. I didn't think I had it in me to experience that intensity of emotion about a man, but Carlos opened my heart like a flower. Kind and sensitive, he showered me with affection and attention. Confident and wise, he seemed so much older to me than his twenty-eight years.

To complicate matters, my father and uncle worked for him, so he was effectively their boss. Once again, and for entirely different reasons, I was asked to keep yet another situation secret from my parents. I knew they'd disapprove of it because of the age difference and the fact that Pops worked for him. If it had been anyone else, I would probably have walked away, but I'd known Carlos for years and—I now realize—I'd always loved him from afar.

He was touring a lot at that time, too, and whenever he took off on the next leg he'd tell me to "be good," which always shocked me. I was a one-man woman. If he thought I'd see anyone else while we were apart, then he didn't know me at all.

Turns out it was *me* who didn't know something.

I had no idea at first, but I was participating in an extramarital affair. It was a devastating shock to find out I was deeply in love with a married man. Even though I'd known him for so long, he never spoke of his wife to me, and no one else did, either. I don't remember how I discovered the truth, but when I did, I immediately told him it was over. A part of me had already starting pulling back anyway. As much as I was in love with him, I was still so young. About a year into our relationship, he'd proposed marriage to me—the first time anyone had asked me—but the thought of settling down with him was scary. It was so unfamiliar to lose myself in somebody, even somebody whose love of music was as all consuming as mine.

I wish my memories of this time were clearer. I don't know why there are so many gaps, especially about something as significant as finding out I was the "other woman." For whatever reason, while some images are as clear as yesterday, I seem to have blocked out a lot of the chronological details surrounding this time, maybe because it was too painful to acknowledge that I'd been the source of someone else's pain. These are issues I'm still working through today.

What I do know is that Carlos told me he was in love with me and that he and his wife were essentially separated. I wanted to believe him. How was I able to be at his house so often and never see her, after all? It seemed to me like he was totally single. All those times he was taking me unusual places I thought he was sweeping me off my feet, not hiding me from public view.

Once I found out the truth, I didn't know what to think. My world was shattered. I couldn't stop crying. I couldn't eat and I couldn't sleep. I needed to leave him, but I also yearned for him to comfort me, to make my pain go away. It only made matters more difficult that Pops was in his band. Always intensely private about relationships, I hadn't talked to my parents about our affair, and I certainly couldn't once I knew there was even more to hide.

When Carlos told me his wife had left him, I was still trying to wrap my head around the fact that he had a wife in the first place. I knew it was my fault—she left because of me. I'm not sure what transpired next. I can only imagine that my mind has tried to do me a favor by pushing away the bad stuff. This is one of those chunks of time that I've lost, as if I blacked out.

The next time I came to, he was picking me up at the house in his Jag to take me to the Day on the Green concert, where he'd be performing. The event was part of a series organized by Bill Graham at the Oakland Coliseum and was a sell-out show featuring Carlos, Lynyrd Skynyrd, Peter Frampton, and the Outlaws.

I know from video footage of the concert as well as photographs from that day that I was wearing a white, tight Wild Cherry T-shirt and black pants tucked into maroon platform boots. As we wandered through the back entrance of the Coliseum, Carlos held my hand. He felt we had nothing to hide. We were a couple now.

He was still holding my hand when we entered the VIP area, and I looked to my left and spotted members of his family. My heart dropped. They stared at me with an intensity that I interpreted as pure hatred. They didn't have to say a word; their eyes said it all. My stomach lurched. He held my hand tighter, sensing my discomfort and trying to reassure me, but the horrific reality had already crashed down upon me.

I had broken up a marriage.

I had destroyed a family.

I was "the mistress."

It was all completely wrong. This was not the person I'd been raised to be.

Carlos seemed intent on proudly displaying our love for one another. When it was time for him to go on, he walked me to the side of the stage, sat me down on an Anvil guitar case, and gave me a kiss.

"I love you, Cho," he said.

"I love you, too."

He walked away.

There I was, sitting on a guitar case, suddenly on my own. My world collapsed in on itself, and as I looked within myself, the applause of forty thousand people seemed to fade, quieter and quieter with every step he took away from me. I was alone in a crowd of thousands. Silenced in a sea of cheers. In an atmosphere of open celebration, I was grieving.

It's a different kind of hurt when you know you've done something to cause another's pain, even if you hadn't known what you were doing. Furthermore, I'd never caused that kind of pain before, the kind that has ripple effects.

Carlos eventually called me onstage to sit in. I got up reluctantly and walked slowly toward him. As he was waving me over I was drowning in ambivalence—relieved at the thought of being close to him again, but hesitant to emerge from my moment of self-reflection. I walked on timidly, my shoulders hunched in defeat. Carlos met me at the timbales, and we played together.

I always loved playing with him, but this time I gave minimally, just enough to get by. My heart was so heavy that it felt hard to breathe. I was trying to focus on the music, but the expressions on his relatives' faces and the thoughts of his wife haunted me. It was like that moment at San Leandro High when I suddenly saw myself from another perspective. From every angle, I didn't like what I was seeing.

I tried to enjoy the moment, sharing the stage with Carlos Santana at this legendary festival—the Bay Area's equivalent to Woodstock. But I couldn't let go of my guilt and shame. Even playing percussion, my reliable source of salvation, couldn't provide me with what I needed. The song I sat in on that day said it all—"Soul Sacrifice."

I went back on tour with George Duke during the middle of my inner turmoil and found some comfort in being away and losing myself in music again. It was 1977 and we traveled all over the US and to Europe, where I sat in with the Jackson 5 (renamed the Jacksons) in Germany. That was such a trip to hang out with those same kids my brothers and I had mimicked when we were younger. I told them what fans all my family had been: "We copied every move you guys made!"

They were sweet and humble, getting a kick out of my stories about how their band had so influenced our family "performances" in our Oakland front room. But despite these wonderful moments, I couldn't quite escape the heartache, and I knew it was only a matter of time before I'd have to walk away from Carlos for good.

He had given me a beautiful ring that had an iridescent turquoise stone and that I'd worn on my engagement finger as proudly as if it was a three-carat diamond. Even that seemed suddenly tainted, and I slipped it off one day and put it away.

Our breakup was difficult and drawn out. We'd been together, on and off, for two years. As I see it now, we were doomed from the beginning; our very foundation had a crack in it. As much as I wanted to be happy, I couldn't release the darkness, the heavy-hearted burden I'd felt on that stage.

I had to let my first true love go.

Once I finally made the break, Carlos asked Pops to leave the band, because it was too difficult to be around him. Pops had been soaring with one of the biggest groups in the world, and he was suddenly out of work.

He and Carlos didn't speak to each other for more than twenty years after that.

Neither did Carlos and I.

As always with me, I threw myself into work to distract myself from my heartache. From that moment on, it was like Carlos had left the planet.

The Bay Area was a very small world of musicians, though, so at times I'd inevitably wind up in places where Carlos was. Whenever he and I crossed paths, we avoided eye contact and didn't speak.

It wasn't until twenty-two years later, at the first Latin Grammy ceremony in 2000, that we finally broke our silence. We'd both been invited to play in a tribute to Tito Puente, who had recently passed away. My "godfather" had died after a show in New York, at age seventy-six.

I was overwhelmed with emotion already. My beautiful Tito was making music in heaven. As I walked down the corridor to the stage for rehearsal, my heart started beating a little fast in anticipation of seeing Carlos again. I adjusted my timbales and was talking to the director when I saw—or first felt—him walk onstage. We gave each other a cordial hug and said hello. I pretended I wasn't nervous.

The performance schedule shifted, so we ended up playing the tribute without Carlos. Right after the show, however, I saw him in the hallway.

"You look beautiful," he told me, those big brown eyes staring at me again after so many years. "And you look happy."

"I am."

Several years later I caught his show at Madison Square Garden. His percussionist and musical director, Karl Perazzo (my "little brother," whom I once stole from a rehearsal room so he could join my band in another), waved me over to join them onstage. I was nervous, and not just because I didn't have my in-ear monitors. I hadn't shared a stage with Carlos since that Day on the Green in 1977, but Perazzo kept waving me on.

"Mama, come on!" he yelled.

Carlos's back was to me when I started playing congas. He immediately heard the extra rhythms and spun around to see who it was. He had the biggest smile on his face once he saw it was me. Then he announced me to the crowd and gave me a nod, that nonverbal blessing for me to take a solo. I played feverishly, overcome by a sense of relief.

"Sheila E!" he kept saying to the crowd.

I stayed for another song.

We were giddy backstage afterward and so excited to have played together after so many years. Our friendship has been strong ever since.

In 2009, Carlos presented me with an award for Women in Latin Rock, along with Wendy Haas (from Azteca), Linda Tillery (who sang with Uncle Coke), and Lydia Pense (from Cold Blood). Before giving me the award he acknowledged Pops for his contribution to Latin music and Moms for being the heart of our family. I was humbled both by the award and by having it presented to me by Carlos. That meant the world.

Ours was a life-altering love, and it taught me an invaluable lesson. I vowed to never again be involved with a married man or even a man whose relationship status was the least bit complicated. I carried regret and guilt for many years, wishing I could take back all the hurt I caused his family.

I am eternally sorry to them.

Years later and after Carlos divorced his wife, he proposed onstage to his drummer, Cindy Blackman. When we played together again the following year, I congratulated him on getting remarried. Laughing, he told me, "I couldn't wait for you, Cho. I guess I got another drummer! I like drummers."

I guess he does.

And with those few words, he finally released his butterfly—his little Cho Cho San—into the big blue yonder.

16. Syncopation

The displacing of accents
or beats in music

I had some problems and no one could seem to solve them
But you found the answer
You told me to take this chance and learn the ways of love,
My baby, and all that it has to offer
In time you will see that love won't let you down

"ALL THIS LOVE"
PETE ESCOVEDO

In late 1977, I overheard Tom Coster—the keyboard player for Santana—excitedly telling Pops what had happened at the Record Plant in Sausalito that day. When the band took a break, they heard a ridiculous rhythm guitar part coming from the room next door.

"There's this young kid," Tom said, "and he's playing all the instruments, he wrote all the music, and he's producing the entire record."

"Who are you talking about?" I asked.

"This kid!" said Tom. "He's doing his first album for Warner Brothers."

"All by himself?" asked Pops.

"Yes! I've never heard anything like it."

"Wow," I said. "I want to meet him. What's his name?"

"Prince."

I never did make it down to the studio to meet "the kid," but a few months later, in April 1978, I was at Leopold's record store in Berkeley browsing through records when I looked up to see a new poster. It featured a beautiful young man with brown skin, a perfect Afro, and stunning green eyes. The word *Prince* was written in bold letters at the top. That was the guy Tom was talking about!

I found his album *For You* in the rack and immediately looked at the credits: "*Produced, arranged, composed, and performed by Prince.*"

The staff at the store, whom I'd known for years, let me take the poster home. Before I'd even listened to his record, I'd taped the poster above my waterbed. Then I lowered the needle onto the album on my record player, sat on the floor, and listened to it in its entirety. Tom was right. I immediately heard that funky rhythm guitar part he'd been talking about. It wasn't only on one song, but the whole album.

I stared up at the poster and told him, "I'm gonna meet you one day."

Fast forward to September 17, 1978, and an Al Jarreau concert at the Greek Theatre in Berkeley. I was wearing my trademark platform boots, bell-bottoms, halter top, and of course no bra. I rocked my 'fro, my big hoop earrings, and lip gloss. I looked like Angela Davis, but I felt like Foxy Brown.

I stood in the backstage corridor chatting with friends. The place was jam-packed with all the great Bay Area musicians who'd come to check out the show. Back then, everyone who was anyone played the Greek. It was the best outdoor venue around. When we heard the stage manager's announcement—"Five minutes, Mr. Jarreau"—we all rushed to find a spot on either side of the stage.

The crowd was pumped that balmy fall night. I heard a few people scream my name. "Look, it's Sheila Escovedo!" I waved and smiled. It was fun being recognized.

When Al hit his first note, we all went crazy. School was in session. I bopped on the side of the stage, ever the student, ready to absorb all of his goodness. That's when I suddenly spotted a man leaning against the wall across from me on the other side of the stage. I knew him immediately. He was *that* guy, the one in the poster on my bedroom wall. And he was staring right at me. Our eyes locked, and . . . *Wow!* I'm not somebody to often skip a beat, but in that moment, my heart sure did.

Only the previous night, before falling asleep, I'd stared at his poster, gazing intently at his striking hazel-green eyes. And now those same eyes, decorated with more eyeliner than mine, were staring right through me. I'd always thought beauty was an attribute reserved for women, but he was proving me wrong. I'd never seen a man so beautiful.

Oh, Lawd! Help me, my mind cried out. *He is fine. And he plays guitar. What? It's over now.*

That day we exchanged no words, only eye contact. But for me, that was more than enough. I knew it was only a matter of time before we'd connect again.

The next time I saw Prince was several months later when Connie and I went to see him play live at the Circle Star Theater in San Carlos, California. This theater in the round was another of *the* places to be. On any given night you could go there to see artists like the O'Jays, Gladys Knight and the Pips, and Diana Ross. Since I had played and visited there so many times, management hooked me up with tickets and a backstage pass. But I hadn't thought to ask for a parking pass, so when we got there we spent half an hour trying to find a spot, ultimately having to park across the highway since the regular lot was filled.

We were late. We ran across the highway, me pulling Connie hard as she shrieked and squealed, "Slow down, Sheila!"

"Come on! Let's go," I yelled.

I was so frustrated that we were missing the beginning, not only because I didn't want to miss any of Prince, but also because as a performer myself, I really respected the totality of a show. Showing up late to anybody's performance just wasn't cool.

We rushed in through the backstage entrance, and as we ran down the aisle toward our seats, the music, just like his record, was slammin'. I looked onstage and I could hear him singing and playing, but where was he? Where was the guy on the poster? I couldn't for the life of me figure out which one was him. Was he the bass player? The guitar player? The fact that he played every instrument didn't help me narrow it down. There was a second guitar player who I thought might be Prince, but that wasn't him, either.

And then I realized he was the guy on lead vocals singing "Soft and Wet"—that wild and crazy black man with long flowing hair, no shirt, thigh-high leg warmers, ankle boots, a short scarf, and a trench coat.

What the heck?

Not only did he look totally different from how he'd looked at the Greek Theatre, but he looked totally different, period. His look was as unique as his music, and he was killing the stage. And while his performance was mesmerizing, I began to entertain thoughts about meeting him afterward. I hoped I'd finally get to introduce myself to the man on my bedroom wall.

After the show I made my way toward the rear of the theater. I pulled back the black curtain, hoping to find somebody who could direct me to him, but that wasn't necessary. There was his reflection right in front of me. He was looking in the mirror, slowly combing out his long, straight hair. Those perfect eyes caught mine in the mirror, and he gasped before turning around.

I stepped a little closer, butterflies dancing. I could finally introduce myself. Reaching out my hand, I began, "Hi, I'm . . ."

"Oh, I know who you are," he said, taking my hand and holding it for longer than the usual shake. "You're Sheila Escovedo."

I stopped and stared at his lips. *Did my name just come out of his mouth?* "I've been following your career for a while," he added.

Wait a minute. He's been following me?

I guess it made sense. I'd already released my first record with Pops and had performed on multiple records for other artists, in addition to being on national tours and television shows. It dawned on me then—I didn't need to be nervous. I suppose I was a "somebody" before he was.

"Me and my bass player, André Cymone, were fighting about which one of us was going to marry you."

I laughed. "Oh, really?"

He told me he'd watched me play drums with George Duke on *Midnight Special* and *Don Kirshner's Rock Concert*.

"Oh, really," I repeated nervously, thinking that was pretty cool.

"How much does George pay you a week?" he asked.

I told him my salary.

He paused, crestfallen. "I'll never be able to afford you."

"You never know," I said. "Things could change."

He walked me toward the dressing room and introduced me to the band. By the end of the night we'd exchanged numbers.

In the ensuing weeks, Prince and I gradually became friends. We started out talking on the telephone, and then I invited him to come over and hang out with me.

Signed by Warner Brothers as an artist and their youngest-ever producer, he never seemed to stop working. Whenever he came to town I'd pick him up at the St. Francis Hotel in San Francisco or at the studio. I'd proudly drive him all over the Bay Area, showing him the coolest haunts, the prettiest scenery, and my former houses and schools. We'd get sandwiches around Lake Merritt and doughnuts at the famous Colonial Bakery. Mostly, we'd chat for hours.

Unlike me, Prince was a multi-instrumentalist who had played just about every instrument you could think of from an early age. Plus, he could sing—I mean, *he could sang!*—and yet he had such humility about his talents.

I was in awe.

Of course I bragged to him about Pops and his band and how we kids would often sit in and play with him and his legendary friends. Prince didn't believe it until he saw it—a father who plays timbales with his daughter and two sons. It was unheard of.

"Prince of what?" Juan asked when I first introduced him.

When Pops and my brothers saw how well he could play every instrument, they were pretty impressed. This man was a prince of music. He got along well with my family, and we welcomed him into our jam sessions. I liked that he showed so much respect to veterans like Pops.

My new friend from Minneapolis was impressed by our Latin jazz sound and loved coming to our gigs or just jamming in the front room with our family band.

For the next couple of years, as we each toured and I was getting over my split from Carlos, he and I would meet up whenever we could—but always just as friends. I'd been too deeply hurt by my last relationship to even begin to contemplate another, and certainly not one with another ladies' man and guitar player.

The cords that had bound us from the beginning, though, gradually drew us closer. We loved the same kind of music and shared a respect for each other's talents. We were checking each other out—seeing what the other one knew. We would jam at the house where I still lived with my parents off and on, due to touring some two hundred fifty days out of the year. I thought it silly to spend money on a place of my own for such short stays.

We'd hang out in my bedroom—which was a pseudo–recording studio—and jam for hours. The decor reflected my growing obsession with music. The walls and ceiling were covered with various posters I'd begged, borrowed, or purchased from record stores. (I took down the one of Prince before he came.) I wasn't really interested in posters of the standard teen heartthrobs, actors, or even pop singers. All of my posters featured musicians like Earth, Wind & Fire, Stevie Wonder, the Jacksons, Parliament-Funkadelic, James Brown, and every Motown artist you could think of. I had no idea that I myself would be on a poster in someone's room one day. I had no desire for fame. I just loved being surrounded by the faces of all my favorites. By this time, music was far more than a hobby or a means of paying the bills. Music was my life.

The rest of the room was all about the sound. Inspired by Pops's office, I had my collection of LPs and a piano, bass, and guitar along with virtually any percussion instrument I needed. I'd harbored dreams of writing my own songs, so I invested in the latest recording equipment, including a reel-to-reel four-track and a huge stereo system. On days off I'd record myself and listen back—my first attempt at being more than a player. Musician friends as well as Prince often came by our house to jam for hours. It didn't hurt that he was beautiful to look at.

Ever the workaholic (like me), he locked himself away in studios all over the country to continue to craft material for his next few albums, most of which were destined to go gold.

I was thrilled for him and enormously proud of my new friend.

I, too, kept working steadily, fulfilled and happy by gigs and tours, playing whenever, wherever, and with whomever I could.

I was getting more and more studio session work as well. When Quincy Jones called me in to provide percussion on a Michael Jackson song, "Don't Stop 'Til You Get Enough," which would soon be the number-one hit from his *Off the Wall* album, I contributed the distinctive percussive sound. It was the perfect song title for my pace at the time—I wasn't stopping, and I was nowhere near getting enough.

We were going after a particular sound on that number, and after trying various instruments I ended up putting water into a glass bottle. Once I'd pitched the key, I tapped it with the metal beater from my triangle. If you listen closely, you can hear that exact sound.

I'm not credited anywhere—the recording process took so long and the engineers chopped and changed around so much of it that they forgot to put my name on the record—but it was cool to be a small part of such a great song. And I was thrilled to contribute to one of Michael's tunes. He was one of the great entertainers and had become someone I enjoyed being around whenever possible.

Continuing to record fervently, sadly my work schedule—coupled with Prince's—meant that we didn't get to see very much of each other for a while. For anyone else that might have been the end of a beautiful friendship, but Fate had something else in mind.

17. Time Signature

An indication of rhythm following a clef

Sometimes love has no rhyme and no reason,
Even if we try to be cool
At the strangest times, love can make a connection

"NO RHYME, NO REASON"
GEORGE DUKE

I was a huge fan of Herbie Hancock, master of jazz funk, so getting to tour with him was a big deal for me. He was right up there on my list of greatest musicians. Herbie's an amazing instrumentalist, and nobody does what he does with a piano. Playing that kind of straight-up jazz is beyond me.

He and I had been on the same bill a couple of times when I was with Billy and George, and then one day in 1979 he called me up and asked me to play with him. What an honor. The first recording I did with him was for his twenty-ninth album, *Feets Don't Fail Me Now*. I played the congas and was in good company with family and friends including Uncle Coke, Bill Summers, and Ray Obiedo. I went on to feature on several of his other albums over the years. One of the things that most impressed me about Herbie was his self-care regimen. He was always taking vitamins and herbs and eating really mindfully, which wasn't the norm at all for musicians on the road, where fast food was the typical choice. Herbie ate the kinds of foods Moms would bring home from her job at the health food store. He showed me that even on tour one could maintain a healthy lifestyle.

I was getting more exposure, and with the increased attention came increased criticism. The more I took my music into the world—out of my house and out of the Bay Area—the more I found myself faced with either outright negative reactions about being a female drummer or at least a frosty reception. I was starting to understand that a lot of folks—particularly guys—considered the music industry a "man's world" and thought I was unusual for playing a "man's instrument."

Pops was the only one who seemed to understand what I was facing, and he helped me deal with all the negativity by encouraging me to shift my perspective. "You have to let your own light shine, Sheila," he told me. "Don't dim it just to make the guys around you feel more comfortable." The judgment from others had nothing to do with me, he said. He advised me to let go of any urge to explain or prove myself, and his words of wisdom helped me ignore the negative comments.

"Just tune in to your love of percussion. Focus on playing from your heart. When your heart says 'Go,' you *go*! Learn your music and be prepared so you walk in with confidence and ease. Be on time or be fifteen minutes early. Don't burn any bridges, because in the music business you never know when you'll have to work again with those same people you harmed." He was right. Whenever I played from my heart, I felt invincible. My music could speak for itself.

I always came prepped and with a good attitude, but this often made the other musicians mad, since a lot of them were late and didn't always come so well prepared. So they snickered in the corner or they teased and gossiped about me, trying to make me feel bad for doing the right thing and for respecting the craft like Pops had taught me.

In addition to the general sexism, I continued to contend with directly inappropriate behavior from some of the guys. They would hit on me daily, even after I'd been clear and direct in turning them down. It was just so disrespectful. And I knew their wives! I wouldn't have wanted my father to do that to my mother. After Carlos, that whole cheating thing was such a no-no for me. I didn't want to degrade myself, and I made sure to go back to my hotel room each night on my own. Sometimes I'd organize a girls' night with the background singers, but mostly we just made sure everybody was cool and stayed out of everybody else's business.

These men were my colleagues, and I wanted us to get along but remain professional. But for some of them, that wasn't enough.

It's true that I sometimes performed with barely any clothes on, which some might say provoked them, but I saw my dress choice as my prerogative. No one ever commented on how tight the guys' pants were or the fact that their shirts were open to the waist. But they thought whether or not I wore a bra was a hot topic that deserved lots of airtime. Backstage after a gig, the fellas would flatter me and say, "You were amazing, girl!" Then they'd offer me drugs and alcohol. Eventually, their talk would turn to sex.

Really? I'd think. *Are you guys for real?*

My disdain wasn't always enough for some of the men, though. One night we were leaving a venue in New Orleans, and a few of us had to squeeze into a car full of equipment because the van had left with the rest of the band. I had no choice but to sit on the lap of one of the musicians in the backseat.

A few minutes into the journey he started groping me and made a nasty comment about what he wanted to do with me when we got back to the hotel. The others in the car laughed, but I was enraged.

Something inside me exploded. Without skipping a beat, all of my built-up frustration from similar incidents in the past just exploded. I turned around and slapped him across the face.

Hard.

He was shocked to silence.

And I was too.

I guess I made my point, because—once he'd recovered—he apologized for what he'd said and vowed never to do it again. I accepted his apology and nodded to the reflection of the concerned driver in the rearview mirror. "It's all good." We sat in awkward silence for the rest of the ride, but I felt a great sense of calm come over me.

While I hadn't exactly articulated my point in the most civilized of manners, word soon got out about what I'd done. I'd made my point. These guys weren't accustomed to that kind of response. Some women in the business chose to sleep around, but not me. I took my romantic relationships very seriously, and for me, physical intimacy was only for two people in love.

It was all part of my determination to maintain my boundaries and the sanctity of my personal space. Nobody was messing with this lil' mama.

While working with Herbie, I was still on the lookout for other great musicians I could learn from and jam with. One night I went to the Circle Star Theater because I heard a singer named Chaka Khan was playing with her band, Rufus. I was such a fan and had studied her album closely, trying to figure out how and why they played what they did.

My friends at the Circle Star let me backstage and introduced me to Chaka. She and I hit it off immediately. She was a party girl and her band was funky—they had such great songs and arrangements on numbers like "You Got the Love" and "Tell Me Something Good."

Chaka's such an amazing singer and a downright powerhouse of a woman. Nobody sounds like Chaka. I liked that she dressed sexy while belting out her hit songs with confidence and strength. When she asked me to sit in on one of her shows, it was another dream come true. We especially bonded because she was one of the first professional female musicians I'd ever worked with who could play drums *and* sing.

My new "sister" knew all about being a woman in a man's world, although it was sad to watch her descend later into alcoholism and drug abuse. I screamed at her dealer once because he'd given her something that wiped her out so bad she became almost unconscious on my shoulder and nearly burned a hole in my jacket with her cigarette.

"What the heck did you give her?" I yelled. "Leave her alone!" I always felt terrible when I saw her like that. I didn't know how to help her. She was someone I looked up to, and I felt powerless when she was so weak. Even my Oakland attitude didn't have much sway over the cunning force of alcohol and drugs. Chaka and I have stayed close, and I love her dearly. She has been clean since 2005 and looks and sounds even better now. How is that even possible?

Music was all my friends and I talked about. "Have you heard of this band?" and "Let me play you this song" or "Watch this new pattern I came up with." The Bay Area was still buzzing with great musicianship. A project would come along and turn into another project, and then a third. It was nonstop. I took it all on and loved each opportunity because they were all so different.

I had a couple of boyfriends then (musicians, of course), but music remained my one true love. As far as I was concerned, it was all I really needed. If someone came along and swept me off my feet, then that would be fine, but I wasn't going to seek anything out. I wasn't pushing love away. Rather, I was just enjoying the healing power of music and relishing everything it provided me.

Back then I was steadily working out what was appropriate in terms of my look and my stage presentation. I saw what Chaka got away with—often little more than a decorated bra, pants, and a bare midriff. I was still learning how to define myself as a professional musician, which also meant learning what being professional was all about. But I still had a lot of growing up to do, and my attitude wasn't always as mature as my musicianship.

One day I got an urgent call to play percussion in Diana Ross's orchestra for a set of dates at the Circle Star. I was replacing someone who'd dropped out at the last minute. Ms. Ross was a personal idol of mine—everyone wanted to be her! I went to the rehearsal, where I caught on pretty quickly and never once let on that I couldn't read the music they'd handed me. I was really looking forward to the public performances.

As I left the rehearsal, someone from her management team told me I should dress in all black for the shows, since I'd be playing in the pit along with the rest of the orchestra. They didn't specify anything else.

I'd figured out long ago that my arms needed to be free or I'd feel uncomfortable. My biceps would pump up the more I played, so an outfit with sleeves that might start off loose before a show would be horribly tight by the end. I was also coming to learn that it felt nice to dress sexy. I mostly wore halter-neck tops or sleeveless blouses, some of which were see-through. That was my look.

I turned up for the show with a low-cut halter-neck top and black pants. I was excited about the gig, so I'd called up a few of my friends to come and watch us play. When the members of the orchestra were announced, I was surprised to get a noisy round of applause, and not just from the friends I'd invited along. That was probably the first time I realized that I was developing a name for myself in the Bay Area, because this was a gig without Pops. The biggest thrill for me, though, was to be playing with Diana Ross.

As we were tuning up, a few of my friends started waving at me and screaming my name, and I could see Ms. Ross wasn't happy. There was a moment when I thought, Uh-oh, this could go badly.

The show went great, though, and I did all I was asked to do and more. I was happy and looking forward to the rest of the gigs. But just as I was packing my instruments, her manager came over and asked me to wear something less revealing the following night.

I was shocked. Sure, my top was low-cut, but not excessively so. Instead of just doing what I was asked, I adopted my default position of "You can't tell me what to do!"—a rebellious streak I hadn't yet shed from adolescence.

"You hired me for my musicianship," I told him indignantly. "I was on time. I played well. I wore black. You didn't tell me I had to dress like a nun!"

Then he told me, "Ms. Ross wants to speak with you."

Feeling like a naughty schoolgirl, I went sheepishly to her dressing room and stood right outside the open door. She sat at her dressing table, chatting to a friend. She could surely see my reflection in the mirror, but she kept me waiting for almost twenty minutes. I knew my friends were outside, and I started to get mad.

Even though I was a lowly percussion player, I decided that it was disrespectful for her to ignore me. Finally, and with a dramatic sigh, I turned to head back down the corridor. Her musical director called me back and asked me where I was going.

I turned and told him, "I'm out of here!"

Diana stopped chatting and called, "Excuse me, can you come here for a second? I'd like to talk to you, young lady." In front of her friend she let me know I did a great job, but I sensed that wasn't what she really wanted to say. Her director grabbed me afterward and said, "Ms. Ross would appreciate you wearing something more covered up for tomorrow's shows."

I was so mad I just walked off, saying, "Really? First she made me wait twenty minutes, she disrespected me, and now you want me to calm my look and play it down? Well, how about this? I quit!"

"Wait a minute, you can't quit!"

"Watch me."

Can you believe I walked out on Diana Ross!

Man, I was crazy. I didn't care who she was, or how famous. I did not like how she treated me.

I guess I hadn't quite fully taken on board all of Pops's advice yet, and I'd completely forgotten the part about doing what I was told to do and remaining humble.

Fortunately, Diana didn't hold my youthful hotheadedness against me. Years later we were playing on the same bill at the American Music Awards and everybody was in the green room together, including Bruce Springsteen and Lionel Richie. It was so crowded that there was nowhere for me to sit. Diana spotted me standing awkwardly in the doorway and cried out, "There's my baby! Come and sit on my lap!" So I did.

Over the years we've frequently crossed paths, have many mutual friends in the industry, and have become—I'm proud to say—friends.

18. Metronome

A device used by musicians to mark time

No one could speak of passion and touch her
Touch her the way he does . . . It was him (life without love)
or a life without love

"MICHELANGELO"

SHEILA E

On Valentine's Day 1982, Prince was booked to play at the San Francisco Civic Auditorium as part of his *Controversy* tour. Eager to see him again after a couple of years in which we'd lost contact, I bought tickets and took Connie and my girlfriend Karen, who'd been dating my brother Peter Michael.

We watched the show from our balcony seats, screaming and hollering along with every other woman in the place. I knew all the songs; I'd bought all four Prince albums. My old jamming buddy was mighty fine and hecka sexy. The sheer spectacle of his show was amazing, and I loved everything about it.

Prince hit that stage singing, dancing, playing piano and guitar. I think he could play something like thirty instruments in all. He was so talented, and at the time there was nothing like him or his show around in terms of the lighting, stage presence, songs, and showmanship.

He was on fire, and watching him made me feel starstruck, nervous, and excited all at once.

Afterward, I talked my way backstage as usual, which wasn't so hard to do since most of the crew and security knew me. As I walked down the long hallway toward his dressing room I tried to play it cool, but inside, my butterflies were all aflutter. My head was buzzing with images of his performance, and his music was still ringing in my ears. I couldn't wait to see him again.

It was difficult not to blur the line between being a fan and a friend.

I spotted him backstage talking to his musicians, just like before, and—once again—our eyes locked.

Smiling, he said simply, "Wow!"

"It's been a while," I said, feeling unusually bashful.

We hugged, we caught up, and we acknowledged it had been far too long since we'd seen each other. There was that familiar sense of intimacy and the immediate ease that comes when you feel connected to someone. Words are secondary, and it's the *being together* that becomes paramount to the talking.

I felt like I'd known him for a thousand years.

Trying to snap myself back into normal social etiquette, I gushed over his performance and told him I was "awestruck." He thanked me sweetly, but his eyes just kept on boring into me like he was staring into my soul.

I was so fascinated by what he was doing musically and so proud of him, but because we hadn't seen each other for so long it was almost like I didn't know him at all. We had to start our friendship all over again.

Apart from anything else, he looked completely different. His hair was very short this time. He wore tight black gymnastic pants straight to the ankle with stirrups at the bottom. They were high-waisted and sexy, and he wore a big white shirt open to the waist. He looked strong and handsome and his cologne was—well—his own natural musk.

Now it was my turn to have the bigger crush, but I had no idea where that might lead because Prince was now a huge star, a top platinum-selling artist. I didn't feel worthy of him.

We swapped numbers and started talking on the phone again, but our schedules conspired against us once more. I'd get days off here and there, but his schedule was seriously nonstop. I half resigned myself to the fact that our paths would drift apart again and that we would always be long-distance friends.

Once again, I had other things to distract me because I'd been invited to go out on tour with the Motown legend that was Marvin Gaye. I could hardly believe it when I got the gig. I mean, man!

Juan, Peter Michael, and I had worked out dance routines to "I Heard It Through the Grapevine" when we were kids fooling around at Moms and Pops's house. Now, I was actually going to be on the same stage with this genius, playing percussion while he sang: *I guess you're wondering how I knew* . . . Sadly, Marvin's personal life had been dogged with tragedy and other problems. At forty-four years old, he had some major drug issues, suffered from paranoia and depression, had twice attempted suicide, and was a tax exile for years due to the millions of dollars he owed to the IRS. Having straightened himself out a little and finding some spiritual relief in returning to his faith, he had a massive global hit with "Sexual Healing" and negotiated to return to the US, where he would work his way out of debt.

Rehearsals were due to start right away for the Sexual Healing tour, which would last from April to August 1983. I had to fit them in between my increasingly demanding schedule of recording work as well as gigs with Pops and my brothers.

I was playing with Pops during a show at Redondo Beach one night in 1982 when we heard that Lionel Richie would be coming to watch me perform because he was looking for a percussionist for an upcoming tour. His tour manager was a guy from Marvin's tour, and he'd told Lionel about me.

Knowing that it could be a great opportunity for me, Pops let me sing up front that night and feature a bit more in the show. To our disappointment, Lionel never showed, but his wife, Brenda, did. I think that when she heard he was considering bringing a girl percussionist into the band she probably wanted to check me out. She helped run the business for him too. Brenda listened to me play, and then we met afterward and she interviewed me casually. I liked her, and she seemed to like who I was too.

Finally, she told me, "Okay, Sheila, you've got the gig." She went home and told Lionel that she'd hired me. Thanks to Brenda's vote of confidence, I was in!

The plan was to start rehearsals with Lionel toward the end of Marvin's tour and then start touring with Lionel as soon as Marvin's ended. But first they wanted me to appear in a video they were shooting to accompany Lionel's latest hit single, "Running with the Night." Music videos that told a story to accompany a song were a relatively new concept back then, and this was my first. Although I was excited to be part of it, I had no idea what to expect.

Once I got into hair and makeup at the studio, I started learning bits and pieces about the story line. The backdrop, I was told, was a joyful wedding, complete with a dewy-eyed bride and groom cutting the cake and a roomful of dancing wedding guests. Everyone was over the moon, except for the lonely bridesmaid sitting alone at a table—cue Sheila.

My character, I soon discovered, would not be anyone I could relate to. I wouldn't be holding drumsticks or commanding some conga drums. Sitting alone in my cheesy dress and heels—not the kind of thing I'd ever really wear—I was told to look sad. I felt like a pitiful little Mexican at her quinceañera. Lionel would play a street-smart dancer who, with his gang of dancers from the street (a version of those ubiquitous gangs of dancers in nearly every eighties music video), would crash the wedding and beckon me to the dance floor.

When I met up with Lionel on set and we got a look at each other's costumes, we were already in giggles.

For Lionel we used the nickname "Lonnie Bistro," or "Lonnie B" for short. The Escovedos and Garderes are big on nicknames. If we give you a nickname, you're in the family. I myself have seven nicknames, which alternate depending on if I'm being addressed by my family, my friends, or my godchildren.

When the director, Bob Giraldi (who'd worked with Michael Jackson), told us the concept of the video and that Lionel—ever the jokester, the hilarious storyteller—would be playing a serious, sexy man and I would be his love interest, we cracked up. We were like sister and brother. How in the world would we keep straight faces once the camera was rolling? There were so many takes, mostly because we had such a hard time gazing earnestly into each other's eyes.

My kid sister, Zina, was cast as an extra in the video (this is a family show, remember?), and, a natural on the dance floor, she took to it better than I did. Even though I'd always thought of myself as a good dancer, on this video set I suddenly felt so stiff and without coordination. It was nothing like doing Jackson 5 numbers with my brothers in our front room or hitting the dance floor at San Francisco clubs with my girlfriends. These were not your normal dance moves. They were official dance routines choreographed by Michael Jackson's choreographer, Michael Peters.

I thought I was a good dancer until I started trying to do as I was told. There were so many formations and step sequences—stuff I'd never do in real life. It just wasn't natural. Plus I was wearing a fluffy off-the-shoulder red dress and having to stare at Lonnie B like I was in love with him. The whole thing felt so goofy.

Filming the video for "Running with the Night" is an experience I'll never forget (and not just because it's always a few clicks away on YouTube). I got to work with the best producers, directors, choreographers, and dancers; share the experience with my little sister; and hang out with Lonnie B, the World's Most Famous Negro, as he used to call himself.

And on top of all that, I was about to go on tour with Marvin Gaye. Best of all, my family friend Tony Flores (whom we call our cousin, or more accurately *cuzzin* or *cut'n*—so ghetto I can't even spell it) was in Marvin's band too. None of my relatives had auditioned for Marvin's show, but I had a secret plan. I encouraged Peter Michael to come with me to hang out and crash the rehearsals. We could show up under the pretense that we were just visiting Tony.

The band was already huge: four singers, three guitar players, five horns, multiple keyboard players, and one vibe percussionist. So I figured, why not have more percussion players? I'm an Escovedo, so the more percussion, the better. Besides, I wanted some family with me. We always had so much fun and played well together.

Days went by, and I kept asking Peter Michael to just sit in with us while we rehearsed.

"Sheila, they already have a band," he said. "You want me to sit in when I haven't even been invited? That ain't cool."

"Trust me," I told him. "It'll be fine." It took all my powers of persuasion and big-sister bossiness, but I eventually talked him into sitting in during rehearsals. When I make up my mind that something's going to happen, it usually does. And I had made up my mind that my brother was going to join the tour with me, before Marvin or the tour manager had even heard him make a sound.

We set up at rehearsals with three sets of congas, three sets of bongos, and three sets of timbales. This might sound excessive, but keep in mind we were complementing a twenty-three-piece band. The sound was fat. Once we all started playing together, it was clear to everyone that we enhanced the sound and that their absence would've been felt.

It went well, but there was no direct offer of work for Peter Michael, and I was disappointed that my plan looked set to fail. After all the rehearsals, we were ready for the customary dress rehearsal. Peter Michael came to the theater and sat in the audience. We ran down the show, and when it was done, Marvin said, "Where is Peto?"

Wilbert, the tour manager, explained, "He wasn't officially hired. He was just sitting in at rehearsals."

"No," said Marvin. "Go find him and get him, we need him."

Since Peter Michael was right there in the building, Wilbert didn't have to look far. Peter Michael was pulled out from the audience and told to call the designer so he could be fitted for a tux immediately. He'd be joining the band for the tour. I had to smile.

The tour started on April 18 that year in San Diego. Musically, it was a wonderful experience, and my playing grew by leaps and bounds. Professionally, it was one of my most challenging tours. Marvin was beset with problems and surrounded by all kinds of unsavory characters. Thank God I had family with me. We had each other's backs and got to share the honor of working for one of our musical heroes.

He was such a gentleman—funny and sweet. His talent blew me away, night after night. During the first couple of shows, once he started singing—especially when he was sitting at the piano—I was so swept up in his delivery, so lost in his unearthly talent, that I literally forgot I was onstage with him and missed my cues.

Peter Michael would subtly walk over and nudge me. "Sheila, you were supposed to play that beat!" or "Sheila, hit the chimes!"

"Oh, shoot!" I'd say and start playing.

I was so lost in Marvin I sometimes felt like a fan at the concert, not a part of his band. Sharing the stage with him, one of the musical greats I'd always looked up to, was utterly surreal. He had a lot to teach me. One day during an on-the-road rehearsal, I learned an important lesson about what it meant to honor the integrity of a song. When we were running through "What's Going On," I was so feeling the groove of that song that I had to start dancing. Then Peter Michael and I busted out some of our old Jackson 5 moves, both of us always wanting to add a little spice. It was our own little dance fest. Tony joined in on the dance moves, and soon the horn players were doing our steps, too. Section by section, the whole band started grooving.

Marvin sang his heart out, and everybody felt it: *Mother, mother, there's far too many of you cryin'*.

Then, as I was playing the simple conga rhythm of that song on the high lead conga drum (quinto)—*boong boong gah, boong buh-doong gah, boong boong gah, boong buh-doong gah*, you know the one—I was so into the song that I got happy and hit an extra beat (*donnnng!*) on the low conga drum (called a tumba). That extra hit is *not* a part of the song.

Wrong move.

Immediately Marvin yelled, "Stop!"

The whole band stopped. It got quiet, real fast.

Marvin, a very softly spoken man, never yelled, so we knew

something was wrong. He scanned the room, looking at all of the musicians and then focusing his attention on the three of us.

"Who hit that extra drum?" I was speechless, afraid to confess and praying my brother and cousin wouldn't tell on me. I felt like a little girl again, being interrogated by Moms after one of us kids did something bad.

Marvin waited.

Without thinking, I pointed to Peter Michael and tried to blame him for it. Old sibling dynamics die hard. I did get him the gig, after all. Maybe he owed me this one.

But when my brother looked at me with utter shock, his eyes said he wasn't having it. His look said, *How you gonna call me out like that and it ain't even true!* Rather than tell the truth and let Marvin know that I was the one who hit that extra beat, though, Peter Michael let me blame it on him. He took one for the team.

Guilt was eating me up, though, and I realized how wrong it was for me to have blamed him.

"Okay, okay, guys. Sorry. My fault!" I said, hands in the air as if I was under arrest. I admitted to Marvin and my fellow musicians that it was me who'd mistakenly thought it was cool to accessorize an already perfect rhythm line with that extra beat. Most everybody thought it was funny, but I dug into some serious humble pie that day.

As is usually the case with embarrassing blows to the ego like this one, I ended up learning a very important lesson. Only play what is supposed to be played for the specific song you're supposed to be playing. Knowing when not to play is in some ways more important than actually playing. My extra little beat didn't even sound right. Everyone knows that song right away from that perfect conga rhythm—just as it is. Less is more.

I've come to think of percussion as the last color added that turns a pretty painting into the most beautiful painting in the world. Percussionists are those extra crucial colors. But which color should a percussionist choose? And where should it go? And how light or heavy should the stroke of the paintbrush be? Percussionists should be selective. They don't have to play just because there's a space to play.

One of the most valuable things is knowing not just how to play, but when *not* to play. That is key. Fledgling percussionists tend to want to play during the entire song. They want to be heard. But being a good percussionist during a song is like being a good listener during a conversation. You're not going to create a very fulfilling dialogue with another person if you're talking over them, interrupting them, or, instead of actively listening, just waiting for your chance to get a word or two in.

A good listener is an active listener who stays present and doesn't step on the speaker's words. It's the same thing with percussion. A good percussionist knows when it's time to listen and when it's time to play. And a very good percussionist doesn't just listen for a good spot to play; a good percussionist is present for the song, listening for a chance to enhance it rather than crowd it.

The same goes for drummers. I've played with both drummers and percussionists who don't know how to solo that well, or don't know a lot of licks and fills. So technically, they end up playing less than someone who knows more. But those who play less actually make the song sound better. Those are actually the ones I'd prefer to work with. It's a question of quality over quantity.

When I'm auditioning a drummer for my band—believe it or not, I'm not always on drums, so I need a drummer behind me when I'm out in front singing and/or playing percussion—I'm more interested in the one who plays less and keeps time more. In other words, I need a drummer who can set the foundation for the band.

If you're busy playing a bunch of fills, then you may be looking cool and sounding cool, but you're missing the point. Just because you know all that doesn't mean you should play all that. The drummer needs to be steady, reliable, and on time—and, above all else, to stay out of the way.

A good drummer drives the bus instead of running up and down the aisle distracting all the passengers. This comes back to something that I think all musicians in a band should keep in mind. To go along with the bus analogy, passengers can't all get on at the same time. There's a narrow entryway and a narrow aisle. You have to fall back to give someone else time to get on, walk on, and sit down.

Whenever the E Family performs, we still have to take time to negotiate this seemingly simple guideline. We can't have my father, my two brothers, and myself all showing off our tricks at once. Back in the day, my brothers and I didn't quite get this. We'd be in the garage or at house parties, all trying to take the solo. Juan and Peter Michael would each want to take a timbale solo, one after the other. And then me.

While that's fun, and the solos might even be halfway decent, we had to learn how to give each other space, how to be not only good musicians but good musicians who know about musicianship. Talent and musicianship are two very different things.

When I was on tour with Marvin Gaye, my contact with Prince was pretty minimal—though often when I opened the door to my hotel room after arriving in a new city, I'd be delighted to find a beautiful bouquet of flowers, accompanied by a really touching card. Such surprises certainly provided a happy distraction and made the challenging times on the tour more bearable.

Every person on that tour has a different story to tell, but I think we can all agree that as lucky as we were to be there, we were equally stressed. Our beloved drum tech, Eric Sharp, so young and vital, was found hanged in his hotel room during the tour. His loss was traumatic to Peter Michael, Tony, and me. I often think of him and will always miss him. After his death, it felt like a dark cloud was hanging over the entire tour. There was such a strange energy, and I never felt completely safe.

Some of the attention I was getting from men only made things harder. Playing on that tour signified another level in my career, and yet I quickly discovered that with these new opportunities came new challenges. Once again I had to navigate around some unsavory invitations from various music-industry insiders who attended the shows.

Different tour, same proposal: sleep with me and I'll advance your career. The proposal was the same, even if now it was more frequent and more dressed up.

I was now being told that I could have money, drugs, cars, houses, and record deals if I would just give up my body for the night. Turning down offers like this was a no-brainer. I became increasingly grateful for my upbringing, for Moms and Pops raising me with such a strong moral code. Besides, I wanted an honest man with a sense of humor who would sweep me off my feet. And, of course, he had to be fine!

Even though I was still pretty young at twenty-five, I was getting better and better at trusting my instincts about people—who would support me and uplift me and who was there to use me or bring me down. I'm grateful that my devotion to the music kept me focused and kept me from straying from who I really was and what I felt I was called to do. While my increasing resolve didn't stop guys from making aggressive pitches about how they could make me a star, I was becoming better at defending myself against the onslaught of disingenuous lines. I just wasn't interested in that kind of pitch. I was satisfied with where I was in my career and constantly excited by all that I was learning.

While I was creating the foundation for being more than a backup singer and featured percussionist, I didn't have any conscious plan for anything more. Divine timing was working it out for me.

By this time I was already writing my own songs—carrying around notebooks and journals filled with lyrics, experimenting with music, playing with my drum machine and keyboard, navigating the gear, working my four-track and my eight-track. So I'm sure it was in the back of my mind somewhere: being a solo artist or, more vaguely, moving beyond whatever constraints band membership might create. And yes, it did occur to me that I could maybe solo one day, but I didn't have a conscious plan. Besides, there weren't any women who were solo percussionists/singers/ drummers who played different genres of music while integrating dance routines.

A few friends had small studios in their homes and were making demos, so I taught myself to do the same. No one ever sat me down and showed me how to make a demo, and I didn't like reading a manual. I just bought the most professional equipment I could afford at the time and started to play.

Being on tour with a Motown icon like Marvin, I was exposed to lots of perks like extra amenities or special access to restaurants and clubs—just special treatment all around. Sure, I thought, I can get used to this. But I was also being exposed to something greater that I wanted to get used to: respect for the artist.

While intellectually I understood that Marvin was a huge star whose songs affected so many, I was continually blown away by the reaction he'd get onstage. Hearing people sing along to his music and thank him for his impact on their lives, I was beginning to fantasize about somehow doing the same.

Of course, it'd have to be my unique version of the same. Can't nobody even touch Marvin. But he inspired me to want to continue being the best Sheila-artist I could be. What lyrics and arrangements and showmanship could I develop within myself? What if my own music could move people? What would it feel like to inspire others—to allow for even just 1 percent of the kind of inspiration Marvin provided? I didn't know how any of this would actually happen, but I was more than ready—thrilled, really—about the prospect of finding out.

Toward the end of Marvin's tour, my schedule got crazy: I'd fly to Los Angeles to rehearse with Lionel during the day and fly back to whatever city Marvin and the band were playing in that night. Only when the tour finally ended was I able to practice full-time with Lionel and his band. It was during one such rehearsal with Lionel's band that I learned the shocking news of Marvin's murder, an unthinkable tragedy only compounded by the horrifying detail that it was his father who had pulled the trigger. I kept thinking about how much security he had with him when we were on tour. There were always four or five bodyguards protecting him. Then he went home and was killed by his father.

The thought haunted me—how home, what should be the epitome of safety, was the place he was ultimately the least safe. Perhaps something about that was painfully familiar to me. Marvin's death continues to evoke a sense of horror within me—the loss of this gifted man and the reminder that regardless of environment, safety is never a guarantee. I suppose that's one of the reasons that developing my spiritual self began to feel so crucial. Within the realm of spirituality, there is everlasting safety.

Rehearsal was canceled that day out of respect for our beloved Marvin, and because we were all too upset to continue. Although there had been some dark omens on the road, none of us could have predicted that that was his last tour, that those would be his final performances.

As the days passed, my grieving only intensified. The pain of his loss is still so profound for me. And the grief has given way to a deeper understanding of my purpose.

Peter Michael, Tony, and I would come to understand the true honor it was to play together in Marvin's last tour; to share the stage with a musical genius gone much too soon. I got to play with someone I idolized. But I didn't know the amount of pain he was living with, all the internal suffering he was enduring. I would later come to learn about his financial, spiritual, creative, and professional struggles.

His legacy has been a blessing to so many, and I can only pray that he had a glimpse of understanding his purpose in his lifetime.

May he finally rest in peace.

19. Brushes

A drumstick with long wire bristles to
make a hissing sound on cymbals

Ain't no turnin' back now, got my whole body sweatin'
I can do this all night, ain't got long before the last song

"DO WHAT IT DO"
THE E FAMILY

Working with Lionel Richie couldn't have been a more different experience. He had a wealth of experience from his time with the Commodores, and now as a solo artist he was unstoppable, soaring up the charts with his latest blockbuster album *Can't Slow Down*, which featured the Grammy-winning hit "All Night Long."

His on-tour rehearsals were a revelation for me because for the first time I was working on a proper soundstage that had to be built months in advance. The stage show was much more of a spectacle than Marvin's: so many more technical effects and lighting cues. Not that it's better—I'm also all for simplicity and purity—it's just a new level and different.

That tour was just like the tours you hear about or see on TV. Lionel was even more popular than Marvin Gaye at the time, and once I saw him in action I realized why. He's not only an amazing songwriter, but he's also funny, personable, and charming.

It was while I was working with Marvin and Lionel that I made the decision to leave home and move to Los Angeles with my friend Connie. I didn't want to go alone, and since she had great business instincts and a desire to build upon her skills in the entertainment industry, it wasn't too tough to convince her to make the move with me.

We packed up our belongings and hit the highway. Six hours later (maybe less, because I like to drive fast), two brown girls from East Oakland were taking pictures of each other at all the major tourist spots like the Walk of Fame, plus a few of the lesser-known ones. Hollywood was a dream come true, just like I'd pictured it.

I'd been to LA before—for gigs and on road trips with my family—but now I'd made the leap to live there officially. I loved the idea of having a roomie, but it didn't last longer than twenty-four hours. On the day we moved in, after we'd just finished unpacking the truck, it was time for me to go out on tour again and for Connie to begin working as a studio assistant for George Duke.

The people who toured with Lionel were an intimate bunch made up of band members, security, crew, and relatives. We were family.

Mideighties fashion was all about shoulder pads and big hair, all glitter and glam. The show featured synchronized flashing lights and multiple stage levels, with dancers and ramps. The greatest thing for me was being allowed my own little spot where I could play a solo, sing along with Lionel, or be featured in some other way. Everyone was so gracious; they really allowed me to shine.

Even though Lionel's tour was pretty grueling and I didn't get the rest I needed, given that it came on the heels of so much else I was doing, I loved every minute. This was what I wanted. It was 1983 when I first toured with him, and even though my solo success was a few years away, I was getting some invaluable experience and a taste for a certain kind of life. The most obvious step up for me was that I went from traveling in a car or a van and commercial flights to private buses and then—my all-time favorite—a private jet. Now, don't get me wrong. I loved having my own tour bus and the experience of traveling with all the other artists—I almost sold my house once to live on a bus. I loved the simplicity of having your transport and your home as one, and not having to worry about anything else. No mortgage, just gas. (These days, I'm not sure there's much difference!)

Private jets, on the other hand, made a whole lot of other fun stuff possible. There's no security at the airport (and therefore no flashbacks to Colombia); you never have to wait in line; there's hot food once you get on the plane; you have the option of sitting with the pilot during takeoff and landing (feeling a bit like the astronaut I'd always longed to be); and you can help yourself to hot chocolate-chip cookies, in-flight massages, and glasses of wine. I would gaze out at the sky in wonder and count the real stars as well as my lucky ones.

Sometimes I had to pinch myself when I realized that the high school dropout whose family occasionally had to rely on welfare stamps was now enjoying the kind of life I'd only seen in movies. I was living larger than I ever could have imagined.

I was so busy and having so much fun that there wasn't room in my life for anything but work and music, which was just as well, because Prince was co-coordinating three or four projects at a time, including several protégé bands.

We spoke when we could (before mobile phones, e-mails, and Skype), but each time we did, he slowly chipped away at my defenses. He was very smart. On the Lionel Richie tour, he sent enormous bouquets to every hotel room in every city where I stayed.

There was definitely some serious wooing going on.

It's a good thing I didn't suffer from hay fever, because he'd send an embarrassing amount of blooms. The different arrangements had cards that read HAVE A GREAT SHOW or LOVE YOU, PRINCE.

With every bouquet I'd wonder where all this was leading. We had always been such good friends and, although he'd hinted at moving our relationship to another level, I was happy for things to stay as they were—for now. Not only was he as busy as I was, traveling and working, but women constantly surrounded him, and that wasn't the kind of relationship I wanted with anyone—especially after Carlos.

Inhaling the scent from his bouquets, I'd think, Heck, what am I going to do with this huge arrangement? The band members would have to make room for my flowers and me—even on Lionel's private plane.

I continued to be privately delighted each time, though, because every arrangement was different, outdoing the last. Each time I saw them, my heart skipped a beat, and I couldn't deny that my feelings were growing. He was so darn romantic. I think I was falling in love with the concept of Prince more than I was with the man himself—whom I hardly ever saw. What with the flowers and phone calls telling me how much he cared, he was wearing me down. He was also hugely popular at that point, and everyone was talking about him, which made him seem even more powerful and sexy. I was starting to think, *Hmm. Maybe.*

My collection of cards from him was growing too. I treasured each one, carefully storing them in a large envelope that became worn and wrinkled as it moved from city to city with me, safely tucked inside my luggage. I still have them all somewhere.

Prince's strategy worked. I couldn't get him off my mind, even to the point that when I bought myself a new racquet for racquetball (which I played ferociously and competitively in every town where I could find a court), I selected a brand based on name alone: Prince.

I liked looking at his name.

When he could, he'd fly out to visit me on tour with Lionel—which always gave me such a thrill. He'd turn up in some amazing outfit and hang out on the side of the stage with the enormous bodyguards he now needed, watching the shows (and my playing especially) with a forensic eye. He and I also started hanging out a lot between touring, and much of our time was spent in the studio. He was working with a camp of people, developing artists and producing their songs.

In one studio he might be rehearsing or recording something for himself, such as his upcoming Purple Rain tour and the accompanying rock-musical movie; in the next studio he might be laying down some tracks for somebody else; and in the third he'd be producing a new group he'd put together. He had a female vocal trio called Vanity 6, another female threesome called Apollonia 6, and a separate band called the Time.

He hired engineers in shifts because no one could stay up or go the distance the way he did. Music is what kept him awake. He was practically living at Sunset Sound Studios in LA and, since I was with him so much then, so was I.

That man never stopped. Everybody wanted them some Prince.

One day in December 1983, he called me up and asked me to join him at the studio.

"Sure, what do you need me to bring?"

"Don't worry about it," he replied. "Just get down here."

I was intrigued.

Sunset Sound was on Sunset Boulevard, not too far from my

new home. The first time I walked through the gate I saw a basket-ball court and thought, *This is my kind of place.* Ever the Gardere, I looked at the musicians and technicians hanging around and asked, "Who wants to shoot some hoops?"

Once I was in the studio that night, I figured it would be the usual format, with me providing drums or percussion to one of Prince's tracks. It would be a late night or an early morning, de-pending on which way you looked at it, but I didn't care; I was just happy to be with him.

I walked in to find sweet-smelling candles burning and the whole place impeccably clean, as usual. Prince had set up the stu-dio like a living room—all comfortable and cozy as if we were at home. It might as well have been—if he wasn't playing live, he was in that studio, so it was "home."

As ever, he was a real gentleman, and he asked me what I wanted to drink or if I was hungry. He always wanted to make me feel comfortable. Most of the time, like on that particular night, there'd be no engineer. If there was, he or she would leave the room whenever someone else came in. Prince liked to record on his own.

I expected to walk into the studio and find drums or percussion set up for me as normal. All I saw, though, was a solitary micro-phone.

"Where's my gear?" I asked, confused.

He chuckled and said, "We don't need that tonight."

We sat down and talked a little, and then he played me some new music he'd been working on. One of the songs was the unfinished—although already funky—"Erotic City," intended as a B-side for "Let's Go Crazy."

The song began, *All of my purple life, I've been looking for a dame that would wanna be my wife* . . . I loved it.

"That's funky!" I told him with a warm smile.

I looked around for a bag of tambourines or cowbells, but neither was in sight. Not even a shaker.

I felt the butterflies flicker to life in my stomach.

Prince smiled, and my butterflies danced.

"I want you sing with me on this track," he said. It was the last thing in the world I expected him to say.

"Oh, okay. Backup?" I asked hopefully, fearing his answer.

He shook his head.

Whenever I get nervous my throat constricts. If I don't breathe and relax, then I can't speak, let alone sing. I sound all choked up and tiny. In a voice that was already several octaves higher than usual, I squeaked, "Um, you know I don't like singing."

"You've been singing behind everyone for years, Sheila," Prince said softly, brushing back a fallen strand of my hair. "You know just what to do."

His suggestion that I sing a duet with him (one of the biggest stars in the world) was made with such nonchalance, as if it was an everyday offer. There he was, an amazing singer with a range from low to high falsetto—whereas all I'd ever done was croon a little background. "Come on," he said. "Let's just do it."

"Ah, really?" I had a lump in my throat and was so nervous.

I tried everything I could to wriggle out of singing with him. I reminded him that backing other people was much easier for me. I told him that what he was proposing was the most intimidating prospect of my life. Despite my usual confidence, I didn't even know how to begin. Even though he was my friend (with increasingly romantic undertones), I felt suddenly self-conscious and half scared to death.

"But we sing together all the time," he soothed, pushing me gently.

"Sure, when we're just hanging out and jamming—but to sing in a studio and have you record it?"

I had been recording my vocals for years in my own home studio and also doing vocals with my dad on our records. This was different, though.

My knees were shaking at the mere idea of standing in front of a microphone. What in the world would I do with my hands, which were always moving at a hundred miles an hour?

But Prince is a hard man to say no to. Before I knew it I was just where he wanted me, in front of the mic, my hands clamped rigidly to my sides as I waited to hear what strangulated sound would emerge from my throat.

The answer was almost nothing. My throat closed. He was so patient with me, and the more I tried, the more my confidence grew—well, a little. He told me to sing like I do with everyone else. After a while, my nerves began to dissipate, and I even started to enjoy the process, although I'm not sure I ever got that comfortable that night.

One unexpected hurdle, though, involved his lyrics, or rather one word in one line of the chorus. I looked at the sheet he'd scribbled them on and told him I really wasn't happy about singing the f-word.

"My mother would have a fit!"

He smiled at me as if indulging a child, then worked out a compromise. He would sing "We can f— until the dawn" while I sang "We can *funk* until the dawn." Which is what we did, and then later he laid the two tracks over each other.

In the finished song you can hear both words, which ended up becoming a bit of a mystery for Prince fans. People were asking, "Are they saying 'funk' or are they saying the f-word?" Most DJs claimed it was "funk" so that they could play the track and not get into trouble. My moral shyness had inadvertently not only got people talking about the double entendre, it started a buzz.

Although it was the eighties, society hadn't yet been inundated with the kind of overt sexuality in songs and videos that came later. Prince was really pushing the envelope in "Erotic City," and it was still a big deal back then to hear that word (or even *think* you'd heard that word) on the radio.

I'm relieved to say that, to this day, Moms never seemed to notice. If she had, I'd have been in big trouble.

People still comment on how "sexy" I sound on that song, which always makes me laugh, because if you had been in the studio with Prince that night, you'd sound sexy too! I have no idea what time we finished recording in that windowless space, but it was late. Oftentimes we'd walk out of the studio and I'd be surprised to encounter daylight and have to reach for my sunglasses.

In the weeks we lived at Sunset Sound, we grew closer and closer, and I fell a little bit deeper in love with him every day. I knew now it was love, and had gone beyond our deep friendship. He made a few moves on me, but I kept pushing him away in a kind of power play between us. Despite how I felt, I still didn't want to spoil our friendship, and I was afraid of what might happen if we took things further. He still had all kinds of women in tow and I didn't want to be just another number. Plus, I'd been badly burned and the memory still stung. The last thing I wanted was to walk into another relationship with another famous guitar player that women drooled over.

So ours was a slow burn. But one day much later on I couldn't say no anymore—and I guess we really did "funk until the dawn."

20. Click Track

A series of audio cues used to
synchronize sound recordings

I gave my heart to you and I'm in heaven
I know your love is true 'cuz I'm in heaven

"HEAVEN"

SHEILA E

Music had saved me when I was a child, and it continued to save me, giving me a reason to get up each morning and to keep on living and loving. To share my passion for it with someone who felt the same way was one of the greatest privileges of my life.

Working with Prince was the beginning of a fabulous musical relationship. He loved the music and the musicianship I brought to the table, so he gave me a lot more work. And we had so much fun! For Prince, making music is the most fun in the world. While we were collaborating we'd stop to eat. Or we'd play Ping-Pong or basketball—and I gave him a run for his money, even though he won't admit it. We were like a couple living and working together and enjoying ourselves. It didn't feel like work at all.

One day at Sunset Sound he turned and asked me, "So, do you want to make your own record?"

I laughed and said, "It's that easy, right?"

He shrugged and nodded.

I knew I could play percussion well enough—that was a given—but to come up with material that was more commercial than my daddy's music would be a serious challenge for me. To be able to perfect it, perform it, and go out with my own band was something altogether different.

It was definitely something I'd considered after all those hours I'd put into recording my own demos, learning how to write songs, and finding my own sound. I just hadn't done anything about it yet.

"Do you have any songs?" Prince asked.

"Well, I did another demo since the last one I gave you."

"Okay, let's hear it!"

He had his own production deal with Warner Brothers, so he suggested I sign to him. I met with Prince's manager at a hamburger joint to go over the contract.

I was so thrilled.

My own manager!

My own contract!

I signed on the dotted line before my burger and fries even came to the table. I didn't even read the small print.

In March 1984, I began recording vocals on some songs that Prince and I had chosen for my album. As always, we worked together really well, so it was easy to meet in the middle. The next few days were a mix of writing, recording, singing, playing, and staying up all night. That was what was so cool about us being together. We were influenced by each other's music. Prince was not used to leaving his other artists in the studio by themselves, but since I was a seasoned session player, I didn't need babysitting. It seemed like only five minutes ago that he'd persuaded me to sing a duet with him. Now he'd convinced me that I should be the lead singer in my own band!

We worked three days solid without sleep because we were both so excited about the project. Prince was a machine: he was still working in two or three rooms at the same time. It was organized chaos, but always exciting and cool. His no-nonsense attitude was "Okay, let's go!" I was the same way. I don't believe he ever had a woman around him before who could hang like I did—I mean musically, athletically, creatively, and competitively.

It seemed like we recorded my album in about a week. The songs were all long versions too. There were no three-minute numbers for Prince. I've never even come close to recording an album in such a short amount of time since. It was crazy and a lot of fun—just the way I like it.

The secret was that we'd record and semi-mix simultaneously. Prince taught me that if you record it right in the first place, there's not much mixing to do—so there was very little mixing done afterward. I had never recorded that way with any other artist.

Many people have come up with different stories about how my professional name became Sheila E. Well, here's the deal.

Escovedo has never been an easy name to say or spell. Since middle school, people referred to my brother Juan as Juan E. And soon I was Sheila E. If you listen to the videoed studio session of George Duke's *Dukey Stick* in 1978, you can hear George call me E when he sings, *What you gonna do now? Tell me about E, E?*

Prince and I had talked about a stage name for me. When I suggested my childhood nickname Sheila E, he said that was perfect and far more commercial than anything he could think of. We both thought it was catchy and easier for people to remember than my real last name. He then flew me to Minneapolis for some parties and jam sessions, where we tested the waters to see how people would respond to my new name.

"I want you to meet my new artist, Sheila E!" he'd announce. (Coming from Prince, that was some introduction!) The crowds seemed to like it.

So when he presented the final cut of my first album to Warner Brothers a couple of weeks after I'd agreed to make it, Sheila E was born.

Between us, we had come up with the concept of presenting me on the album cover as a glamorous Hollywood film star from a by-gone era. We were both very visual people and wanted to make this album both different and entertaining. As far as we knew, there had never before been a woman who led a band playing timbales. The idea of a film star dressed in a mink coat singing about wanting a glamorous life seemed kinda cool.

"The Glamorous Life" was the last song we worked on. In fact, we weren't even going to include it on the album. It started out as an instrumental, and I couldn't think of any lyrics for it at first. Once I got started, though, the words came quickly.

She's got big thoughts, big dreams, and a big brown Mercedes sedan. What I think this girl, she really wants is to be in love with a man. She wants to lead the glamorous life. She don't need a man's touch . . . Without love, it ain't much.

After rearranging the music and adding other musicians to the song, we were really happy with it. It was very percussive and it had a catchy melody, incorporating all the black keys on the piano so that it almost sounded like a nursery rhyme. And the song was sim-ple. Commercial music—even if it's funky and soulful—sometimes needs to be simplified in order to appeal to a broader audience. Simple melodies and simple rhythms often create hits because they're easy to remember.

When Warner Brothers heard the album, though, they weren't

quite so enamored. They wanted "The Belle of St. Mark" to be the first single. Prince and I fought hard for it to be "The Glamorous Life," which we also wanted as the title of the album.

We won.

On May 12, 1984, my single was released and became an almost immediate club hit. The album followed a few weeks later. "The Belle of St. Mark" (which I wrote about Prince) was released as a single in due course, along with "Oliver's House." To my amazement, my first album eventually reached number 28 on the pop chart, was nominated for a Grammy, and went gold.

In keeping with the cinematic theme, the liner notes said that the record was "directed" by Prince's Starr Company and me. (Prince sometimes called himself Jamie Starr, along with Alexander Nevermind and other monikers.) It was Prince's idea that his name didn't appear at all, even though he'd coproduced the entire album, cowritten most of the songs, and performed on almost all of them.

Another song he and I cowrote was "Noon Rendezvous," which was about our relationship at the time. The words included the lines: *I've been wondering what to wear. I love our noon rendezvous. I know you tell me you missed me, and I want to make love to you . . . The words are all over your face, my love. What shall you or shall I do? You could show me some new tricks, my love. I'd love to be taught by you . . .* We started writing "Noon Rendezvous" when I let Prince listen to a ballad I'd written and played castanets on. We talked about it, and I told him my dream was to write a song commercial enough to be played on the radio, which was something totally different for me. I was hoping this one might make it.

Prince was excited by the idea. He loves being inspired by other people and opened up to things he might not have thought of on his own. I had always collaborated as part of a family band and was brought up to be a team player (despite my independent streak).

It was nice to see him influenced by my musicianship as well as my family's musical bond. Prince had begun spending more and more time with my family, and he remarked that he'd never seen a father and his children jamming together, exchanging competitive licks, and communicating seamlessly through melody and rhythm. We exposed him both to our music—a completely unique blend of percussion, Latin jazz, and melody with syncopated rhythms and different time signatures—and to our unabashed expression of family love. I think it was this latter aspect, the bond between us—onstage and off—that truly struck him. It was the joyful public affection between Moms and Pops and their children, as well as the family's capacity to extend unconditional care and compassion to anyone, that Prince was especially moved by. He's one of many who have responded to the warmth our family shows one another. It's feedback we're humbled to receive quite often—how refreshing and inspiring it is to see such a tight-knit family that makes their work and play one and the same.

It's no wonder there are a gazillion honorary Escovedos. In a world of broken homes, family grudges, and tragic disconnects between relatives, I suppose a family that plays, prays, and stays together provides something much needed. Since I've always been in the middle of it, I didn't always realize what a God-given blessing it was to be in a family so overflowing with love.

Now, thankfully, I'm well aware.

Once my album was made, I then had to focus on the video to promote it. I knew from my time with Lionel Richie that music videos were becoming a major part of popular culture in the eighties and one of the best ways to promote a song, album, and persona. So when it was time to shoot the footage for "The Glamorous Life," I wanted to approach it strategically. It would, after all, be the first image people would put to my music and my debut exposure as a solo artist. Like everything else within my career, I took it very seriously.

As I didn't have an official band by the time we were ready to shoot, I held auditions. Ever-inclusive Moms suggested (i.e., *commanded*) that Zina, still a teenager and to me always the baby, had to be in the video. I told her, "Moms, I'd love to have her, but she doesn't play any instrument, and I need real musicians that can actually play so it looks totally realistic."

Moms, who lives by the all-for-one-and-one-for-all principle, pointed out that Zina already had experience being in Lionel's video with me. I tried to convince her that this was different—I needed a musician front and center, not a background dancer. But more important, if I was going to use my sister, I needed to prove to the record company that she was as capable of doing the video as any professional. I couldn't just hire her because she was my sister.

Moms didn't take no for an answer (see where I get it from?), so I agreed to let Zina audition just like everyone else. Since she was an Escovedo, we were pretty sure she'd come through.

Zina, meanwhile, wasn't too happy about having to audition. She had to get up on the stage in front of me, Moms, and the rest of the musicians who'd already been hired—including Juan and Peter Michael—as well as some serious record company executives. But then she did such a good job faking the guitar playing, and her dancing skills have always been ridiculously good. She didn't look as young as she really was because she assumed her role with such conviction. She also dressed the part. After she did her audition, everyone applauded.

I couldn't deny it—my sister turned it out. "You're hired!" I cried.

Now I had Juan, Peter Michael, and Zina by my side. And while I was playing it cool about the whole video shoot, it was something new, and the stakes felt high. Having my siblings with me would make a world of difference.

The final band lineup was Benny Rietveld on bass, Juan on keys (which he really didn't play), Lee Williams Jr. (Zina's boyfriend at the time) on keys—which he didn't play, either—Scott Roberts (an ex-boyfriend of mine) on drums, Zina on guitar, and Peter Michael on soprano sax (which wasn't even an instrument in the song, but he said he could dance better with a straight sax).

We were all nervous and excited. How were we going to make this work? The answer was practice, practice, and practice. And then some more practice. That's how I roll. The band rehearsed a couple days in advance, because I wasn't taking any chances. Zina needed to practice holding her guitar in a way that looked like she was really playing it. She then played the parts that sounded like guitars but actually weren't (they were keyboard parts that Prince had recorded). We were going to have it down solid before anyone from production even got a first glimpse.

When we showed up and presented our routine for the director, he was pretty impressed. (I guess he didn't know about all our years of dance routines and band-formation practice on our back porch and in our front room. We had this thing locked down!)

The director had some great ideas, like putting glitter on the head of the low drum for a shot. They also poured water onto the glitter, so when I kicked the cymbal there was a cool effect—magic drums with a splash of glitter straight into the camera.

Someone in production created the story line of the video, inspired by the lyrics. We filmed it at the Wiltern Theatre on Wilshire Boulevard in Los Angeles. Instead of doing the band shots on the actual stage, we ended up doing them in the lobby, with its great colors and amazing architecture, which came across even bigger and more impressive on film. While most of the video was shot in LA, there were a few San Francisco shots as well.

As the music blasted out of the speakers, I lip-synced to my own voice, which was easy for me because I'd grown up lip-syncing to all my favorite artists like Sammy Davis Jr. and every Motown artist under the sun. As a young girl I loved to practice mouthing the words just right, trying even then to be convincing.

On video shoots they want you to really sing and play your instruments so that it looks real. To complicate matters, I had to do all that while dancing. This was a challenge, but I wanted to show people that it was possible to do all three things at the same time. I wanted to be a *triple* threat.

So at the film studio on the lot with a background similar to my album cover, we worked hard replicating everything as best we could; doing the same thing over and over and over and practicing our dance steps for hours on end—the same way we had done since we could walk.

I didn't want a choreographer, because I didn't think we needed one. I told the record company, "Why would you want to hire someone else when I know what needs to be done? Plus, there isn't a woman in the world who's doing all this at once and who can do what I do."

There still isn't.

I knew instinctively that I'd be the best one to choreograph my own video, since it was my song and I knew better than anyone the kinds of steps my feet could do while my arms were drumming. Later on I saw people in the clubs, even in cities where I didn't speak the language, not only singing along to my words of "The Glamorous Life" but also mimicking those very steps. They had taken on a life of their own. Who knew that the little girl who loved to imitate other artists would one day be imitated herself?

Despite my insistence that she wouldn't be needed, a professional choreographer was brought in for some additional exterior pickup shots. She had the extras do a small part in the beginning where they're kind of tripping over each other as they run down the sidewalk. Imagine my surprise when she got an MTV Music

Video Award nomination for Best Choreography. I found out the night of the awards show. When her name was called I thought, *Who is that?*

My managers should've informed me who'd been nominated, not to mention the fact that they should've submitted my name in the first place. That was a trip, and one of many music-business lessons learned about making sure management does what they're supposed to.

It was a given that I'd wear my long mink coat to match the story line and the lyrics, as well as the covers for the album and the 45. The off-white-and-gray mink was perfect for the black-and-white sequences. But what would I wear for the color shots? I worked closely with the design team, creating items that would be different, provocative, but also movable. We came up with reddish-pink satin culottes with pockets long enough to accommodate the sticks for my timbales.

I wore a revealing leopard-print bustier underneath a jacket, which I eventually threw off. It was *very* revealing, and my brothers—who always kept it real for me—gave me a hard time about it. "Sheila, you're going to wear *that*?" they cried. "Are you serious?"

I liked my outfit, and they weren't my personal stylists. I was playing a role and feeling more and more comfortable in sexy clothes. But the only problem with my less-is-more outfit was that whenever we filmed the outdoor scenes, I was freezing. I had to keep warm by running through our dance moves. We practiced dozens of shots of me throwing my timbale stick in the air and then catching it behind my back. Sadly, they didn't make it into the final cut, although they did keep one of me bouncing the stick on the ground and catching it midair. And there were also lots of shots of me kicking the cymbal, which became a signature move.

To provide moral support (even though he was so busy), Prince came by during rehearsals and dropped in one day of shooting. He liked what we were doing; he thought we had our own very sexy look.

In a few shots, Peter Michael played my love interest, which was kinda weird. He and I were cracking up during those scenes. My brother as my lover? Oh, my God! Talk about low-budget restrictions. And on the second day of shooting, which Peter Michael couldn't make, they had to shave the head of the stand-in so he could wear a wig that would better resemble Peter Michael's hair. He's the one who pulls my hair back in a quick shot. I felt bad—that guy had a beautiful head of long black hair, but he said he was okay with it. I wonder how long it took to grow back. Zina appeared in the black-and-white segment as a young girl selling flowers. They had to reshoot the scene over and over again because she kept making me laugh. The camera was behind her, and she was making crazy faces—sticking her tongue out, going cross-eyed—anything to make me lose it. It didn't take much for any of us to break character. We didn't even quite understand what her character was all about, since it sure wasn't a part of the lyrical content. Why was the guitar player selling flowers to me? Fortunately, it looked cool in the video, thanks to the magic of editing.

As is usually the case, my brothers and sister kept me grounded, comfortable, and, above all else, they kept me laughing. Plus their excitement about everything made me forget about the potential seriousness of the whole endeavor. They were all still living up north, and this was the first time they'd worked professionally in LA, which felt like a big deal to them.

Zina, especially, couldn't get over it. When we all went shopping on Melrose Avenue she was beside herself, because the very name conjured up every fantasy of Tinseltown for her. "Walking down Melrose!" she kept saying under her breath. "This is the life."

At one point during the shoot the band took a break to grab some sandwiches across the street. And we were all trippin' because the guys were fully dressed in their costumes, their faces covered in foundation, full-on eyeliner, lipstick, and mascara, their hair teased high like rock stars'. They were nervous to venture outside dressed like that. If it had been Oakland, they'd have been stopped in the street, laughed at, and beaten up!

They made it through the store, in line at the cashier, and back across the street into the Wiltern again without anyone giving them a second look. Juan and Peter Michael couldn't believe it. "I guess that's just LA," they told me. "Everybody looks crazy, so we fit in."

By the time the video finally came out in the spring of 1984, I was in Europe, hustling hard to promote my album, and had pretty much no idea that MTV and other video programs had played it in heavy rotation. Unbeknownst to me, the video gave me immediate global visibility, which catapulted me to superstardom.

It was all a big blur, but I do remember a funny conversation I had with Juan. He'd gone back home to his family after the video shoot, where he was juggling gigs at night and landscaping during the day. One morning, wearing his jeans, T-shirt, and sneakers, he was inside a client's house discussing what kind of look they wanted in their yard when our video came on TV.

The woman who'd hired him kept looking back and forth between him and the TV. "Wait a minute! Isn't that you?" she asked in total disbelief.

"Yeah," he replied.

"Oh, my God!" she exclaimed. "Can I get your autograph?" After he signed her notebook, the woman asked, "So what are you doing here, then?"

He thought it was a good question. Later that day, he called me up. "Sheila, this ain't cool. I'm in your pretend band on MTV, but in real life I'm digging backyards in the hot sun, making a dollar fifty. You need to put me in your band."

He had a point. I'd always loved the way he played percussion, and I was about to start rehearsals. "You're hired," I told him. He was thrilled to let go of his nine-to-five and play music with his big sister. Now he could finally tell people, "Yes, that's me in the 'Glamorous Life' video, *and* I'm on the tour."

21. Accents

Notes played louder than normal

She's got big thoughts, big dreams
And a big brown Mercedes sedan
What I think this girl
She really wants
Is to be in love with a man

"THE GLAMOROUS LIFE"

SHEILA E

After the fun of the video shoot, I knew I needed to find a real band with proper musicians to complement my brother, so I started rounds of auditions. Musicians came from all over, and the line outside the SIR rehearsal studio was down the block. I laid out an intricate and strict auditioning process. There were four rooms to get through, each indicating a different requirement.

Room A was where my staff took all the information, including how willing candidates might be to travel far from home. This was important to me because I knew I would be out on the road for much of 1984 and 1985, a long time, and it's hard to be away from friends and family that long.

Room B was where the musicians played their instruments. Room C was where they had to play their instruments while singing. Room D was where they had to play, sing, and dance all at once, which was necessary for the gig. I assured them, "If I can do it, so can you!" If you made it through to Room E—you guessed it—that's where you'd meet me, Ms. E.

As part of my decision (encouraged by Prince) that we were all playing a theatrical role in the whole *Glamorous Life* event, auditionees also had to agree to change their names as well as their appearances, which might mean cutting or coloring their hair and wearing their assigned costumes 24/7. I felt that people had to look the part to believe the part.

So my brother Juan became J. E., Sir Dance A Lot, because he was known not only for killing the percussion but also for dancing his butt off. Saxophonist Eddie Mininfield became Eddie M, and his look was a cape, no shirt, and coins wrapped around his chest. I knew the girls would love that.

I found most of the band members quite quickly, but I didn't have a drummer yet. I knew the drum chair would be challenging: if a drummer couldn't do it better than me, there was no need to make the hire. I didn't want to babysit and carry the band. One day I heard a band playing in an adjacent studio. Despite the sign on the door that said CLOSED REHEARSAL, I walked right in.

I had no idea who was playing, but there were horns, percussionists, and singers all playing amazing salsa music. Heading the band was my honorary "brother" Karl Perazzo, whom I'd virtually grown up with. Karl was known as one of the baddest timbale, percussion, conga, and bongo players around. He and his brother Gibby, also a percussionist, were well respected in the Latin community. They were just little boys when they sat in with Tito Puente.

I saw Karl sitting down playing timbales, reading a chart, and conducting his band—another kind of triple threat. He looked up and waved me over with a smile. "Mama, come in." I gave him a huge hug and said hello to the band. "Perazzo," I said. "Come here for a minute. I wanna talk to you."

We walked out of his rehearsal and into mine.

I pointed to the drum setup on the stage.

"I want you to go play those," I said.

He shook his head. "I don't know how to play drums."

"You can keep a beat, so I know you can play drums."

He just stared at me.

"And by the way," I added. "You have to stand up and play."

He started laughing and clapping his hands while walking to the drums. "Okay," he said. "What do you want me to do?"

I turned the LinnDrum machine on and watched him play the two and four like nobody's business. Now it was my turn to start laughing and clapping my hands. "Do you have a passport?" I asked.

"Yes," he answered. And then, "Why?"

I turned, put my arm around him, and walked him back to his room.

Before he could say anything, I gave him an instruction: "Tell your band you quit because you're going out on tour with me, and you start right now."

He burst out laughing and then said, "Really?"

I looked at him like, "Yeah," already knowing it would be done. He packed up his timbales and moved them to my room.

Because my record first broke in Europe in the spring of 1984, my managers sent me there multiple times to promote it. I was used to international travel from previous tours, but this was different. It was my first solo album, and it was crazy what went into pushing it—not just the rehearsals but also the nonstop promotion, interviews, and performances. It was beyond grueling. There was so little time even for eating and sleeping. Like anything I commit to, though, I was determined to give 150 percent and I expected everyone else to do the same. The managers set everything up and schooled me in every aspect of the business of promotion. It felt like performer boot camp. Sadly, I don't see this kind of all-inclusive coaching happening for new artists anymore.

Each day, I'd be booked for up to ten hours of back-to-back interviews. My band did half that. During the day we were on almost every popular television show, and at night we'd play wherever we could to create a buzz in the club scene. Sometimes our gigs would start at midnight or one A.M. We were spreading the word that Sheila E, the Queen of Percussion, had a hot new dance track, "The Glamorous Life." It was more than a full-time job.

Despite how much work it was, I found the transition from band musician to solo artist surprisingly easy. From the age of fifteen, I'd been a percussionist behind the main artist. It seemed that whatever artist I performed with, they'd always given me a chance to do my thing and be featured. I guess I was used to the attention of the spotlight. But being center stage was a whole new deal, and the responsibility was a little intimidating. All eyes were on me not just for a song or two, but for the entire show, and I was responsible for setting the tone as well as leading my band.

It didn't take me long to become quite comfortable in the role. I harnessed my memories of being the oldest sibling in my family or a ringleader in everything from street gangs to our family dancing at parties. I remembered how I even once led an expedition through a creek looking for special rocks.

The older I got, the more I liked to be in charge. I had a vision for how things should go, and I enjoyed feeling responsible, even as a young girl. When Moms and Pops returned home from a night out, they'd often find a handwritten letter from me waiting for them by the door. It was my "official report" of the evening—what they'd missed, what chores we did and didn't get to, and which of us kids should be punished.

Sometimes I'd even tell on myself: "Sorry, Mommy and Daddy," one of those letters read. "I didn't get to fold my clothes like you asked, and now I see why you asked me to do it before going out to play."

My reports weren't all business, however. They always ended with my sincere plea that they'd wake me up and give me a good-night kiss.

Similarly, in Europe, I took my leadership position seriously. The band carried my name, and it was important I led it and also recognized that each individual was an essential part of the group. I told my musicians that we needed to approach the press as if we were in a gang. "We have to be loyal and strong, but most of all we have to watch each other's backs."

We each embraced our respective roles—with the heavy makeup, crazy hair colors, and carefully planned costumes. And even though we really didn't have the money yet for the costumes we'd have liked, we did the best with what we had. Image was a crucial part of our promotion. Even for print interviews, we had to be in full costume and own our roles as if we were actors. This, as well as the physical requirements of playing, soon became exhausting. Choreography was an important aspect of our stage performances, so we rehearsed twelve-hour days until all of the band members played, danced, and sang together perfectly.

"We can't do this anymore," a few complained. "We need a break."

I didn't blame them. After leaving a late performance, we'd hit the road for the next city, get maybe a couple of hours in a hotel room to eat, sleep, and shower, then do another show. We'd go back to the hotel around three or four A.M. and try to unwind so that we could catch maybe two hours of sleep before being driven to the airport at five A.M. It all took a toll on me, but I needed to do every photograph, TV show, dance show, and magazine and print interview until I couldn't do any more. This is what it would take to be a star.

For me there was no choice. My journey as a solo artist had begun, and there was no turning back. A lot of times, promotion is about investment—which means working with a limited budget and bringing in little to no money. So often artists don't feel all that motivated, because there's not always an immediate reward. But I was already rewarded, getting to do what I loved. It was my life. So not only did I say yes to every single offer that came in, I aggressively pursued every possible platform for self-promotion that I could find. With the same conviction I'd felt as a teenager, working my way backstage and then onstage, I would do whatever it took to make it as a solo artist and make *The Glamorous Life* successful.

As a female percussionist fronting a band, playing timbales and singing songs I'd written, produced, and arranged, I was a novelty—something fans hadn't seen or heard before. Of course, it didn't hurt that I was associated with Prince. Every show was packed.

I had no idea what a hit my song had become or how much airplay our video was getting until I got back to the States. There was no Internet or digital radio, so no one was tweeting or trending about seeing my video on MTV or hearing my song. I was so busy, and everything was happening so fast, that I really didn't understand that I was coming back as somebody famous. As soon as I returned, I was booked for more shows and couldn't believe the response and support. All the hard work was paying off.

Periodically, Prince would show up and jam with us. We had a blast. One night we were performing at a sold-out show in New

York at a club called the Ritz. Prince came onstage and we played side by side. The crowd was going wild. You couldn't squeeze a fly into that room. If felt like 120 degrees, and everyone was soaked from the funkiness and the heat. There were so many photographers right up front that I couldn't see a thing because of all the flashbulbs.

I danced over to one side of the stage and saw that people were going crazy. I thought to myself, "Wow! I am really throwing down! They love me!" The flashing of the cameras was blinding. Why were they taking so many pictures of me all of a sudden? I knew I could dance a little bit, but I wasn't that good. I couldn't believe how much everyone was looking at me.

Prince was playing his heart out, and yet all eyes were on me. I remembered to freeze-frame the moment and told myself, *This is incredible.* I saw about five people trying to get my attention, but I just kept singing and dancing. The flashes from the camera were even more intense the more I danced. I finally realized why. One side of my lace blouse had fallen down, and my boob was out in the open and having a good time. One of the girls had come out to play. I had no idea!

Once I realized, I pulled the blouse back up quickly, using the Velcro straps I had made for quick changes. It didn't bother me too much; I just went on about my business, playing some "fonk-E" music.

And so the craziness continued, and all I knew was that I felt like I was living in a dream. In fact, I was so convinced of it that once I asked a broker friend of mine who rented cars for the rich and famous if I could have a Mercedes—convertible and red—just to see what would happen.

The answer was, "Sure, Ms. E, anything you want."

I had to pinch myself once again.

It was a beautiful day, so I took my handsome new car for a

cruise east along Sunset Boulevard. I was headed for Greenblatt's Deli in West Hollywood, on the corner by the Laugh Factory. I was craving a slice of their lemon cake.

Just as I was in the middle lane waiting to take a left across two lanes of traffic to turn into the parking lot, my single suddenly came on the radio. This was the first time I'd ever heard it played.

"What?" I cried. "Oh, my God!"

I started screaming. I turned the volume up to the max and started waving my arms in the air. I was so excited. I was yelling hysterically at fellow drivers, "This is my song!"

I couldn't believe life was so good.

I had a hit single.

I was falling in love.

I was lemon-cake bound.

I was not paying attention.

The cars all stopped, and I crept into the third lane, still whooping and hollering and singing along to "The Glamorous Life." I didn't see a car coming up on the inside lane.

Bam!

Of all the times to be hit—while listening to my first single on the radio for the first time!

The other driver was coming fast, and he hit me right on the passenger side. My shiny red Mercedes was totaled, but all I could do was laugh. The driver was stunned and simply couldn't understand why I was laughing so hard. The traffic backed up and everybody was leaning on their horns, but I just sat in the middle of the road listening to the end of the song and laughing my head off.

A while later I called up the guy who got me the car and, still giggling, I told him, "You know, Randy, I don't think I like red cars after all. Can you get me a black one?"

22. Fulcrum Point

A fixed point of support
on which a lever pivots

There's a nasty rumor that's goin' round
People think that U and, U and I are goin' down
They insist that we're more, more than just friends
So I'm gonna stick around until this movie ends

"SISTER FATE"

SHEILA E

As if my life wasn't crazy enough, Prince had asked me to open for him on his forthcoming Purple Rain tour, starting that November in Detroit. He could have asked just about anyone in the music business and they would have jumped at the chance.

Instead he picked me.

Prince was smart. He made sure that anyone he was producing stayed around him, as it made him and his company sell more records.

As soon as the Sheila E tour was over, I flew to the Bay Area to rehearse my band at SIR studios San Francisco. I wanted to add a few more players, so I made some calls.

Then Prince came up with the idea that I give my first performance as a solo artist in the US at the *Purple Rain* movie premiere party on July 26, 1984. Based loosely on his own life, the movie was to be shown at the famous Mann's Chinese Theatre on Hollywood Boulevard.

The after-show party was in the nearby Palace Theater—and the whole event (including my performance) was to be televised live on VH1 and MTV.

No pressure, right?

Purple Rain was one of the biggest movies to be released that year. For a few weeks that summer, the man I was falling for had the number-one album, the number-one single, and the number-one movie. Not bad for the kid from Minneapolis whose poster I'd drooled over six years earlier.

We both decided what we'd wear and how we'd behave that night. The planning helped me keep on top of my nerves. We even decided to match our clothes to the colors of our two stretch limos. Mine was turquoise, so my outfit was in sparkly turquoise with fuchsia. I had a designer make it for me, but it didn't fit great, so instead I wore a jacket with massive shoulder pads (which I took off to play), a corset, and a V-neck top with only one sleeve.

Prince's outfit matched his limo: purple. He wore a frilly white shirt and a piece of fabric—originally a belt I'd bought for him—around his head. "What if I wore it over one eye?" he asked me.

"Yes!" I told him, usually a bossy know-it-all when it comes to fashion (and a few other things too). "You have to do that!" So he did.

I was petrified that night at the Chinese Theatre; it was one of the most nerve-racking performances of my life. Even arriving at the premiere was scary. The limos were inching along Hollywood Boulevard, which was lined with screaming fans and news vans. I walked in on the arm of my makeup artist, James, trying to act like I was totally used to all the cameras.

Prince and I watched the movie, and then as soon as the final credits rolled we rushed around the corner to the Palace, where I was to start the after-party.

The small theater was packed with a thousand people: all the hottest celebrities, top record company executives, and industry insiders. Standing room only. Before I went on I had to answer rapid-fire questions from reporters and MTV VJs. My hands trembled, but I was well rehearsed: *Don't reveal too much. Keep them wanting more.* When it was time to go on, there was nothing to do but take the ride. Looking across at my brother Juan, I nodded, and we started to make some music. We played about forty-five minutes straight. I don't remember much about the show except not being able to hear that well over the monitors and sensing that it wasn't my best performance. But we'd gotten through it, and the crowd was pumped. When applause replaced the final note, I scanned the crowd—all strangers clapping and cheering—and tried to catch my breath. I looked at Juan, who was taking in the applause himself. He must have felt my eyes on him—that special peripheral vision he has—because he turned to me almost instantly.

We were just a six-hour drive from Oakland's Ninth Avenue and East Twenty-first Street, but on that stage, in that moment, we were worlds away.

For a moment I wanted to slip away somewhere quiet, far away from the noise in the theater and the noise in my head, but there was no chance of that. The crowd was pressing forward. More camera bulbs popped in my face, and bright television lights made it hard to see. Security was a little slow on the uptake, rushing over to block me from the crowd just a few seconds too late. Prince pushed through the melee to congratulate me, and suddenly the press was all over the both of us.

"Who is she?" people were asking. "Is she *with* him?"

When we left the party I heard fans screaming not only for Prince, but also for me. I was exhilarated, exhausted, and floating on air. Plus I was hungry. All I wanted to do was go back to the hotel, eat something, and take a bath. But police had shut down the streets, and crowds were still swarming.

"It's Sheila E!" I heard people yelling. "Sheila E! Over here! Pose for the camera! Sheila E! Can I get your autograph?"

I knew it would be a while before I could get back to my room, get back to Oakland, and get back to being Sheila Escovedo.

That night marked the beginning of a decade of madness. Up until then I'd been happy to be in my father's bands or to be a background percussionist, drummer, and vocalist for Billy, Herbie, Diana, George, Marvin, Lionel, and others. That night I felt a deep gratitude for where I'd been, and I knew the butterflies were telling me something good about where I was going. But I didn't know yet how many true blessings were in store, or that I was one step closer to discovering my purpose.

After the *Purple Rain* premiere, I went straight into rehearsals with my band, and I was very demanding about what I wanted to achieve and how it should happen. This time I was the one in charge. We were going on a major tour with money in our pockets, and things would change. I needed to get new wardrobe and update the look of the band.

Once again, our rehearsals took a minimum of twelve hours a day for the tour. We'd have to be reminded to break for a meal. Each song had to be broken down to parts, vocals, and dance routines, and we had to place each member in position during each song. The staging was very important. I wasn't playing around, and

I whipped them and myself into shape by making them dance even if they didn't know how.

I came up with a list of rules that applied to everyone involved—including me. No drinking, no smoking, and most of all, no being late. You were excused if you were late one time, but the second time you'd be fined. If you were late a third time, you'd be fired.

I didn't play around. The final rule was about making mistakes that might complicate my tour. Being late three times meant that the musician was getting lazy, didn't care, was drinking or taking drugs. My message was: if you are serious about your craft and give it all you've got, then there will be no mistakes.

Prince flew to the Bay Area to one of our rehearsals to see how we were coming along. Little did he know how serious I was about being a solo artist and putting together the best band. If you were going to open for him, better be good. In fact, we were so good that once he checked out my rehearsal and watched the show, he walked out to the car and called his tour manager to arrange an emergency meeting with the Revolution at his rehearsal spot.

When he got home four hours later, he apparently told them he was changing the entire show. "Ain't no way Sheila's gonna have a funkier band than me!" I heard he told them.

I gave him a run for his money. Bay Area musicians weren't messing around. We meant business. Every single person in the band played their own instrument and would possibly play another as well as sing, dance, and look good.

I didn't have a Hollywood clue about what was about to hit me.

All this time, I was still saying no to Prince as far as starting an intimate relationship was concerned. Even when I flew across the country and ended up staying with him in New York, I was trying to keep our friendship platonic. It wasn't just about me trying to stay in control as far as men were concerned—something that dated back to my childhood—but wanting to keep my own power and identity now that I'd finally found it. Prince was a huge star, and had so many other women around him a lot of the time. I didn't want to be part of a harem.

I also continued to fear that if we slept together, it would only mess up the great relationship we already had. Although I was crazy about him and amazed by his talents and his sexiness, I valued our friendship above all else. He definitely knew how to pursue me, though, and we both knew it was only a matter of time before I'd say yes.

The Purple Rain tour began, and so did our romantic relationship. It was as simple and as sudden as that. Thrown into close proximity with the man who'd been wooing me romantically for years, and in the high-octane environment of a world tour with all its attendant madness, my defenses were finally broken.

We were working hard and playing hard, throwing ourselves into a nonstop, exhausting, and creative explosion of living, loving, performing, and recording. Plus we were doing our best to keep our fledgling relationship a secret. There were many levels of secrecy here. We couldn't hide it from those in our inner circle, but like any relationship that begins in the workplace (however untraditional our workplace might have been), we knew it was best to keep things private for professional reasons.

There was, of course, lots of speculation among the crew, the fans, and within the media. "Are they or aren't they?" was a question floating in the background throughout the whole tour. He didn't do interviews, but I did. And when asked about our relationship, I never verbally confirmed it, but you could tell by my smile, my avoidance of eye contact, and that twinkle in my eyes. I never did have much of a poker face.

Other people figured it out by finding out which hotel we were staying in and somehow which room too. It got to the point where our security guards had to make an extensive sweep of our room each night so that Prince and I wouldn't be surprised if we found a fan or two hiding in our closet.

Even before we were famous, Prince and I had both been very private people. Back in my teens, I only told one friend about my first boyfriend—the one with whom I shared all those long telephone conversations watching *Love, American Style*. Having our most intimate moments scrutinized so closely by the media and fans was painful and awkward for us both.

Meanwhile, I was contending with an onslaught of media attention for breaking down assumptions about what it meant to be a woman *and* a percussionist. I was just being me, playing from my heart like Pops had taught me, but now, with a hit record, I was being asked to explain, defend, and make sense of something the public had never seen before—a woman leading her own band, singing, dancing, mixing musical genres, and playing an instrument lots of people had no clue about.

They were constantly pointing at my timbales and asking, "What are those things called?" (I still hear that.) This instrument had been a part of my life since forever. It's an extension of both my father and my heritage. Timbales were a common fixture in the small, impoverished, mixed-race neighborhood around Ninth Avenue and East Twenty-first Street in Oakland—where I could jam for hours on end with friends and family, pounding out beats without my gender being a factor.

But now I was being asked to account for myself as a symbol of something, as a fixture within the context of the feminist movement and as a representative of something much larger than I could fathom at the time. I felt the responsibility to continue my father's legacy through pop music without losing my integrity. It was a lot of pressure.

Getting through the concert and after-shows night after night, then the after-parties, the after-after parties, and the after-after-

after-parties, was an ordeal. My body was bruised and aching and my mind foggy from jet lag, but that part was easy compared to managing this overlap of my public persona and my intensely private relationship.

I was fighting to keep control of the (good and bad) emotions while simultaneously adjusting to the (good and bad) implications of my increasing celebrity. All parts of my life were colliding. And they were colliding loudly—my career, my love life, my well-being, my spirituality, and my identity as a woman. My anonymity was gone. My heart was wide open. It was full exposure on every level.

Remaining sane required a lot of compartmentalization. I had to keep my vulnerabilities in check while simultaneously running the machine that was my life. On top of everything else, I was writing and recording my next album, *Romance 1600*. Sleep wasn't a priority. Needless to say, over time I became exhausted. Learning to navigate the press machine and some unexpected aspects of celebrity was often exciting and certainly necessary, but it added to me feeling generally drained. My body was tired, of course, but it was the mental fatigue that was getting the best of me.

The tour ended in Miami after a full year on the road, and all I wanted to do was lie on a beach and do nothing before I had to go out and promote *Romance 1600*, which was set to be released in August of 1985. So I took my first week off in over a year.

I had worked so hard to be successful, and suddenly I had the financial means to not only give myself a little vacation at a luxurious five-star hotel, but to also do those things I'd always dreamed of doing. So the band and I flew to Florida and rented speedboats and motorcycles, went deep-sea fishing and parasailing. When I had time to myself, I made sure to savor those delicious moments of quiet and calm—enjoying the feeling of my feet in the hot sand and the soothing sounds of the ocean waves.

During one of those blissful vacation days in Miami, a friend dared me to cut my hair. Of course the Gardere in me said yes—never one to shy away from a dare, and knowing I needed a new look for the next album anyway. And, as usual, I took it to the extreme—telling my hairstylist to cut it real short. It was a cool, asymmetrical cut, but it really threw me off for a minute. Once again I had leapt before I looked. The *Glamorous Life* image was now gone. I suddenly had to re-create my entire wardrobe to match both my new cut and my new album.

I looked less feminine, which made me feel like I wasn't sexy anymore. I was used to flipping, teasing, and twirling my hair. All men say they love women with long hair, especially seeing it strewn across their pillow. So were they still going to see me as sexy? When I walked into a nightclub a few days after the big chop, the owners recognized me and led us to our table. I could tell that heads were turning. I wondered, *Are they looking at me because I'm Sheila E, or because they still see me as sexy, short hair and all?* I found myself trying to act even sexier, strutting harder toward the VIP booth, swishing my hips to compensate for the fact that I had no hair to flip.

It was during my much-needed mini-vacation and this haircut meltdown that I got the call to audition for a movie called *Krush Groove*. Designed as a vehicle for some of the new young talent coming out of New York and based loosely on the early days of Def Jam Recordings, *Krush Groove* was produced by Warner Brothers and went on to become one of hip-hop music's most iconic films. If I got the part, my costars would include Run-DMC, LL Cool J, the Fat Boys, New Edition, Kurtis Blow, and the Beastie Boys.

This would be my second movie audition—the first being for the film *Cocoon*, which I'd sabotaged because I was too nervous about my reading comprehension and didn't have enough time to prepare my lines. I talked myself into a panic. Also, I was auditioning opposite the actor Steve Guttenberg and knew I had to wear a bathing suit and shorts for most of the movie. That freaked me out, since I had bad eczema at the time—red and white spots all over my body, most likely a stress breakout.

When it was time to read with Steve, I didn't really read my lines at all. Instead, acting silly and unprofessional, I tried to distract everyone from my insecurity. Needless to say, I didn't get the part. So when the *Krush Groove* offer came up, I was anxious to redeem myself. While they had me in mind for the lead female role, before officially offering me the part they wanted to make sure I had chemistry with the male lead, the up-and-coming actor Blair Underwood.

At first I was pretty hesitant about the whole thing. It was an exciting offer, but I was unfamiliar with auditions of any kind. Flying to New York for a screen test felt really strange. Even the word *test* made me uncomfortable. Having to prove my talent in a whole new realm made me pretty nervous.

On the day of the screen test, my hands were shaking and my heart was beating out of my chest. This was a huge career opportunity, yet I was terrified because it was all so new. While I was totally cool with my hair by now, I woke up that morning with a new problem: a huge pimple on the tip of my nose. I guess all the stress and fatigue were showing up in my complexion. This pimple had a life of its own. It looked like a thumb, or a third elbow. I told Connie that they'd be expecting a glamorous Sheila E but they'd be getting an unglamorous unicorn instead. I didn't realize that I could have visited a dermatologist for a cyst injection, so I did it the ghetto way—by putting a big glob of toothpaste on it. Of all days to do a screen test. I couldn't have felt more self-conscious.

They handed me the script just minutes before the test, so I didn't have any time to prepare my lines. Then I met Blair, who was very sweet and seemed excited to work with me. He was a real actor, so I felt out of my league. I like to feel confident and comfortable in professional settings, and I usually did. But there I was—a fish out of water (and a fish with a humongous pimple).

Despite my nerves, Blair and I had chemistry on screen, and the feedback was positive. Soon I was officially offered the role and moved into the Berkshire Hotel in New York for the duration of shooting. I couldn't believe I was actually going to be acting in a movie. I was thrilled, but still nervous. It wasn't the good kind of butterfly excitement. It was total fear of the unknown.

I always felt more comfortable with my family and friends around me, especially in new situations, so when I didn't jell with the woman who was cast as my best friend/manager, I told the long-suffering director Michael Schultz that they'd have to fly my friend Karen to New York to replace her if they wanted me in the film.

They did as I asked, and things were looking up. I had my band, Karen, and a great costar. Once I got on set, however, events took a turn. Some of the East Coast rappers in the movie didn't like that I had been given the role. I had recorded one rap song, "Holly Rock," that was to be featured in the film, and since I was from Oakland, they thought I was some West Coast wannabe rapper who didn't know her place and should stick to one genre of music. Little did I know, but the hip-hop community was on the defensive at that time. They were being attacked by critics and musicians for being nonmusicians—often accused of being a fad or just talking into a mic. They weren't being acknowledged for their poetry as artists and the musicality of their beat making.

Then I arrived with my band, my timbales, and my proud musician identity, and they wanted to know what I was doing in a movie about rap music. I didn't fit into their box. I often felt ignored as well as looked down upon and ostracized. It was pretty hurtful. Being on set was just like the times in my adolescence when I was told I had to choose, black or white. I couldn't just be me. Of course I wasn't trying to present myself as a rapper like them, and even the script of the movie depicted my character as a singer-percussionist who is encouraged by Run of Run-DMC to give rap a shot.

I think the fact that I came from a successful world tour and was confident and clear about what I wanted might have contributed to the divide. Just like always, I had my dressing room set up the way I liked it—as in a five-star hotel, complete with rugs, lamps, couches, paintings, and even a popcorn machine. I always wanted to bring my home with me wherever I went, and I made sure my assistants dressed my hotel rooms before I checked in. But on the *Krush Groove* set, the guys didn't have their rooms pimped out like mine, so they dogged me for being some kind of diva. In some ways I was.

Some of the guys, like the members of the Fat Boys, Run-DMC, and the Beastie Boys, were a lot more supportive. Kurtis Blow especially seemed to notice the cold reception I was getting. One day he pulled me aside and told me not to worry about it. "Don't take it personally, Sheila. You just keep being you."

In the last scene, while the final credits rolled, each cast member was supposed to do a little dance. Blair asked me to help him with some of the moves, so we worked out a routine. Once the camera rolled, we were supposed to be first or second, but we kept getting pushed out of the way, eventually ending up in the back. I couldn't believe they were being that rude to us. In between takes I told Kurtis Blow what was going on. "Don't let them run you over," he said. "Just do your thing." So during the next take, I took his advice. We literally shoved them out of the way.

The worst day of shooting was when we filmed the "Love Bizarre" performance. Like the "Holly Rock" scene, I took it really seriously. I had them bring my microphone stand, my mic, my guitar, and my timbales into my hotel room so I could practice in front of the mirror. Everything was tightly choreographed, and I was probably better prepared for these scenes than for the acting ones.

When it was time to film, the band and I took our places on-stage. It was a club setting with several hundred extras hired to be our enthusiastic audience. Once the cameras started rolling, of course we threw down because we were used to recording in one take. But at the end of our performance, you could hear crickets. The audience was just standing there, arms crossed, unimpressed.

The director was furious.

"Cut!" he screamed. "Do you guys understand that we're shooting a movie here and you're supposed to clap when she's done, like you really enjoyed it?" Then he stormed out.

I was so hurt, embarrassed, and ultimately really mad. I knew the song was a hit, but apparently not everyone was a fan. We had to film it again. My band and I gave a slammin' performance the second time, too, despite the hostility from the audience. (I've watched this scene several times over the years, and the wall be-tween them and me is clear. My I'll-show-you attitude is on full display.)

That's the night I started drinking on the set. Nobody knew Karen and I were pouring Heineken beer into our apple juice cartons. Drinking was the only way I could get through some of those difficult days, and it continued until the director shouted, "That's a wrap!"

The stress continued, too, as I was fighting hard to take a love scene out of the script. Sure, I was half-naked in some of my stage outfits, but I was transitioning out of that look and was feeling less and less comfortable showing so much skin. Plus the idea of having a shot of my booty preserved forever on film was pretty daunting. And most important, I knew that by making out with another man on screen, I would be hurting the man I loved.

Prince was across the world in Monte Carlo shooting *Under the*

Cherry Moon, and he'd told me he didn't want me to do the scene. But in New York, I had the movie executives in my ear every single day telling me how crucial the scene was to the plot. I couldn't take it anymore.

I became so overwhelmed with all of the pressure—the schedule, the anxiety about memorizing lines, the relationship drama, and the haters on set—that I quit the movie. I walked off. I was done. People around me reminded me that I had given my word and should honor it. After a few days of rest, I knew they were right. I had to finish what I started, and I couldn't let the production down.

On my first day back on set I downed some "apple juice" and said, "Fine! Let Blair suck on my neck."

Blair was very respectful and sensitive to my concerns. With enough "apple juice," I got through it, and I think it actually turned out pretty tasteful in the end.

While Blair was wonderful to me, Run of Run-DMC was another great person to work with. Director Michael Schultz pulled me aside before one scene in which I was supposed to get really mad at Run and encouraged me to improvise so that it felt real. Poor Run was completely unprepared when I slapped him. His knee-jerk reaction was to flinch, almost like he was going to hit me back. We cracked up laughing. We had to film that scene a couple of times, and the director encouraged me to slap him even harder each successive time.

Time and hindsight is a wonderful thing, and I'm cool with all the guys now. Some have even become good friends. To those we've lost along the way, including Jason William Mizell, aka Jam Master J of Run-DMC; Adam Yauch, aka MCA of the Beastie Boys; and Darren Robinson, aka Buffy the Human Beat Box of the Fat Boys, it was an honor to have known you.

God bless you and may you rest in peace.

Those of us still here laugh about those days—all of us so young and so unaware that *Krush Groove* would become a cult classic and such an iconic piece of hip-hop history.

Ultimately, I was proud of myself for getting through the film despite all the obstacles. I rented out the Grand Lake Theatre in Oakland so that my friends and family—most of whom couldn't make it to the first New York screening—could see it in a movie-premiere setting. I think half of Oakland High School was there.

Watching that love scene on a huge screen in front of my siblings and parents and grandparents felt ridiculously uncomfortable. I had to laugh, though, when my grandmother Nanny (the wild one) started squealing with childish delight. She loved that part the most.

23. Hi-Hat

A pair of foot-operated cymbals

Just realize it's an image before it goes too far

"SEX CYMBAL"

SHEILA E

If someone had told me back in the seventies when I'd gingerly sneaked my foot across the boundary of a curtained stage that I would end up playing for a billion people worldwide, I'd have laughed in their face. And yet that's exactly what happened.

Working day and night, including weekends, holidays, and birthdays, had allowed me to follow my dream.

Wow. Was it real?

I'd gone from wearing tennis shoes and shorts to romantic and beautiful seventeenth-century-themed swashbuckling costumes. I was writing songs, making movies, performing at sellout shows, and breaking fashion boundaries. It was crazy, but crazy good.

And then there were all the amazing people I met along the way. It was at the American Music Awards that I first met Whitney Houston, whose star was on the rise. I loved her voice—angelic and powerful, soulful and sweet. Connie and I had been working on a few songs with my sax player Eddie M, and we had an idea. At the after-party I told Whitney about the song.

"We wrote a song for you," I told her, smiling. "It's called 'Touch Me/Hold Me.' It would be an honor to have you sing it on your next record. Can I send it to you?"

"Sure, honey," she said, a sweet grin on her face.

She never did pick up on our song, which was a shame, but I heard from her hairstylist later that Whitney had misunderstood my pitch.

"Sheila E tried to hit on me!" she claimed. "She told me she'd written a song called 'Touch Me' or something—but I knew what she meant!"

Fortunately, we met on many occasions in the following years and always laughed about it. She even came to see Prince and me play only a few months before she passed. I'll always remember her standing there in the wings, telling me she wanted to get up onstage and hit some drums with me. I'll never forget her vibrant smile, her warmth, and the purity of her relationship with music. It was something we shared—our true love of music. I threw her some sticks that night and she caught them before blowing me kisses. She beamed up at me, head nodding to the beat, tapping out a rhythm on the floor.

The pace never slackened as I began 1986 by filming a concert at the Warfield Theater in San Francisco for my *Live Romance 1600* video, as well as working at Sunset Sound Studios on my third album, *Sheila E* (due to be released in February 1987).

Choosing our outfits for the tour was a high point. We had the finest designers, stylists, and pattern makers create clothes for everyone in my band. They decided to dress me in matching (or at least color-coordinated) fabrics to complement the six-inch heels I wore. I'd usually step onto the stage in a coat that lit up, but after that I chose to wear all kinds of different outfits—usually something new, tailor-made, tight, and sexy.

Inspired by the 1984 movie *Amadeus* and its bejeweled eighteenth-century costumes, I had a lot of fun coming up with all sorts of crazy variations on the *Amadeus* theme. The famous Patti LaBelle, a friend from my teen years, was the one who suggested a stand-up collar for me, which was a look I wore for years.

The designers played with ideas and tried out different concepts. I'd see things I liked in all the hippest fashion magazines and tear out the pages to show them. "I like the look of that one in *Vogue*," I might say, "Can you copy the neckline on this?" or "This would look great in blue silk."

There were no rules, and if there were, we broke them.

My main concern was that whatever I was wearing be easy to get on or off because I had to do so many quick costume changes. Everything had to have Velcro or snaps—there could be no buttons or zippers in case they got stuck. Between us we figured out what made sense. Some of my outfits were very risqué and had little more than doilies over the spots that needed to be covered. I took it to the extreme.

There were times when even Prince looked at me as if to say, "Are you sure you want to wear that?"

The media was picking up on my over-the-top-sexy outfits, too, and the critiques confused me. I was either being called a role model for being a woman who could play a typically "male instrument" or being judged for dressing too sexy. At the time, I viewed both playing drums and wearing revealing outfits as ways of celebrating my womanhood. Even though I was very much a tomboy, I still loved being a woman.

During the song "Next Time Wipe the Lipstick Off Your Collar," I started to lure men from the audience up onto the stage and sing to them as a security guard tied them to a chair. They were not allowed to touch me at all, but I got to tear their shirts open, buttons flying, then sit on their laps, straddle them, grope their crotches, and rip their belts off. This was long before Janet Jackson or Madonna started acting out bondage scenes onstage, and it was all my own idea.

I guess the act was all about being in control of a man—something I had never once been as a little girl—and I loved the power and the freedom of it. I went through that routine in almost every show, so at least ninety-eight men must have been publicly humiliated (and/or enticed/aroused) by me. But at some point it started to feel wrong to me. I felt empty and dirty.

Word got out about the kind of thing I was doing, and people soon started coming to see me in my own right and not just as an opening act. The downside was they also started to comment about how I looked. I read what they wrote, and I wasn't sure how I felt about it at first. I wasn't even sure who I was anymore. The Sheila E I'd created was up-front, provocatively dressed, and playing with men like toys. I wasn't even playing the drums so much anymore. I was getting further and further away from my craft.

More and more, people began writing not about my musical abilities but about my outfits. The tone was, "I wonder what she's going to wear or *not* going to wear tonight?" I started to feel naked in the wrong way. That really bothered me and made me begin to reevaluate the image I wanted to project.

One night in a city somewhere in the middle of the tour, I looked into the audience and spotted dozens of young girls dressed like me, which really alarmed me. I was half-naked a lot of the time, and I didn't want teenagers who weren't yet aware what men were capable of to have anything happen to them because they were trying to emulate me.

It was time to reconcile my public and private selves. From then on, I started to wear more and more clothes in public.

Prince was intrigued by me both as a musician and as a sexual being. He made me feel empowered and sexy, and part of that process had made me dress the way I did. I think it worked both ways too. I doubt he'd ever met anyone, especially not a woman, who could stand up against him the way I liked to. That was part of my attraction. I was always so competitive, and we were testing each other to see who could stay up the longest, work the hardest in the studio, or win at basketball, pool, or Ping-Pong. He was up against the wrong person. I was a part-time boy and competitive as hell thanks to my mother.

Prince wasn't great at relaxation, either—he always had so much stuff on his mind that even eating a meal seemed a waste of time. As he said in one interview: "Sometimes I can't shut off my brain, and it hurts. . . . Do I have to eat? I wish I didn't have to eat!"

It didn't help that people went so crazy for Prince and me that we couldn't go anywhere; we couldn't even walk the streets or do something as mundane as go for a coffee or to the mall. Fans would tear at our clothes the minute we stepped out in public. It was like being back in Colombia—only all the time. I hadn't been prepared for that. We were constantly surrounded by bodyguards, many of them hulking professional wrestlers.

One way I could get him to relax, though, was to watch a movie, either in our hotel room or—if we could manage it—by sneaking out to a theater very late at night so that no one would spot us. Occasionally we'd hire the whole movie theater so we could watch a show undisturbed. His normal wasn't my normal, because he couldn't even go out in daylight anymore.

I was dating a vampire.

After a while I found I couldn't keep up with the relentless nature of my new life, especially as I'd just come off a couple of big back-to-back tours with Marvin and Lionel. I was massively grateful and happy for everything Prince was doing for me, but adjusting to the way he pushed himself and everyone around him was a tough transition.

When I was a kid I'd wanted to run in the Olympics and win gold for the United States. Those first couple of years with Prince felt to me like the kind of physical and mental training that an Olympic athlete must have to put herself through. And like any athlete, I knew in my heart that there had to come a time when I would crash and burn. My moment in the spotlight would inevitably come to an end. Pushing that thought as far from my mind as I could, I somehow found the reserves of energy to carry on.

Even when I wasn't with him, the partying never stopped. I guess it wasn't that easy to kick the habit. Some of the craziest things we did were when we were on days off between gigs. Just like Moms, I was always looking for fun—especially as an antidote to the stress. I'd be in a speedboat with the band in Miami with me screaming, "Go faster!" or we'd go Jet Skiing in the middle of the ocean.

We might be somewhere in Europe with a bunch of friends and I'd say, "Let's get on a plane and have lunch at the Eiffel Tower!" I'd ask my secretary to find me somewhere hot to take a break if we had a few days off. She'd suggest somewhere, and I'd check the weather reports *USA Today* for the hottest place of all—Hawaii or Florida—and then I'd change my mind and fly there instead.

While touring in Chile, someone offered us a helicopter ride. "Hell, yes!" was my response. "Fly over the beach!" But the chopper went into free fall, and my stomach ended up in my throat. The band was all screaming and yelling. We flew over the venue at the Vinca del Mar Festival we were playing in, but then we got lost as the fog rolled in. The pilot had instruments, but he didn't speak English very well, and we were terrified as we watched him guessing in broken English where to land. Another time we visited the Olympic equestrian team and went horseback riding, and I just took off. Everyone panicked because they thought my horse was out of control, but it wasn't—I was.

Someone else took us parasailing, and I told them to let me out as far as they could. I went up so high I couldn't even discern the motor of the boat anymore—all I could hear was silence and my own heartbeat. That completely freaked me out, and I waved at them to get me down.

All my life I'd never heard silence like that—there was always a tone of the world, always something—and it didn't sit well with me. That surprised and scared me a little, because I'd thought I wanted silence. I was beginning to find the constant throng of people and demands way too noisy. There was no time to be on my own, and there was never any peace. We didn't stop, and the madness of the life we were leading almost began to feel normal.

The loneliness of never being alone started to get to me.

I could never seem to find a quiet place for myself. I'd grown up in a house full of noise and should have been used to it, but my life was different then.

Even more confusing was the growing feeling that I could have anything I wanted, whenever I wanted it. People were buying my music in droves, and my fans really did love me and my work. They were singing along to songs I'd written, and that seemed crazy to me. Sleep deprivation didn't help. Nor did the intensity of being in a full-on relationship with someone I was not only working with every day but who was constantly surrounded by people, especially other women.

After a while, I started to become paranoid that I could no longer do things by myself. Fearing that I was close to losing my mind, I asked Connie and Karen to join me and found them jobs as assistant tour managers. It felt so good to have my friends around me, and they helped me enormously. They were surprised by how quickly I'd gone from being the tough Sheila they'd always known to being a semi-helpless celebrity.

We were in New York doing a movie shoot one day when I admitted to them that I didn't feel I could even walk down the street on my own anymore.

"That's crazy!" said Connie. "Right now, Sheila, you are going to walk to the corner of the block by yourself, go into that deli over there, sit down, and eat a meal by yourself."

I swallowed my shock and shook my head vehemently. "No way!" I said. Then, in a tiny whisper, "I can't."

Karen took my hand. "You can. You have to learn to be by yourself again, okay?"

I felt naked and vulnerable without security and was afraid everyone was looking at me. I couldn't believe how scared I was to do the most normal thing in the world. But I was grateful to have my good friends support me and give me some tough love.

Connie and Karen remained several paces behind me as I put one foot in front of the other and headed toward the deli.

"Table for one, please," I stammered. I was so embarrassed as I sat down. Did I look stupid in a restaurant all by myself? I was so out of touch with reality that I'd forgotten that eating alone was perfectly normal.

My girlfriends followed me in and sat at a table on the other side of the room. I kept looking over at them longingly, but they deliberately ignored me. It took all the strength I had to sit there and try to eat a little something. I don't think anyone really recognized me, but I felt like everyone did. I thought they were all whispering about me behind my back. I couldn't stop thinking about what people thought of me. It was insane.

The girls made me do that kind of simple task a few more times until I began to feel more comfortable in my own skin. It was like exposure therapy. Their leveling presence also made me painfully aware that by being surrounded by people whose only job was to say yes to whatever I wanted, I was at risk of becoming an egotistical monster.

In an environment where everybody led me to believe there were no limits, I only had to ask to get what I wanted. If I wanted my sticks to light up when I played them, I could have it. If I wanted two two-thousand-dollar outfits for every show, that was fine too. The response was always "Sure!" or "No problem! We'll get that sorted for you."

The sky was the limit—I could have anything I wanted—and, in that environment, I became increasingly impatient for that "anything" to come to me *now*. In my extreme moments of delusion, when they told me that the fabric I wanted for a coat was French, I'd say something like, "Well, then fly to Paris and get it for me!"

I became mean, demanding, and angry. I stopped asking and started telling. I began to see my team as a group of people working *for* me, rather than as individuals who worked *with* me. I didn't give them the acknowledgment and appreciation they deserved. I didn't say "please" and "thank you." I was becoming a nightmare.

In turning into a diva, I was a million miles away from the Sheila Escovedo my parents had raised me to be—the kid who bought her Christmas gifts at the ninety-nine-cent store and needed nothing but a trash can and a few spatulas to make some satisfying beats. I take full responsibility for becoming this person, and when I began to do some soul-searching, I realized I had a lot of apologizing to do.

I'm still apologizing. I think that, for the most part, my diva ways are a thing of the past. However, my experience in an elevator relatively recently taught me I still might have a ways to go.

I was with a guitar player I hadn't seen for a while, and we were in a five-star hotel. Dodging paparazzi when we got out of our limo, we eventually made it to the elevator breathlessly, but then stood there for a minute or so before I realized that it wasn't moving. I looked at him.

"Is it broken?"

"I was just wondering the same thing," he said. "Why aren't we moving?"

We looked to the floor buttons. None were lit up.

Then we looked at each other.

"Wait a minute," I said. "You didn't push the button."

"You didn't, either?" he asked.

We suddenly cracked up, realizing that we were both so used to having assistants or security push the elevator buttons that neither of us had even thought of doing it ourselves.

"Which one of us is going to press it?" he asked.

"Which floor?" I asked.

"Penthouse."

"But of course." I leaned in to press the button. "I got this."

Fortunately, when fame struck and then threatened to spoil me, I always had my friends and family to keep me grounded. They knew how to make me remember who Sheila Escovedo was, even as Sheila E's star was on the rise. When I flew back to LA one day midtour, Moms came to meet me. I walked through the airport looking every bit the star, taking my *Glamorous Life* role a bit too seriously—flanked by security, wearing a fur coat, sunglasses, and in head-to-toe couture.

That's when I spotted a crazy lady running toward me shouting, "I'm Sheila E's mama! I'm Sheila E's mama!" Moms was dressed in red onesie pajamas with the back flap open, multiple Pippi Long-stocking braids sticking out of her head, and a blacked-out front tooth. She had a sign taped to her behind that said, I'M SHEILA E'S

MOTHER in big black ink. She was jumping up and down with bells on her ankles so everyone could hear, laughing and waving for all to see—including the press. Zina was running alongside her, laughing so hard I thought she'd fall over.

Welcome home, Sheila. Back to *The Goofy Life*.

The trouble was, no matter how normal my life away from Prince was, I was madly, crazily in love with the guy who had shown me what it was like to live in that kind of rarefied world.

On tour all of the girls had hooked up with someone, and Connie started dating one of the security guards, Gilbert. None of us had any inkling back then, but it was the love of a lifetime for Connie and Gilbert, and they ended up with six kids—my godchildren. Connie and Gilbert's relationship was surely one of the best things ever to come out of *Purple Rain*.

When the tour finally ended (with plans for the next already in hand) and I returned to LA to recover from the madness, I didn't have anywhere to call home. Connie and I had given up our apartment because we were never there, so my life was packed in boxes. Luckily, I had plenty of friends and stayed in close touch with Lionel Richie and his wife, Brenda.

She and Lionel had been teasing me over the fact that I didn't have my own place, and she suggested I move into one of the empty wings of their house in Bel Air. I wasn't sure at first—it was very different from what I was used to, but at least my months in fancy hotel rooms had prepared me a little. In the end, though, I thought it would be fun. I hated being on my own and was used to being surrounded by a lot of people.

Taking me in meant taking in my family, too, of course, as we were virtually inseparable. Not that Brenda and Lionel minded one bit. They had tried without success to have children of their own, so they loved having a big family around. The Escovedo entourage generally included my whole family along with Connie and Karen, with her two-year-old daughter, Nicole, my adorable niece—known to everyone as Nikki.

Although Karen and Peter Michael weren't together anymore, they were still a big part of our lives—not least because of their much-loved daughter.

Brenda adored Nikki, too, and suggested that my niece stay with them whenever Karen was on tour with me. She insisted it made sense. She provided her with a beautiful bedroom and showered her with toys and clothes. She even bought her a puppy.

As a single working mom, Karen was extremely grateful, but very torn.

Brenda enrolled Nikki at a local primary school, where she was getting a great education. She had everything she could possibly need. Peter Michael (who'd married someone else) visited whenever he had breaks from his music career too. If Nikki stayed where she was, rent-free, then Karen could earn enough for their future without disrupting her child's life. It seemed like letting Nicole stay there was in her best interests.

Things changed, though, once I moved away to Minneapolis to work and rehearse for the next big tour. Nicole stayed in her pretty pink bedroom and Karen kept visiting. When Brenda started to talk about adopting Nicole, Karen didn't know what to do. Lionel, who was Nicole's official guardian, would do anything to keep Brenda happy. In the end, the Richies convinced Karen and Peter Michael that they could give Nicole the kind of life her birth parents never could. They told us that we would all be in her life as much as before, and they acknowledged that we were always her family.

The heartbreaking part is that once Nicole Escovedo legally became Nicole Richie, it felt like we lost her. We all lost her—me, Karen, Peter Michael, Patrice, Moms and Pops, Juan, and Zina.

People have lots of questions about Nicole. There's been a

ton of false and upsetting information put out there by the media from completely inaccurate sources surrounding Nicole's early life and the circumstances around her open adoption. While there are many more things I could share from my personal perspective, out of respect for Nicole and others in the family, as well as out of respect for the Richies, I have to emphasize that the rest of the story isn't mine to tell in a public forum.

I can, however, share this. She's my niece, whom I love to pieces. She's my brother Peter Michael's biological daughter. Her mother was and is a good friend. Lionel and Brenda Richie adopted her and gave her a life full of love and great privilege. She was a precious little girl and has grown up to be a remarkably intelligent, talented, creative, funny, and beautiful young woman. All of the Escovedos love her madly and always will.

The rest, as I say, is not my story to tell.

24. Drum Break

An instrumental or percussion section
or interlude during a song

You don't have to send me flowers like you used to,
You don't have to buy me candy, I'll still be your fool
All I ask for is a little decency and class

"NEXT TIME WIPE THE LIPSTICK OFF YOUR COLLAR"
SHEILA E

There was no jumping off the juggernaut that was Prince's life. In 1987, the industry rumors were confirmed when he officially separated from the Revolution and promoted me to the role of band drummer for his next tour, Sign of the Times, which was due to begin that spring.

Being Prince's drummer was a position I'd hold for two crazy years during another of his most intense and creative phases. As well as writing and playing music on his next album, I was asked to contribute to the songs of his latest protégé band, Madhouse, and be the musical director of his backup band, the New Power Generation.

Sign of the Times was a double album on which I collaborated with him on a number of songs, at the same time releasing singles and videos from my third album. My single "Hold Me" did well on the Billboard charts and continued to improve my reputation as a solo artist.

My hunger for the work wasn't purely creative. When I came off the Purple Rain tour, I believed that I'd be rich. I'd been working flat out for well over a year on the biggest tour in the world. I never did it for the money—that was never what had motivated me—but it was comforting to think that I could maybe find myself a nice house and really fill the family fridge.

So it came as the most dreadful, terrible shock when Prince's account managers told me that I was a million dollars in debt. "You owe us a lot of money, Sheila," they said. "How do you want to start paying us back?"

I was shattered.

It turns out that every time people told me, "Sure, we'll fix that for you," my account had been charged. I'd been so naïve. I thought all the expenses for costumes and hair, equipment and staff would be covered by Prince and his team as part of the tour—as they had been on my previous tours with Lionel and Marvin.

I had no idea I was expected to pay for it all myself.

Prince's managers were my managers, and yet nobody had advised me separately. I bear full responsibility for the bills I incurred, but I have to say it hurt to think that neither Prince nor his team came off that tour in debt, as I did.

When I went through the final accounts for equipment, wardrobe, hairstylists, flights, food, and drink, I realized that they'd made me pay for everything. They even charged me to use sound equipment that was already there.

I felt like such a fool.

As with all big music events (and I'd seen it with Marvin Gaye

especially), there was a lot of stuff going on behind the scenes that I didn't understand or want to know about. I never worried about it because I didn't think it related to me. Now I realized that some of it did.

There was no escaping the truth—I owed the money, and that was that. I was still signed to Prince's management company and to Warner Brothers. He had casually told me at the start that it would be easier to go in with him. It never even occurred to me that I shouldn't, or that there might be a conflict of interest. I didn't even ask anyone to study the paperwork for me.

Not checking the small print was a salutary lesson for me, and one I paid dearly for. I spent years paying back what I owed. This meant that—whether I wanted to or not—I'd have to carry on working at that level and that pace for some time to come.

Creatively and personally, that was a bitter pill to swallow.

People are surprised to learn that I'm not what they would consider "wealthy," even though I am rich in other ways. What is rich? In truth, I have turned down more than I've made. In the early nineties, I was approached to participate in a TV infomercial about psychics. I declined, explaining that I didn't believe in their product. They assured me that that part didn't matter. They just needed my name, offering half a million up front and another half a million once they filmed the ad. It was still easy to say no.

All money is not good money.

"You know," I told them, "if you guys wanted me to endorse Tupperware, I would've taken the check, no problem. I believe in Tupperware. It keeps my food fresh. And me and my mom are big on leftovers. But I don't believe that you're offering something valuable. So thanks, but no thanks."

I called Moms and Pops immediately.

"I just turned down a million dollars," I told them.

"You what?" they asked.

"I don't believe in the product they wanted me to sell."

"Well, can't you believe in it just a little bit?"

It took a minute, but once I really explained where I was coming from, they were proud of my conviction. I never would've imagined that turning down a million dollars in an instant would be such an easy choice.

I guess that for me, chasing the light of stardom was never that important. And chasing the money wasn't, either. I think at times I got off course, rerouted a bit. Fame can be intoxicating, and it's easy to misplace your moral compass. I definitely made some mistakes along the way and had to learn some valuable lessons about maintaining my personal values. But ultimately, when it came to the big decisions, it was always more important for me to maintain my integrity. I can't bear the thought of doing something I don't believe in. Whatever decision I make, I want to be able to sleep at night.

I was also offered a lot of money to pose naked for *Playboy* and quickly turned it down. The offer made sense, given that I was being paid to be half-naked onstage every night. So what was the difference? It's a question I'm still asking myself.

It's hard to remember some of the thoughts I had back then, since my spirit has changed so much. But I can recall thinking that posing half-naked for a magazine seemed like a very different thing from being half-naked while making music, which was an expression of my soul.

I didn't know when I turned down the offer that I was still going to get my *Playboy* money one day—playing under the stars at the Hollywood Bowl for the annual Playboy Jazz Festival. It's one of my favorite gigs. And they let me do it fully dressed!

While Prince and I were crazy for each other back in the day and worked together constantly, we were not a constant couple. I tried to ignore the sadness I felt about not being the only woman in his life, but I learned to deal with it early on.

I'd been placed in a similar situation with Carlos and had spent years watching so many people around me being unfaithful. As I approached my thirtieth birthday, I was beginning to think that, given my profession, my hopes of finding a one-woman man were unrealistic. My old-fashioned notions of fidelity seemed completely out of kilter with what was going on all around me.

And I wasn't sure if I could have been with him nonstop and permanently anyway. Although we were with each other on the road all the time and did end up living together for a while, it was never going to work. We both liked our own space too much.

We were in London filming a show sometime around that tour and staying at the Dorchester Hotel. When I was walking through the lobby on my way to sound check, I spotted someone ahead of me. My heart stopped. He had his back to me, but the silhouette was unmistakable.

"Oh, my God!" I cried, clinging to a friend for support. "That's Sammy Davis!" I was nervous about approaching him, and so I hovered on the periphery while he talked to some other people. "If I don't say something now, I'll miss my chance and regret it for the rest of my life."

I stepped closer but didn't want to be a pest, so I waited for the right moment. I had a newfound appreciation for what fans must go through when they're hoping to meet me. I'm not saying I'm anywhere near Sammy in the celebrity department, but it was somewhat of a wakeup call. It's nerve-racking!

While waiting, my mind flashed back to one morning when my brothers and a few friends skipped school and actually drove six hours south in a Monte Carlo to Los Angeles—the glittery city of Tinseltown—for an adventure. We bought one of those celebrity maps that showed us where the stars lived. We drove around for hours gawking at all the Beverly Hills mansions. These were houses I'd only seen in movies, and they looked more like museums than places where people actually lived. Not even Pops's rich and famous celebrity friends in Marin County and San Francisco's Pacific Heights had mansions like those.

As we sailed along Mulholland, I thought of my ultimate idol. "Hey! Let's find Sammy Davis Jr.'s house!" I cried. We couldn't believe that it was actually cited on the map, and when we realized we could actually drive right up, I nearly fainted. I wanted to preserve this moment in time—my being in such close proximity to the actual home of my Sammy.

"I have to have something of his," I said as we pulled even closer. Then I spotted his mailbox. My brothers looked at me with dropped jaws as I ran up, dug my hand in and retrieved a few envelopes. I leaped back into the car and we sped off.

"Sheila!" Peter Michael cried. "You could go to jail for that!" It was only a few pieces of junk mail, but it was an illegal prank, not to mention immoral, unethical, and just plain wrong.

There in the lobby, I thought about telling him that story, but my heart was beating so fast I wasn't even sure I could talk. When his conversation finally ended and I spotted my opportunity, I walked right up to him, still trying to figure out what to say. "Sir? My name is Sheila E and I'm in town playing. You have no idea how much I love you. I mean, I am, like, the biggest fan!"

He smiled at me with such warmth. "Oh, Sheila honey, that is *so* sweet!"

I couldn't believe my ears were hearing *that* voice talking to me—the voice I had mimicked with such dedication day after day, family gathering after family gathering. I couldn't believe my eyes were looking into the face I had studied so closely as a child.

We chatted for a few minutes, and I could have stayed talking to him all night, but my driver kept telling me it was time to go. Sammy Davis Jr. placed my hand on his arm and, like a true gentleman, walked me out to the Bentley that was waiting for me. I don't even remember what we talked about as he opened the door for me. I just remember thinking, "Sammy Davis Jr. has his arm around my waist!"

That album Pops had brought home when I was nine years old had been so pivotal, so liberating—it had opened me up to music's infinite possibilities. I had learned his every line as he bellowed from the big wooden speakers of our Marantz record player, and copied his every move as I viewed it on our old Zenith set. Now here he was right next to me, as sweet as pie: the courteous and gracious star I'd always imagined him to be.

As I reluctantly stepped into the car, I invited him to the show as my guest. He thanked me politely and told me that he'd love to see me perform, but he never came. I don't suppose he even knew who I was, but he was far too much of a gentleman to say so. The driver started the engine, and off we went.

I should've told him that story, I thought. *I could've finally apologized.*

I floated away on air in the back of that Bentley, my head somewhere up in the London clouds.

Meeting Sammy was far from the only momentous event of that tour, however. One night, somewhere in the middle of Europe, Prince and I were playing when we started in on "Purple Rain." There's something about that song that moves me. It touches my spirit, and the melody is beautiful. It's one of my favorite songs, because as a drummer I get to drive. As always, I lose myself in the music.

Prince was singing at the front of the stage, but halfway through the song and after his guitar solo, he spun around and grinned back at me as he often did when he felt the same thing I did.

I smiled back, wrapped up in that exquisite exchange of melodious connection for which there are no words. But then he found some.

"Marry me?" he mouthed.

My butterflies danced, twirled, and flipped as I stared into those deep green eyes I'd fallen for so many years ago.

"Yes!" I mouthed, without any hesitation.

He blew me a kiss, turned to the audience, and took the most amazing guitar solo ever.

A lot of people on the tour knew we were together, yet few knew he'd asked me to marry him. Again we kept it a secret from the public, because he said he didn't want the extra publicity; that we were hounded enough as it was. It never even occurred to me to ask him for a ring (even though I shouldn't have needed to), nor did he offer one. Besides, I didn't wear rings very often—they only got in the way of my playing. And of course a ring on my finger would have told the world what he didn't want the world to know. So I kept it a secret, even from my family.

I'd been good at keeping secrets since I was five.

I talked to my folks all the time on the phone, of course. Pops was gigging with Anita Baker and Moms was still running around challenging everyone to a game of anything. The physical distance was making me homesick, and as much as I wanted to tell them my news, my private life seemed especially private, so only Connie, Karen, and the band and crew knew.

For the rest of that year my relationship with Prince was a dream. We were very happy together, and even though I had my own tour bus, I usually spent the night in his. We were with each other all day and night, so if he was fooling around on me, he would have had to be quick about it.

"He's crazy about you," one of his close friends told me later. "But it scares him to love someone that much."

Between concerts, I divided my time between Los Angeles and Minneapolis. It was fun hanging out with Prince, especially when he was so fired up about the next tour, the next look, and the next big thing.

"Let's cut our hair!" he'd say one day, so we would. "Okay, now let's dye it crazy colors. Wait, you could go blonde!" So I did.

It was while I was staying with Prince in his hometown that I first met Miles Davis, whose music my father had played almost every day of his life. He came to dinner one night, and I could hardly believe I was sitting across from him. I wanted to call Pops and let him say hello on the telephone, but that wouldn't have been cool.

Miles spoke in an incredibly rasping voice that was almost a whisper. He turned to me and said, "Prince told me he's got this girl playing drums, so I had to see you play," he told me. "I never knew you were such a bad motherfuckin' bitch!"

What do you say to that? Thank him for the compliment? High praise indeed!

Even though Prince and I were happy, after the intensity of touring I decided I needed a place of my own. Ever since I'd moved out of the Richies' house in Bel Air, I'd gotten into the habit of renting somewhere for a few months at a time. It was a way to separate my life "on land" from life on the road—which so often felt like space travel.

Renting strangers' houses in towns or areas I didn't know, preferably in the hills and surrounded by trees, meant that no one knew where I lived. If no one knew where I lived, then they couldn't reach me. And this gave me the silence I craved.

I loved playing pool, so I took my own table wherever I went. Practice makes perfect, and I was determined that one day I'd beat my uncles at their own game. My new home had to have a grand piano and stairs to run up and down, as well as a basketball hoop to keep me in shape. I needed a yard so that I could spend time outside, and I'd look for places in the hills or mountains near Los Angeles, or close to a lake where I could go fishing on my own.

My cousin Ia, who worked for me as well, found a beautiful

four-bedroom house in Minneapolis. In that remote lakeside property, with its own fishing boat, I wrote my own music in an environment of pure peace.

I needed to shut out the noise for a little while.

After so many years traveling with bands, with all that speed and movement, sound had taken hold of me, become a part of me, and I needed some distance.

No sooner had I found someplace quiet, though, than the noise started up again. I had to go back out on the road after I'd barely had time to chalk my pool cue.

There were times when it felt like too much, and I wanted more time to myself. Prince and I never argued or fought (that came later), but we didn't always see eye to eye. At first it was music, the very thing that brought us together, that became our biggest point of contention. He was determined never to copy himself musically, and he wanted to release something edgy and original every time. Even though I respected his artistry, his rich fusion of sounds, and knew his songwriting was nothing short of great, I was increasingly uncomfortable with where that drive to be different seemed to be taking him lyrically.

His songs were getting too dirty for my tastes. There was so much cursing—way past the "funk until the dawn" days. It just wasn't fun to be around. A talent like that didn't need to listen to me, however, no matter how much he may have valued my opinion. He's brilliant in part because he seeks out and soaks up all the great musical influences around him but ultimately does what he feels.

But I sensed he was struggling with his own creative decisions. To follow *Sign of the Times*, in 1987 he created the funky *Black Album* (in an all-black sleeve with no writing, including any mention of him at all, and one of my favorite records). We had a blast recording it in his house and in a warehouse before he had his custom-built studio at Paisley Park. Those were some funky songs we laid down! There was one crazy-sounding one, the finished version of which he played me over the phone.

I said, "Let's name it!"

"Okay. What does it sound like to you?"

For some reason, maybe because I'd seen some stuff on the news that day about gangs in Los Angeles, I blurted out, "Two nigs united for West Compton."

He went with it.

As a kid I used to say "nigga please" to friends. The word *nigga* sometimes bothered me, and sometimes it didn't. I guess on this night, the shortened version didn't. I was in the midst of the very gradual process of cleansing my vocabulary. I didn't like it when women called each other "bitch" as a term of endearment. I understood the importance of context and intention, but I was getting less and less comfortable with profanity of all kinds.

Prince was getting uncomfortable with the album for other reasons. One night he woke up and said, "We need to stop the record." He abruptly withdrew it just one week before its release, claiming it was "evil." The lyrics had gotten pretty dark, but I was surprised he turned on the whole album in that instant.

Having spent another intense period back in the studio with the band and me in May 1988, he replaced *The Black Album* (with the battle between good and evil as its central theme) with *Lovesexy*.

The tour to promote it began in Paris in 1988 with an initial seventy-seven dates planned for the US, Europe, and Asia. It was due to end in January 1989 in Osaka, Japan. There were, on average, twelve dates per month (sometimes seventeen), with a lot of traveling to and from countries in between.

Once again I was on tour doing all that I'd ever wanted to do—playing the drums, performing, singing, playing percussion. But things weren't right. They weren't right between Prince and me, and they weren't right in my spirit.

25. Ghost Strokes

Small, almost inaudible, ghostlike strokes

My love for you will never die
Can't you see the tears in my eyes?
All of the promises that you made
Have all seemed to vanish and fade

"NOTHING WITHOUT YOU"
THE E FAMILY

I t was in the early 1990s when God fully came back into my heart. I was working on my next record, *Sex Cymbal*, which my brother, Peter Michael, was helping me produce.

My life was far less frenetic than in previous years, but still I looked around me and realized that I didn't know very many happy people. Instead we all seemed to be growing older and unhappier. I began to wonder, What the heck are we doing with our lives?

This sense of general weariness didn't come to me in a flashbulb moment; it was more of a gradual realization. I had been physically and emotionally exhausted for several years in close succession, and there came a point when my mind and spirit broke.

After years of punishing beats, by the time I was promoting *Sex Cymbal* my wrists throbbed in pain, and I needed frequent deep-tissue massages. But even the best therapists couldn't release the tendons or stretch my tightened muscles. The stiffness in my neck and shoulders caused me to seek out a rigorous course of acupuncture—with sometimes up to fifty needles at a time.

I'd usually manage to play a couple of songs before I'd be crying in pain. After a while, my hands started to tingle, and almost every part of my body began to ache—my calves, arms, ankles, wrists, shoulders, elbows, and neck. I was a wreck.

I didn't want anyone to know how sick I felt (least of all Prince), but I didn't know how much longer I could contain it all. I was so used to being able to do whatever I wanted whenever I wanted, and now I was feeling unbearably vulnerable. I had known myself as a fearless Gardere, a proud Escovedo, a woman who could do anything men could do—only better and in six-inch heels. But now I was falling apart.

I kept trying to work, walk, and mix my latest record. But a voice inside kept warning me, *Something's wrong. It shouldn't be so hard to breathe.* A few times I felt like I was going to pass out. Then one day I turned around to sneeze and my back went out. My legs gave out and I fell to the ground. I was paralyzed for two weeks. Gilbert had to carry me around like a child.

I was in Minneapolis, so I flew in a trusted doctor from LA who carried out a series of tests, trying to figure out the source of all my physical ailments. His X-rays revealed how twisted my body had become from playing drums the way I did—sitting down, legs spread apart playing two individual kick drums in heels—as if I was driving a car. Every time I hit a hi-hat, I twisted my pelvis. I'd played like that for years, all of it in my trademark six-inch stilettos, so that in addition to skewing my spine, pelvis, and hips, I'd actually shortened my calf muscles. I was twisted and raw from the inside out.

"Your body can only take so much, Sheila," my doctor warned me. "You need complete rest."

I had to face the reality. I wasn't Wonder Woman, and I wasn't a machine. I had pushed myself to the extreme for too long and was suffering the consequences. I didn't know how to relate to myself anymore. Was I really that fragile, damaged, worn-out woman staring back at me in the mirror? Who was I if I couldn't pound away on a drum set? What was I now?

I'd heard of the connection between mind and body, but I'd never before understood how deep that went. Finally, in the solace of my home, my body could reveal all it had endured. And my mind could finally pay attention. Every part of me hurt after too many years of playing so hard without good warm-ups or restorative rest.

I barely had enough breath to walk to the bathroom. It hurt just to sneeze. I would have terrifying spasms and my entire body would seize up for hours. Eventually, a friend whose sister was a nurse advised me to go to the hospital, where the doctors discovered that my left lung was 80 percent collapsed from an acupuncturist's poorly placed needle.

"You're lucky to be alive," they told me. "You could have died." I stayed in the hospital about a week and pretty much shut down. My body had been trying to tell me for a long time that I wasn't invincible. It took me thirty-two years for that whisper to turn into a deafening scream. When I got home, I was sick from all the medication. I couldn't eat and got horribly thin—dropping from 120 to 85 pounds.

My cousin Ia came to live with me and spoon-fed me like a baby. Because I had so little energy, it sometimes took me fifteen minutes just to get down a spoonful of mashed potatoes. I thought I was going to die in that house. Besides Ia, I didn't want my family or Prince to know anything. I told her to promise not to tell Moms and Pops. They would be too worried, and I felt compelled to heal on my own. I longed for the day when it could all be just a story to tell, but I was worried it might never be a part of my past.

I lay in my bed crying and praying to God for another chance: "Please, Father God. I'll do whatever you want me to do." I asked a friend in Israel to send me some holy water. I read my Bible every day and night, looking for a cure in the Scriptures, looking for healing in His Word. And when I slept, I laid my Bible on my chest.

When my body eventually began to recover, I hoped that my mind would, too. But I'd been an invalid for so long that I was now terrified of going outside. My home was my comfort zone, and the thought of going anywhere else totally freaked me out. My faith in myself was wavering. And my faith in the outside world as a safe place was no longer.

Then one day Ia made me get up and told me I had to try and go outside. Somehow I felt the need to do what scared me most. I got in the elevator, and slowly I walked outside. I hadn't felt fresh air in over a month. As soon as I stepped out into the sunny brightness of the day, I dropped to my knees in gratitude and kissed a crack in the pavement. Even that pavement was beautiful.

I never realized how many colors there were in my surroundings—the green of the grass, the rich brown of the tree bark, the white of the clouds, the deep blue of the sky. I ran my fingers through the grass as if it was the first time I'd ever seen or touched it. I walked to a tree and I hugged it like it was a long-lost friend.

The words of the poet E. E. Cummings sprang to mind: *I thank you God, I thank you God for this most amazing day, for the leaping greenly spirits of trees, and for the blue dream of sky and for everything which is natural, which is infinite, which is yes.*

Lying back on the grass, I cast my eyes to heaven. God had given all of this to me. And it took nearly losing myself to truly see it. I had taken so much for granted. I thought I needed money and belongings and applause, but all I needed was this.

Soon enough, my strength and health returned. It was time to start over. I had a second chance, and I needed another beginning. I missed my music. I needed to make some noise, this time on my own terms and at my own—slower—pace.

No job, no relationship, no *nothin'* was worth sacrificing my well-being for ever again.

There was still some heartache to come, though. In the middle of the next major tour with Prince, my Nanny died. Pops's crazy mother with the lewd sense of humor would never make us laugh again. When I heard the news, I told my parents I'd fly home for the funeral. But when I told Prince, he just looked at me blankly and said, "No."

That was the beginning of the end with Prince. I couldn't believe he wouldn't allow me to leave for a few days. He didn't seem to understand how important this was to me, how much I needed my family right then, and how much they needed me. Prince claimed he couldn't possibly get anyone to replace me, even for just a few days. He was my boss, he reminded me. He signed the paychecks.

I screamed and yelled at him for a while, and then I stormed off. I thought about jumping on a plane and flying home to the East Bay right then and there. But for some reason I couldn't let myself go.

There was one thing I could do, though. I told Prince, "Don't even pay me anymore. I don't want your money." Every week for the rest of the tour when the accounts guy came by with my check, I refused to take it.

"You have to!" he'd say, but I'd just tear it up in front of him.

"You have to take your check," Prince would tell me later.

"I don't need your money," I'd reply. "That ain't why I'm here. I'm here to play music and I'm here because I love you, and when people love each other money doesn't matter." We went on like that for weeks.

My heart was hurting. I knew that once the tour was over I'd have to walk away. Leaving the man I loved would be hard. He was my best friend, but if I couldn't get along with my best friend, why would I stay near him just because he was paying me?

When the tour ended, I quietly slipped away to my place in Minneapolis. I took a few months to recover, to savor the silence and space. I still saw Prince from time to time, not yet able to make the final break. But we weren't getting along that well. He was busier than ever and he was seeing other women.

I needed something else to believe in. And then came along a woman who became my dearest friend, Lynn Mabry. Peter Michael got to know her first when they were both on George Michael's tour, and he encouraged the two of us to meet up, sensing we'd get along well.

Lynn and I quickly realized we'd actually met years before, as teenagers, since she sang backup for my uncle Coke. I was sixteen when I went with Pops to a club called King Richard's by our house in Oakland to see Uncle Coke perform. I vaguely remember meeting her then, and she remembered meeting Pops and me. It is incredible that years later we'd become friends, she'd end up being my manager, and we'd compose and create a foundation together.

Lynn had spent the intervening years on the same kind of crazy roller coaster ride that I'd been on. She'd worked with George Clinton, Talking Heads, George Michael, Stevie Nicks, and Fleetwood Mac. Sly Stone was her cousin, and she was the co-lead singer of the seventies duo the Brides of Funkenstein. A single mom, she had raised her daughter and somehow managed to hold her life together and glow with inner happiness in spite of all the touring and the noise.

After I reconnected with Lynn, we decided to go into part-

nership to run my new company, Heaven Productions Music. In the midst of that, she was hired to sing for Bette Midler, but she was also ready to try something different. I wanted a new business manager—I kept firing mine. We got along so well, and she was so great at her job, that she ended up becoming my manager for fifteen years. She was someone I could trust.

Thanks to Lynn, I found work in the late 1990s and early 2000s as a session musician with the likes of Whitney Houston, Mariah Carey, and Gloria Estefan, as well as various television appearances and national commercials. She also helped me launch my next two solo projects, *Writes of Passage* and *Heaven*, on Concord Records with my new band, the E Train, playing a mix of Latin, soul, funk, and jazz and touring Europe and the States.

The more I got to know Lynn, the more I liked her. She had a quiet calm about her that I'd seen and envied in a few people I'd met along my path. It wasn't a surprise to learn that she was a Christian. When she saw the way I lived my life and how I treated people sometimes, she gently encouraged me to go to church with her. Although I wasn't interested at the time, she never stopped asking. I said no to her time and time again, but it was Easter Sunday 1992 when I was so unhappy that I thought, *Why not?*

Lynn attended the Bible Enrichment Fellowship International Church, pastored by Bam Crawford, who had a very intense way of doing things. She'd written books and preached worldwide. She ran her church like a boot camp and didn't mess around.

A few minutes into the service, Pastor Bam invited those in the congregation who wanted a new beginning to come to the pulpit and join her.

Something inside me stirred.

"We all make mistakes and sin every day," she cried. "Don't carry it with you. Come up, leave it all here, and give your heart to the Lord."

I felt a tugging at my heart, and I was strangely drawn to go up with the others around me who clearly felt it too. I heard a voice inside me say, *You can let go. You don't have to carry this around with you anymore. You can be free.*

I was scared, though—I didn't want to go up there on my own. Lynn could see I was struggling as she gently encouraged me, but I kept saying no.

With all of us standing, my body started shaking—my hands and knees went weak. I thought, What is happening to me? I wondered if I was having some sort of relapse, which scared me even more. But the more scared I became, the more I felt the need to make my way to the front of the church.

In the end, I couldn't stop myself.

I couldn't fight it anymore.

The seed of hope from my physical and mental collapse was ready to flower.

By the time I made it to the front of the church, I had purged it all and openly declared my love for Jesus Christ. I sat on the steps of the pulpit and cried like a baby. My life had been out of control for many long years, and I realized it there and then. I wanted to do better and be better. Before I knew it, I had fully redirected my life to surrender to God.

That Easter Sunday in Los Angeles was an intense and personal experience. In the following weeks and months, it became even more so. Once I gave my heart to Christ, it felt to me like all hell broke loose. I felt a negative pull on my life. It was dark—it was the enemy, Satan. The moment I said yes to the Lord, I felt attacked from everywhere.

Strange things started to happen—a series of events and misfortunes that seemed too coincidental to be happening to me and to those I loved all at once. I became increasingly paranoid and felt like something was trying to get to me, and then—if it couldn't reach me—it would try to hurt my friends and family. That really scared me.

Afraid of what I may have triggered by declaring my love for God, I stayed away from church for a year. I slipped back into being my old self and saw Lynn's concern and sadness for me. She shared later how disheartening it was to see me so unhappy and disrespectful to people, including her.

It took a long time for me to appreciate what she was telling me and to accept that I really wanted Christ back in the forefront of my life. Little by little, as I began to read the Bible again, I started to see everything differently. This time, the words of the Scriptures really seemed to jump out at me.

Taking a deep breath, I took that step back to church, and from that day on, I embarked on a walk of faith, peace, and kindness that I would do my best to continue daily.

We are all attacked by sin and temptation, but my daily walk in love shows me how to handle those temptations. Prayer is essential in all that I do. My band and I pray before every show. I have made a personal commitment to be a blessing to someone or something every day, even if it is just by brightening that day with a smile, a kind word, or a good deed. My whole family tries to do the same.

My father was raised Catholic and always had a strong faith, so he was very pleased that I had found the Lord. He was even happier that I started to do ministry work and became a "minister of music." My enthusiasm for Jesus was invigorating—Peter Michael became a minister in another church, as did three of my nephews, which is wonderful; God's love is reaching the young.

Once Pops, Moms, and Zina moved near me, I decided to attend another church so that we could have fellowship together. We have such an enriched spiritual awareness as a family now. Experiencing the power in speaking to Him personally was such a breakthrough, and doing so as a family is even more powerful.

For me, religion is more about following rules and laws. The divine connection is having faith, honoring the Word, and having a spiritual relationship with God.

Faith had always been at the core of my childhood. We went to St. Anthony's church every Sunday and said our prayers every night. I remember saying my blessings before bed and praying for my family one by one. There was always a Bible in the house, though I don't recall reading it. When our stomachs were growling and we couldn't find anything good in our kitchen, we'd knock on our neighbor's door, enduring the Bible readings in hungry anticipation of the peanut-butter sandwiches they would give us. Most aspects of religious rituals felt like a task, though, and I didn't feel spiritually connected to them.

I liked when Pops made enough money at a gig for us to have meat on Sundays after church—great big plates of pork chops and applesauce, which was small compensation for being in that drafty old building singing songs that didn't connect with me at all. When we were younger we didn't have any choice, but as we got older we still endured it because church meant so much to my parents.

The sanctuary was cold and uninviting. The services were boring, and I couldn't hear or understand what the priests were saying half the time. It seemed like church was related to guilt. I dreaded the confession booth, racking my brain for "bad" things to confess to the priest, like not listening to my parents or stealing change out of Moms's drawer to buy candy.

"I'm so sorry, I'm so sorry. God, please forgive me," I would plead. So I talked to God on Sundays, or when I felt I needed forgiveness for some new sin, but I didn't have a personal relationship with Christ like I do now. At the time, I didn't even know such a relationship was possible.

My spirituality is personal, but I gladly share it with others. I hope to inspire others to walk with God, but I have no interest in pushing any agenda. I respect the views and opinions of others, whether they are nonbelievers or they've embraced another spiritual path. My spirituality works for me. And through it, I have found healing and salvation. I don't share the fire-and-brimstone, hell-and-sin talk to minister to nonbelievers. My approach to saving a soul is all about love and being the best you can be. It's not to make other people become Christians.

My belief is that when you find true eternal love, you'll see God and want more of Him. I look at myself first to see where change is needed before I even think about trying to change anyone else. I don't feel it's my job to change anyone anyway. I believe my purpose to make a difference by inspiring others to be the blessing. And when I'm blessing someone, I'm being blessed right back.

I see that there was no choice in my path. If I had kept standing still, nothing would have changed. I needed a major life shift, a spiritual 180. My music is all about change and spontaneity as expressed in my altering the drumbeat. It was time I altered the beat of my own life. My music, like my faith, feeds me. Combining the two made such spiritual sense.

Once I discovered the depth of my faith, everything took on a whole new meaning. Like the stance I usually assume at the end of every intense solo on the timbales: legs firm, right stick pointing straight up. I acknowledge God, from whom my gift comes.

Liza Minnelli was in the audience of a benefit I performed at once and she gave me a great endorsement, telling me she loved that final stance. "It's powerful," she said.

Now, in the midst of prayer, I feel the same intensity. My right stick is in the air pointing to the heavens while my feet are firmly planted on the earth. I'm honoring God, because it's He who lets me do what I do. I'm praising Him. As the audience claps they're thanking me, and I am in reverence to Him.

Thank you, Jesus. Hallelujah. You are worthy to be praised.

Lynn was so important in showing me how to rediscover and tap into my faith. She was also pivotal in helping me move on to the next important stage of my "recovery" from my previous life. Through "walking the walk" and studying the word of God, I came to realize that I didn't want to carry my former self around with me anymore. It was time to face and examine what had happened in my childhood.

I felt the need to forgive myself.

In one of our deeper conversations, Lynn revealed to me that she had been molested at twelve years old. I was shocked and saddened for her but so impressed by how she'd been able to forgive her molester and move on. What a revelation!

With her being a true friend and one I could trust, I took a breath and broke my thirty-year silence to tell her what had happened to me. We cried and prayed together, agreeing to turn our terrible experiences into a positive force. After realizing that our artistic experience was an essential part of whatever we did, we decided to start a movement to help abused kids.

After much discussion, we went on to cofound the Lil' Angel Bunny Foundation (later renamed the Elevate Hope Foundation)—an organization to help abused and abandoned children by promoting self-awareness through music, the arts, and compassion.

We'd hold raffles and auctions after shows, auctioning off some of my equipment to raise money for special programs that cared for disadvantaged youth throughout California. The raffle tickets cost around two dollars each for a chance to win one of my snares or a conga, which were worth $300 to $500. Since we were in small clubs at the time, we'd raise about $200 or so, which we would donate to a preselected facility that helped kids. To raise the stakes, I started auctioning off parts of my drum kit and percussion instruments.

Lynn's role in becoming such a pivotal force in my life and our foundation stemmed back in part to 1996, when she and I were on tour with the queen of Japanese pop music, a teenage sensation named Namie Amuro. I was the percussionist and Lynn was one of her background singers. Namie's band was massively successful and played to sold-out stadiums through Japan. At eighteen years old, she was a multiplatinum recording artist selling millions of records.

There were six Christians in the band and crew, and, as Japan practices mainly the Shinto or Buddhist faiths, we had a hard time finding any Christian churches to visit. We needed to keep strong and maintain our armor of love. We were instructed by our pastor to conduct a weekly Bible-study group during the tour and to meet at least once a week. In this time of study and fellowship, we'd rotate on leading Bible study by picking a subject matter of our choice and sharing related Bible verses. Before we'd begin, we'd have praise and worship together by praying and singing inspirational songs.

After a couple of rotations, it was my turn again to lead Bible study. Having already done it once, I didn't have a clue what to talk about this second time.

Lynn offered some suggestions. "You can talk about God's love, forgiveness, kindness, or even something that you can relate to in the scriptures you read in your own time." I told her I still couldn't think of anything at all.

Gently touching my hand, she added, "If you don't know what to talk about, then why don't you share your testimony with everyone?"

I shook my head. I wasn't ready to *talk* about my rape—it was too private and too painful to admit. Besides, I didn't have a clue how to express it.

Lynn said, "Sheila, you're at a place now spiritually where you can confess it to the world. You don't have to be ashamed of it anymore."

Still not sure if I had the ability to do it, she suggested, "If you have trouble speaking the words, get on your computer and just start writing your experience, and see what comes out."

I placed my laptop on the dining room table, sat in the chair, and stared at the blank screen. My fingers hovered motionless above the keys. It hit me that Lynn was right. How much longer was I going to keep my dirty little secret hidden from the world?

I started to type, and then I held my breath and stopped. I was afraid. I blinked at the screen and read the words, *When I was five . . .* I lowered my fingers back onto the keys and kept going. The next hour or so felt like an eternity of blurred words and feelings as my fingers never stopped typing. I hit those keys with the energy and intensity of a drum solo. The tap-tap-tapping became like a percussion beat in my head—a rising, rousing metronome to the horror story of that part of my childhood.

Finally, my fingers burning, I stopped to take a breath. Shifting position a little, I started to read back what I'd written. The words that filled the screen were like the eyes of my soul, and they tore my heart in two. I had never seen an account of those events in black and white before, and it crushed me. The frightened little girl that I had been back in 1962 was talking to me straight from the page. This wasn't somebody else, though; this was *me* talking about *myself*, and that was what was so horrible.

Every word I read transported me closer and closer to that night when Moms and Pops went out. I could feel myself being carried to their room. I could almost smell the Vaseline. When I remembered the blood, I felt sick. My stomach cramped as I remembered holding everything in and believing that I would die. Reliving my hours in the bathroom snatched the breath from my lungs, and I started hyperventilating.

I was there again, that little five-year-old, scared and helpless. Pushing the laptop away, tears filled my eyes. I was overcome with sadness and fell to my knees. I curled up into the fetal position as the little girl in me started to cry. Memories intensified, and I began howling like an animal in pain.

Lynn came running in from the next room, knelt down beside me, and held me for dear life. "It's okay, it's okay," she kept telling me. "You're going to be all right."

I couldn't speak. All I could do was cry. It was such a relief and a release.

Then, as if she'd read every word I had written, Lynn told me, "I'm so sorry, so very sorry."

I cried for three days straight. This simple preparation for Bible study manifested into the unveiling of the inner pain I'd suffered throughout my lifetime. I couldn't speak. I couldn't eat. I felt as if I was going through a war. Although the continuous sobs were wracking me, the more I cried, ironically, the better I felt. I just needed to get it all out.

For almost four decades I'd buried all that emotion inside. Music had been my only outlet, and it had served me well. Giving my heart to the Lord and surrendering to Him was my saving grace. It was time to exhume the memories, breath by breath. I didn't want to carry the pain anymore—or the guilt, the shame, and the anger. I cried until I couldn't cry anymore.

In a faraway land, with the kindest of friends, I went through a kind of rebirth. It was an agonizing process, but what emerged from a thirty-five-year-old cocoon of sorrow was a butterfly: I finally saw myself as a beautiful, vibrant creature of light.

I knew then that my life had a new purpose: to shine.

26. Groove

A rhythm, drumbeat, or feel of something

It all started when I decided to open my eyes
I am free. And now I see

"HEAVEN"

SHEILA E

Music had given me a purpose and saved me from myself, and others, for so long. Music had helped Pops through the darkest days of his childhood. And, thankfully, it had done the same for me. I now understood music as a gift from God. I was close to discovering a way I might begin to thank Him.

Once I was finally able to face the truths of my past and move on, I knew what I had to do. Pops had planted the seed by taking us to children's homes when we were young. From the earliest age, we'd unpacked our instruments and let unhappy children discover the joy of beating our drums and congas as loud and as fast as they liked. I wanted to show other abused kids that they, too, could find that kind of freedom through creativity.

I had been so incredibly fortunate. I was a drummer, a percussionist, and a singer. I had a loving and caring family, and I felt so humbled and honored to have my parents alive and still married. The love they had for each other opened the door to a world of music. Not everyone had that. The foster kids and those who lived on the streets were the ones I wanted to be able to share my gift of music with—to help them through the arts. I wanted to be their voice.

As a nod to Pops, Lynn and I gravitated toward providing art supplies to several facilities, giving kids the chance to create some color in their monochrome surroundings. It was amazing to me to see how their paintings started so dark and angry but, in time and with some therapy, became lighter and full of color.

We contributed to one facility that taught the kids to grow their own food in their own garden and to cook a basic meal. Many of them didn't even know how to use a knife and fork, as they'd only ever eaten with their fingers. We funded programs that specifically focused on teaching them to cope once they left these state homes.

In setting up our charitable foundation, we realized our mission and set our sights high on creative fund-raising for those children at risk of being lost in the system and not being given the tools to rehabilitate them from the perils of living in foster homes, group homes, or juvenile detention.

There was one five-year-old boy from the Wings of Refuge in Los Angeles, whom I'll call Rudy, who had been so severely abused that he shut down completely. He gave no reaction to anything or anyone and refused to speak. He was in therapy sessions, but I thought he was going to turn out to be one of those kids who couldn't be helped. With the assistance of our donation of percussion instruments and the persistence of a music therapist, though, everything turned around for him.

When he was first shown the basics of how to play the piano, there was little or no response. But Rudy's therapist noticed he loved hitting a box over in the corner, so she encouraged him and sang songs to the rhythm of each thump. Once she saw that he responded to her instruction, she sat him behind one of the drums.

Rudy responded most to the rhythm of the nursery rhyme "Mary Had a Little Lamb." At the end of the last chorus, she would sing in rhythm, "I love you," and smile at him while looking into his eyes. One day, after she sang the words "I love you," he sang them back to her. Those were his first words since his abuse.

When we were told this news, I dropped to my knees and gave thanks. If we helped no one else through our foundation, that was enough. One badly damaged little boy had learned to love and play and communicate again. Since then, there have been some amazing success stories, and a few of the kids who've gone on to work in the music business have told us that if we hadn't helped them back then, they'd be dead.

Music therapy should be government funded in such facilities, but it often isn't. The state does what it can for many of these places, but it doesn't provide nearly enough. That's why outside donors and outsourcing are so important to supplement the need when conventional assistance can't keep up. Some of the facilities we approached didn't like our hands-on approach, or our insistence on how we wanted the money spent. It was our aim to focus attention on the power of music and to raise as much money as we could to promote it.

We rallied as many musicians, artists, and entertainers as we could, including our friends Sheryl Crow, Jimmy Smits, Stevie Wonder, and a host of others. They assisted us in creating fundraisers for more institutions and facilities, both in Los Angeles and the Bay Area.

Visiting various campuses and alternative schools, Lynn and I saw more and more desperation at every turn. The more we observed, the more we realized the need. This far exceeded what I was exposed to when accompanying my dad. There was one facility we visited called Vista Del Mar that housed about two hundred children, many of whom didn't even know who their birth parents were. Most had never experienced living in a real home. What compounded their despair was having very few visitors. They lived in a state of lockdown—physically, socially, and emotionally.

Even though I have a loving family, I saw a piece of myself in them—I *was* them. When I saw how they had turned in on themselves to protect themselves from any more hurt, I completely connected with them and the saddest experiences of my own childhood. It made me even more committed to helping them find a means of processing their pain, which I so closely related to. They deserved the means to release their pain through their creative personal expressions.

No matter how upsetting it was to witness their suffering, Lynn and I made sure we didn't show our emotions in front of them. The purpose of our visits was to encourage the kids to engage, in hopes of reaching at least one of them. Many of those we observed were shut down and rebelled against any contact whatsoever. Some, mostly young girls, just wanted to be hugged. That suited me just fine, as I come from a family of huggers and was more than happy to oblige. The boys were more about high-fiving and less interested in any type of affection.

Our focus was on supplying musical instruments and instructional equipment, electronics and art supplies, and even providing a calm and inviting environment for them in class. We totally remodeled their existing music room and painted and updated their bathroom, cleaning it up and making it a place they'd be excited to enter each day. We purchased violins and electronic drums, percussion and keyboards, trumpets and guitars—whatever they needed. We provided video cameras and production equipment, and we even taught them how to create PSAs and burn their own CDs.

It was overwhelming to see how well they responded. It is surely one of the greatest feelings in the world to view the rewards that this kind of instruction and interaction gives these kids—it provides them with a fighting chance.

An old friend of mine who was a seamstress (formally a member of one of the local street gangs) heard what we were doing and wanted to give back. She decided to make quilts with matching pillowcases, and she also whipped up some warm jackets for the younger kids.

However, our main focus was therapy through music and arts education. We created a pilot program through an innovative curriculum that would ultimately provide them the social skills for a successful transition to the outside world. The power of music had proven its significance in the area of emotional growth and well-being. We secured a music instructor to teach music and video production.

The whole process was an amazing learning experience for both Lynn and me, but it was really hard work. People tried to discourage us, telling us that it couldn't be done, but these kids proved them wrong.

One young boy was a case in point. He had severe emotional issues and was very disruptive and combative in class. Often destructive, he would run away for hours on end. The school was ready to discharge him and turn him over to the state. One of the staff heard that he had a secret interest in playing the saxophone. Learning about our foundation, our office received the request to help him. We jumped at the chance of reaching him when no one else could. Immediately after he was given his own saxophone, his entire demeanor changed. He treasured his instrument as if it were gold, carrying it with him to every class. It was his new best friend.

In a matter of months, he completely turned himself around. He became such a great kid, a model student; his grades improved;

and he stopped cutting classes and going AWOL. One afternoon Lynn and I were called to his classroom, as he had a surprise for us. He had learned to play my song "The Glamorous Life," and he recited it to us note for note. The smile on his face was priceless. We were so proud of him, but better yet, he was proud of himself.

By connecting with the kids musically or in any way that feeds their curiosity and opens their hearts, Lynn and I could prove to them that there is life beyond abuse. I also loved sharing the history of percussion and drums with young children, just as Pops had taught me. I relished describing the hollowed-out gourd called a guiro from Brazil or the shekere drum from West Africa, whose rattling beads always produced smiles.

"Do you wanna play?" I'd ask, and then I'd start tapping out a beat on a drum. I'd invite them to join in, and then maybe get a few of the teachers to jam with me in a way that always takes me straight back to my childhood. While the likes of Tito Puente or Eddie Palmieri made music in our front rooms, we kids would try to keep up on a cowbell or a guiro while Moms laughingly stirred the soup.

It always takes a while to get some of the kids to tune in, but they usually do in the end, and once they've relaxed, I tell them a little of my story. "I understand what you're going through," I say. "I've been through something similar too. I got through it because of music. You can too."

Inspired by these children, I designed a range of percussion instruments specifically for kids that weren't just plastic toys that would fall apart. The Sheila E Player Series of bongos and hand drums in bright colors were designed for children as young as three (the age I started playing), and the range moves all the way up to pro level. I was excited to have TOCA percussion make these instruments for the kids.

We've donated hundreds of instruments to schools all over the Bay Area, including twenty thousand dollars' worth of equipment and money to my old alma mater, San Leandro High School. It felt surprisingly emotional to return to the place where I'd gone through so many agonies of teenage self-analysis and loneliness.

So much of the work I've done with children through the foundation felt like holding a mirror up to my own pain. I could see and feel their anger as I remembered my own. I wished I could make them understand that they cannot fully live a life if they feel ashamed, dirty, or guilty. So many children who've been abused carry the same lack of confidence and live in a state of fear that shackles them to the past.

I knew that as a little girl I became my happiest when I began playing music. When I was taken to that show at Sweet's, I lost myself to the music for the first time. Standing in the spotlight, my heart, arms, and mind pumped with excitement and the satisfaction of knowing I'd done well. That's what I wanted the kids we were trying to help to experience—that feeling of accomplishment. That was the whole purpose of sharing my story.

My life could have been so different, and I was reminded of that every time I talked to kids who'd been abused or were on meds. They had no goals; they were stuck. They either didn't know their parents or they were never around. They'd checked out. I could have gone the drugs route and checked out too, but thankfully that wasn't my destiny.

Music helped me find the way.

Reflecting back on what had shaped and then saved me, I realized that I'd spent far too much of my life allowing my abusers to keep some sort of hold over me. In keeping it all inside, harboring the shame of my past, they still controlled me in some way. I knew I couldn't live my life like that anymore.

It's no wonder it took so long for me to begin to heal, since even well into my adulthood I felt compelled to protect the five-year-old girl within me. I didn't quite realize that I continually blamed myself. And I was protecting the abusers when I often asked myself "What is it about me that made them do this?" The molestation occurred in secret, and I was warned in pressured whispers that it would be bad if I told anyone about what happened in the dark. And so for many years I complied.

Then when I received Christ back into my life and began reading the Word as truth, I found scriptures that guided me in the direction I should go. There was one passage in Ephesians that really struck me. It reads: *Let all bitterness and wrath and anger and clamor and slander be put away from you, along with all malice. Be kind to one another, tenderhearted, forgiving one another, as God in Christ forgave you.*

It was time for me to confront not only the man who raped me, but also the cousins who had molested me. I needed to forgive them, and I needed to let them go. I hadn't seen them for years, and then only at a few family gatherings. Even as an adult, it was always hard for me to look at any of them. On the occasion that I saw one cousin, he behaved as if nothing ever happened. He'd hug me, say hello, and ask me how I was doing, but I'd just stand there stiffly and mumble. I would try to avoid looking at his hands, those same hands that came toward me at night. They looked the same.

As for my rapist, I knew I wouldn't be fully healed until I found him again, talked to him, and offered him my forgiveness. I figured that even if I couldn't face him in person, then I would write him a letter or maybe speak to him on the phone.

I found his sister's number and called her up to get his address. Initially I pretended I was just calling for a casual catch-up. But after a few minutes I heard myself blurt out the truth. It took me a long time to summon up the courage to confront this demon, but I finally found the strength. "I think you should know that your brother raped me when I was five."

"What?" She was horrified.

"So where is he?" I said, feeling very shaky. "I need to find out if he's around young children." And then my voice got quieter. "And I need to forgive him."

"I'm so sorry, Sheila," she said. "He passed away two years ago."

The news filled me with a peculiar mix of relief and sadness, but I was sorry that I had lost the opportunity to look him in his eyes, take those hands in mine, and tell him he was forgiven. I had so badly wanted to feel the profound release of forgiveness. But even in death it felt as if he'd robbed me of something profound.

Instead of wasting time on regret about waiting so long to contact him, I reminded myself that even though he was dead, it was as loving to forgive him in my heart and unto God—and I could still finally have the closure and peace of mind. Just by attempting to reach him, in fact, I actually experienced an invigorating sense of release.

Having experienced this newfound strength and understanding, I turned my attention to the cousins who'd been our babysitters. Believe it or not, I had developed a certain kind of compassion for them, understanding that their actions were the result of their own dangerously unacknowledged pain and low self-esteem.

First I confronted them and described the impact of their actions—how their actions and my innocence left me with invisible scars. They denied any wrongdoing, or at least the memory of it, although one did say, "Man, I don't really remember that, Sheila—but if I did that, then I'm so sorry."

One by one, I forgave them too.

Believe me, as a teenager and a young adult, I never would have thought this could be possible. Nor did it seem like something to strive for. Why would I even consider forgiving the men who had so aggressively invaded my innocence? Well, over time I began to realize that as long as I was still actively blaming these abusers, I would never truly live. It is interesting that prior to my decision, I had this fantasy that when I forgave them, the abuse could magically be undone. I accepted the reality of this part of my past: it happened. Now I had the freedom to move on with total forgiveness in my heart. This was huge for me—an essential component of my healing.

My forgiveness doesn't equal an excuse for their abhorrent behavior. But somehow it has set me free from their grasp. I would have eventually been debilitated by depression or even sought relief through self-destructive behaviors like drug and alcohol abuse.

I have come to learn that, at least for me, forgiveness isn't always finite. Sometimes a memory will emerge when I am sharing my experience in front of a group of kids or even in an interview. For a moment it's as if I'm right back to square one. The sadness fills my heart and brings me to tears.

I have to allow myself to feel these emotions now. And then it is as if a soft wind blows gently over my tears, comforting five-year-old Sheila. And the bitterness I feel turns into the sweet smell of forgiveness. I tap into my heart, forgiving the abusers again. By doing so, I embrace little Sheila, as well as adult Sheila, once more. And all those thoughts and experiences that are not of God disappear.

The conversations I had with my cousins had a powerful ripple effect within my family and eventually led to some much-needed dialogues about putting an end to poisonous family secrets. By my early thirties I began to realize that there were several others in my very large extended family who also had experienced sexual abuse, even intergenerational incest. One family member had been raped at age eight by her grandfather. Her immediate family turned on her when she told on him. Her grandfather was never arrested or went to prison; they just tried to sort it all out within the family.

Not everyone knew about these instances of abuse, and some of those who did know didn't want to talk about it. Discussing it made them sick. It seemed like no one knew what to do about it. But I was done with everyone being so hush-hush about the subject and decided to do my part to bring it out of the darkness, hoping that standing with the abused, I could help both the victims and the victimizers step out of denial.

I began to realize that we could all help each other if we'd just be honest and deal with it. Certainly, I wasn't received as some heroic healer. In fact, my coming forward initially caused quite a bit of turbulence. But I did begin a much-needed process and simultaneously received the kind of support that I needed so much myself.

As I began to experience the relief that came with talking to my family members and trusted friends about the sexual abuse I suffered as a young child, I eventually found the courage to speak about it to much larger audiences. I realized that as a public figure, I have the opportunity to reach many people and encourage them to embark on their own healing process. Just knowing that I have inspired even one person to seek help makes any fame I have more meaningful. In this respect, I have become completely different from the teenager I once was, who tried to ignore the pain of the past and focused solely on the joy of playing music.

Before I felt able to tell my story, it was as if I was carrying around countless heavy bags, so many that I could barely walk. Now each time I share, even to this day, I feel like I'm letting go of another bag. In doing so, I send a message to the little girl in *that* house that none of it was her fault.

My parents always want to support me in all my endeavors, including my ministry work, but, understandably, it's almost unbearable for them to hear about the abuse. Even now, Moms will walk out of the room when I talk about what happened to me. She relives the guilt of her not being there for me. She still blames herself. I wish I could free them from any self-blame. It was such a long time ago and it wasn't their fault, just as much as it wasn't mine.

I am always careful to emphasize that what happened is no reflection on their parenting. They were both wonderful parents who took excellent care of us. We were with them so much: there was no need for babysitters most of the time. If Pops was out, Moms was usually home with us. If Moms was working, we were with Pops. They provided constant care and a home filled with love and laughter. What happened on those distinct occasions was beyond their control. Despite my making this clear, I'm sure it's beyond painful for them to hear me tell my story, since they are powerless to go back in time to protect me from the abuse.

I was so blessed to have come from such a loving, nurturing family. Imperfect as they are—as all families are—they provided me with the foundation for growth and spirituality. They were always providing us with those simple pleasures in life that most could only dream to share as a family. And, last but never least, they passed on their lifelong commitment to fun!

In 2001 I released an album, *Heaven*, inspired by my spiritual breakthrough and my path of forgiveness. On it is a song by Nichole Nordeman called "River God," in which she describes the surface of little stones, smoothed only once the water passes over them. The constant movement of the water from the river breaks down all the rough edges. Some of the words read: *Rolling river God, little stones are smooth only once the water passes through. So I am a stone, rough and grainy still, trying to reconcile this river's chill.*

Love is the water that breaks down everything else. Love is what smoothes it all away. I am imperfect, "rough and grainy still." But I am being cleansed with love—the love of God, the love of my family, the love of my friends, and the love I feel when making music. Thanks to this abundance of love, I have learned to endure this river's chill.

27. E-Drums

Electronic drums with sensors that create sounds

My soul was meant to fly . . .

"GLORIOUS TRAIN"
SHEILA E, ANGIE APARO, JAMES SLATER

Never in a million years did I think I'd ever agree to take part in a reality show. While I'd enjoyed my stint as a judge on a TV show called *The Next Great American Band* (which could technically be considered a reality show), I was jaded by the onslaught of totally *unreal* depictions of folks in "real life" situations.

With this mind-set, I turned down any offers to appear on the kinds of reality shows that featured celebrities thrown together for some contrived reason. And when I was initially approached in 2009 to be a part of CMT's *Gone Country* (which I hadn't even heard of), I didn't have much interest. When they told me that this would involve celebrities living in a house together while competing to become a country music singer, I immediately declined. However, when I found out that it would also mean working with real country music writers in Nashville, I was more than a little intrigued. I actually got a small case of the butterflies—always a sign that something special was presenting itself.

I'm a big fan of country music and had long dreamed of doing my own country music project. I'm moved by the melodies and the expressive lyrics—the honesty, the vulnerability, and the stories. It's both soothing to listen to and comforting to *feel* to—it's down home and it's real. I had a blast performing with Brooks & Dunn at the 2002 Academy of Country Music Awards, and I was waiting for the right time to collaborate with some of the country writers.

On top of that, Nashville has always been one of my favorite cities. Years ago I'd even considered buying a home there where I could live part-time. (There's a lot of cute men there, too, so "going country" in the romantic department was always a possibility. I'm just sayin' . . .)

Before making a decision, I had to do some research. First, I went online to check out the past two seasons' episodes of *Gone Country*. I was surprised and pleased to see that some great artists had participated before, all of whom had been given the opportunity to work with some excellent writers. That was a major pro for sure. The con was huge, though. There'd be no hotel to go home to at the end of a long day of shooting and competing against the other contestants; no private respite where I could—as poet Sara Teasdale wrote—"gather myself into myself again."

Gone Country was one of those live-with-everyone-and-be-filmed-24/7 reality shows. It was to be every man and woman for themselves as they went head to head on physical, musical, and emotional challenges on and off the stage to see who was best suited to pursuing a career in country music. I value my privacy so much—always have. When I was young I begged for my own bedroom (which usually wasn't possible). Although I was afraid of silence for a long time, I still couldn't wait to live in a house by myself one day. And even now, I love socializing, but at the end of the day, give me a quiet space by myself and maybe some music or a drum set or a good poker game to unquiet it with, and I'm good to go. So my first response when Lynn asked me if I wanted to take part in *Gone Country* was, "Heck no!"

But no matter how much the idea of sharing a house with strangers (and the nation!) appalled me, I couldn't stop thinking about the promise of working with great country music writers. And when I did, those butterflies persisted. So I did some more inquiring. The only time they wouldn't film, I was told, was when we were in the bathroom. Yikes. They'd even be filming when the lights were off in our rooms, in case we said or did anything that warranted airtime. If they saw any movement, since we didn't have packs on at that time, camera guys would be coming in with boom mics.

They wouldn't tell me who else was going to be on the show, another aspect that made me wary. That was, they explained, an important part of the filmed surprise: watching each of us discover who else was there.

After much soul-searching, I took a leap of faith and agreed to do season three of *Gone Country*. It was only two weeks, after all, but the opportunities it presented were too great to miss. I was so nervous preparing to fly to Nashville, knowing I was about to throw myself into the world of reality television, but I kept being pulled by the promise of writing a country song.

And from what I gathered while watching the past shows online, the host—singer-songwriter John Rich—seemed like an awesome person to work with. John was the only person I knew I'd meet when I walked into that house, and I was really looking forward to meeting him. He had an impressive career, was a very talented musician, and seemed to command a great deal of respect on the show. I liked his hard-core approach and the way he persuaded participants to rise to the challenge. I didn't predict that he'd have any reason to yell at me, though. I was going to win, or else I wouldn't be going at all.

I was completely self-conscious about the cameras when I first got into the house—a beautiful mansion that had once been owned by Barbara Mandrell. The good news was, the first thing I saw was a drum set. The bad news was that I couldn't get used to cameras following my every move. But once I saw Taylor Dayne inside, I forgot about the cameras for a moment because I was so overwhelmed with excitement. There was my friend from way back, a great woman with some breathtaking chops. Then I saw Micky Dolenz and was thrilled, since I used to watch the TV show *The Monkees*.

When my good friend George Clinton walked in (a man I called Uncle George), I was overjoyed. Seeing him immediately made me feel at home. As a kid, I would do whatever I could to see his group, Parliament-Funkadelic, play live. That man pioneered a musical movement, and Lynn had been in his Brides of Funkenstein band. I was surprised to find out that he was actually a really big country music fan, and he knew a great deal about its history. I also enjoyed meeting the other contestants—Tara Conner, Richard Grieco, and Justin Guarini.

Once the excitement of greeting everyone died down, I was full of questions, wondering what challenges would present themselves and what the dynamics between everybody would be. All the many unknowns kept me on my toes and eager to find out what was next.

When I found out I'd be rooming with the girls, I had mixed feelings. I was excited to hang with my girl Taylor, and I looked forward to getting to know Tara, who was very sweet. But sharing a room? Where would I find solitude and solace? I quickly figured out that I wouldn't.

I'll admit I had some vanity-related concerns, too. Like, how would I manage to look good, television ready, 24/7? Would they capture me looking less than my best? I had brought an entire suitcase of shoes—fourteen pairs (and that was me being conservative)!

One activity that brought me a sense of solace and allowed me to center myself night and morning was reading my Bible. I had a little light and I'd read underneath my covers so I didn't keep anyone up.

There were very strict rules regarding noncommunication with the outside world. We weren't allowed to use our cell phones, and any phone calls we might make from within the house were recorded. (I'd already warned my family that if I called them, they better be careful about what they said or it could end up on TV. That was a mistake, and became an exciting challenge. Just how embarrassing and goofy could they be? They couldn't wait for my call.)

We were given daily tasks that were never revealed until the last minute. They'd wake us up early each morning, sometimes four or five A.M. (which is hecka early to me!), and they'd tell us how to dress. And then, well, let the games begin. We had some amazing experiences, including flying in a Black Hawk helicopter and jumping out of a tree hoping that the team would help with the landing. One task that stands out the most was creating a painting based on the general theme of the song we would write and present in the final show. I love to paint, but I don't have the skills like Pops, who's a professional. It took me a minute to adjust to the canvas and free myself up enough to begin. I painted a train and its passengers going up to heaven. I was moved when someone bought it at the charity auction that is part of the TV show.

Another task that stands out involved the president of the United States. The producers told us to learn a song quickly and that we'd be performing it soon. Little did we know we'd end up on a warship singing for President George W. Bush just a few hours later. I couldn't believe what was happening most of the time. Was this for real? If so, then reality television was starting to grow on me.

I was getting pretty comfortable on the show, but the cameras were still a bit crazy to navigate, especially with regard to changing—which I did in the closet or the bathroom. The days of my skimpy lingerie-like stage outfits were long gone.

I was totally unprepared for the day when we'd meet our writers, friends of John's whom he'd preselected for each contestant. In fact, I was hanging out and eating with them—breakfast that we'd all prepared—before I was informed that they'd be *my* writers.

This was the moment I'd really been waiting for. I loved getting to know my writers, Angie Aparo and James Slater. James told me he'd been a fan for some time and that he'd even won one of my drums from a charity auction. I jelled with them right away and I just loved their enthusiasm as we brainstormed together.

They had some great ideas ready for me based on my thoughts about my father, the *E Train* painting I had done (named after a band I briefly had years before), and my faith. It was important to me that the song be spiritual and inspiring to others. We wrote "Glorious Train" in one hour. It's basically about us all being on the same train, one big love train.

When it was time to showcase our songs to John and the rest of the cast, I first explained a little bit about my background and some of the inspiration for the song. Once I started talking, I found myself overcome with emotion. I was feeling simultaneously vulnerable about my story and moved by the lyrics, the story line, and the notion of the glorious train going to heaven. I was opening myself up to new friends and was just about to perform a song in a genre that was brand-new to me. As I shared about being raped and molested as a child, I began to shake and cry. I was raw.

When we performed it, this time I didn't want to play drums. It was just me and a guitar player and keyboard player. The simplicity felt refreshing and necessary. I wanted to focus on the story the song was telling. And I didn't want to hide behind my instrument. I ended up just miming the timbales part that I'd be playing on the final night when we would showcase our songs in front of the judges and a live audience.

When that night finally came, I was nervous all over again. The venue, a cool country music saloon, was sold out, with thousands in attendance. I don't fancy myself a great singer (I'm no Taylor Dayne), but my thing is always about energy. I wanted to make sure I projected my authentic, energetic self. I definitely had those wonderful butterflies, but I also had a real sense of anxiety about how I would do. I wasn't used to that feeling. How would I represent myself in a country song? How was I going to play timbales—such a quintessential Latin instrument—in a country tune? I wasn't sure how it was going to turn out or how the crowd or the judges would like it, but I knew I had to make it work. I had to do my very best, and with my inherited Gardere competitive spirit intact, I had to win.

Everybody did such a great job. Each time someone went out to perform, we all cheered them on as we watched them on a live monitor backstage. We were competing, but our time together had made us a solid team. I knew that any one of them winning would be something I could be proud of and happy for. I thought it would be between Taylor and Micky. Taylor is the singing queen diva, and I loved her song. It seemed like an instant hit. And Micky brought so much soul and spirit to his performance.

When it was my turn, those butterflies of mine were swarming. I went out onstage, and before launching into the song I started to talk to the crowd a bit to orient them to the background of my song. But people weren't paying any attention. They were drinking, talking, mingling. I couldn't believe it. *These are all country music fans. Don't they realize they're being filmed as part of a song competition for a reality show?* You'd think they'd at the very least just pretend to pay attention to me. I was starting to get really frustrated, hurt, and then angry. I wasn't going to endure this kind of disrespect for a second longer. So I did what I had to do to shut everyone down and get present to my message.

"Does anyone out there have a five-year-old?" I asked. It got somewhat quieter. Some people slowly raised their hands and others looked around to see who had in fact raised their hands. And that's when I got to the point. "When I was five years old, I was raped."

Silence.

I shocked them, but I knew that I deserved to have my voice expressed and my song heard. I had something to say, and it was something worth listening to. *I will be acknowledged. You will respect me.* It was a long road to get to that point. But I got there. *We're all in this together* is a lyric in "Glorious Train." And I needed the audience to be *in this* with me.

Once I had their attention, I cued the band to start. Next thing I know, I'm in my song. *Papa told me there is beauty in the sky. And he told me there is glory in my eyes.* The first line's lyric, which conjured up Pops's belief in me as a young girl, is part of what soothed me in that moment. I got present to it all: the music, the band, the audience, the lyrics. I was also present to my journey—my unexpected journey and all its lessons both on this TV show and my overall life journey thus far.

I've got faith and hope deep down in my soul . . . I belted out the words with all my might. I took off my heels and ran about the stage. And when I got to my timbale solo, first regular time and then double time—faster and faster—my emotions were explosive. During the gospel-inspired ending, my hallelujahs came from deep down in my soul. I was thanking God for giving me this experience and so many other blessings. I was thanking Him for getting me, as the song says, "through the darkness to the light," for allowing me to become who he'd created me to be.

I ended with a scream from deep within me and kicked the cymbal stand over before falling to my knees. I could barely catch my breath. I hadn't held anything back. When the song was over, I threw down the mic, took in the applause, and tried to come back down to earth. I walked back to where John Rich had been sitting in his beautiful white jacket. He was now standing and cheering me with a huge smile on his face as he embraced me. I had given my performance everything I had, and holding back the tears was not an option anymore.

John then brought me back to the front of the stage, where we both raised our pointer fingers upward to God, acknowledging our blessings.

When we'd all performed and were waiting for the results, I was taut with anticipation. I'm always so careful with my manicured nails, but the tension backstage almost made a nail biter out of me. I was thinking about each person's incredible performance—how far each of them had stretched themselves. I truly believed that I wasn't going to win. I knew I put myself out there 100 percent, and I knew the song was great, but I wasn't sure how it sounded to the audience and the judges. I was still convinced Taylor would be the winner. Hands down. I kept thinking, *She had the best song. I would have voted for it. It should be on the radio, like, yesterday.*

The audience cleared out, and the judges got the final say. By this time I'd come to terms with the understanding that I wasn't going to win—something I don't usually do. And I was okay with it, too. I'd had an unbelievable experience and had grown by leaps and bounds as a person. I'd stretched myself further than I knew I could. Aspects of my time spent there interacting with the rest of the cast were like group therapy. I expanded my capacity to trust and I overcame fears. I learned about being a real team player, how to navigate others' personalities, and to surrender to the group rather than always having to be the leader, in control.

Me without control is rarely comfortable, but this experience taught me how easy it really could be. While waiting for the winner to be announced, I could exhale into a deep sense of satisfaction with all I'd accomplished already.

When I heard John Rich say something about my performance, I started sweating and my heart was beating out of my chest. For real. I'd never been evaluated like this—so publicly, and on television! Even after more than thirty years in the business, I felt like a newbie. And then I heard something in John's voice, a tone he took that made me realize—*Oh, my God*—he was going to say I won.

I think I won!

When he finally announced me as the winner, I couldn't believe it. I was overjoyed, but also humbled to my core. It meant so much to me—that I had taken so many risks and had dived into the unknown to be a part of this show. My winning felt like an absolute acknowledgment of that.

Thank you, Jesus. In my heart, I shared my victory with my two incredible Nashville writers as well as every single person on the show. They challenged me to be a better me and created the environment for me to perform the song the way I did. I was humbled, to say the very least.

Back home, I had to keep a serious poker face on. I watched the final episode with Moms, Pops, and Zina as John announced me as the winner. They went crazy—cheering and screaming. Juan claimed later that he had always known I'd won—something about a twinkle in my eye and an extra spring in my step over Christmas.

I must admit, it was a wonderful secret to keep.

The TV show then went to the video for "Glorious Train"—

my official debut in the country music market—that I'd secretly filmed back in LA after leaving Nashville. Pops was moved by the shot in the video where I'm looking at an old photograph of the two of us from way back when we cut our first album together.

Seeing his expression of pride and joy was enough of a prize all by itself.

28. Diminuendo

Decreasing tempo

Sister's very kind so it's never quite a problem
When it comes 2 love
Everything's so easy when we're children
One touch is 2 much

"TOY BOX"

SHEILA E

Whenever I am asked what makes a good drummer or a good percussionist (and I am asked it a lot), I struggle to find the words to describe good music—especially something that comes from the soul. But here goes.

The greatest difference between playing drums and playing percussion is that percussion is all about enhancement. It's as if you're adding a new dimension to something that is already beautiful. And you have to be selective with how much you add, or else you can ruin the purity of the original.

As I already mentioned, I believe that a good drummer keeps good time and has the discipline to know when not to play. You have to have rhythm, of course, and you've got to have some swagger in your walk. It's all about presenting yourself authentically on the drums. Not everyone can drum well in each genre of music. When you play funk, for instance, you have to approach it differently from how you play jazz. But there are many ways to make music. If you drum with a jazz style on a funk song, it changes the vibe on that song, if that's the intention (and, by the way, I have done that). It's like eating soul food with chopsticks. But if the drumbeat is supposed to be funky, then it should stay true to that style or it can sound corny.

I think a lot of it comes down to playing in the pocket—a slang expression that means playing solid but being musically mature; not rushing the beat, neither overplaying nor underplaying. When I play with really good drummers, I tell them, "You are playing the lint in my pocket." That's funky!

A good drummer has to make the drums sing. Rather than always playing at the same level, she or he plays dynamically and is sensitive to the instrument and to what the song needs. If you're always playing at level ten, then there's nowhere to go and no room for movement. But if you're sensitive to the instrument, you can explore the valleys and reach the sky. Knowing your place is equally important. Improvisation within a song can happen organically and effectively when each musician knows when to follow and when to lead. It's a musical conversation, and your communication skills can make all the difference.

You listen to a band member who makes a suggestion. You agree, you follow her/him, and then perhaps you make a suggestion about where to go. It's a collaborative musical journey. And for me, this is the most fun and adventurous kind of journey there is.

When I was first performing publicly with Pops, he and I would ask (or maybe just tell) Juan and Peter Michael to join us onstage and keep time while we did our solos. They'd beat on whatever made sense for that song—cowbells, bongos, drums, congas—while Pops and I did our thing on the quinto or timbales. Sometimes my brothers laugh about this—how in the beginning when we were all much younger and much less known, they'd be the timekeepers while Pops and I got the spotlight. It was the musical family's version of hand-me-downs for younger siblings, I suppose (coupled with the fact that, as the big sister, I had them work as my unpaid roadies!).

Ultimately, though, we all agree that this was actually one of the best kinds of training for a drummer or percussionist. Maybe it goes without saying, but some points need emphasizing: the drummer is driving the bus. Keeping time is an invaluable skill for any musician. If you can't keep time, you're not going to be asked to play with anyone. And if you've been offered a gig and you don't do what is best for the situation and only for yourself, then you probably won't be asked back.

I do believe some are gifted with certain musical abilities, like excellent timing, but you can learn that skill, too. Everybody has the most basic beat: the heartbeat. It keeps you alive. Each person's beat is different, though, for different reasons—literally and meta-phorically. It's fairly obvious that you have to have rhythm to be a good musician, but I'd say it is deeper than that. I think you have to *understand* rhythm to be a good musician. You have to understand what it is to keep time, and if that's all you have, well, then you've got plenty. Keeping good time is one of your best assets, because you can't beat consistency (pun intended). With consistency of rhythm, if you're in a solo battle against a player with amazing chops and less than amazing timekeeping, in my opinion you'll be the winner every time.

I was a percussionist first, which I think benefited me as a drummer. Early on, I learned to feel the song out, find spaces, and splash some color here and there rather than throwing a jar of paint all over the place. Otherwise, you can clutter up the song.

As a drummer, I'm setting the introduction to either the bridge, the chorus, the verse, or someone's solo. So when I play percussion, I'm sensitive to those moments within a song. I've learned to listen to the drummer's introductions and let the drummer lead me.

When I'm expressing all of myself nonverbally, I dig deep down inside and give from my heart. I open myself up to God and let Him speak through me. I let Him let me be the musician He created me to be. And when I let go and let God do His thing, He then surprises me with expressions I could never do myself. This is what keeps me excited, grateful, and humbled to be able to share my gift just as I did when I was fifteen and taking my first solo onstage with Azteca.

There are many successful and talented musicians who read music perfectly. And yet if you take their sheet music away, they haven't a clue how to play. Personally, I like to make creative choices within the song, because then I am truly expressing myself. I prefer musicians who play from their hearts over those who play solely from the page.

I don't use the stage as a place to work out any problems I might have, either. I pray with the band or anyone else who might be around before I go on, and within that prayer I choose to leave everything in God's hands so that when I go onstage I am free to be in the moment, free to let God use me to provide the audience with inspiration and joy.

What makes a great musician has more to do with a positive attitude than playing ability. It's important that everyone, band and crew, gets along, since the majority of the time spent together is offstage. I want to be able to have great conversations, break bread, and enjoy a level of fellowship. A good band member, in my opinion, also has a high degree of integrity. Being on time is especially important, since it's disrespectful to make others wait for you. And, finally, a good band member will do his or her homework and be prepared and willing to give their all in rehearsals, not just onstage. For my bands, rehearsals are very important. The fun part comes when you go onstage to perform. That's when you play and it's easy and fun. But it's not easy and fun onstage if you haven't put in the hard work.

My rehearsal schedules have been called Sheila E Boot Camp because they are twelve-hour days. Overall, I'd rather have a band member be kind, respectful, and prepared than be an amazing musician who comes onstage with a bunch of negative energy.

And don't be afraid of mistakes. After a show one night, a friend of mine (who's an exceptional drummer) asked me my secret for getting such loud applause.

"What are you talking about?" I asked. "You get loud applause. You're amazing!"

"But I don't get the kind of enthusiasm from the crowd that you do," she said.

I told her that while I consider myself a musician first, over the years I've learned how to be an entertainer as well.

During a show early on in my career, I threw my timbale stick up to catch it—a fun visual that the crowd loves. I always catch it on the first throw, but for some reason I dropped it, and then again a second time. I couldn't believe it. What was going on with me? I had to try again. I threw it up and finally caught it. Third time's the charm. What I hadn't expected was the uproar from the crowd. They were cheering and whistling and standing on their feet. I'd never gotten applause like that from catching it on the first try.

I realized that after I'd missed it once, the audience became invested in my success. And after I missed it again, they were really rooting for me. When I finally caught it, they felt like they'd won too. So I actually started to work this into the show—missing it on purpose a few times as a means of building excitement. It was my little gimmick. I've learned that it's okay to make a mistake. Sometimes a mistake can lead you to something far more exciting than perfection.

Even though mistakes can be cool, you should still be prepared before performing or recording. That's what Pops taught me when I was young: be professional, in every sense of the word. When you're about to record or play live or rehearse, arrive early. Know your stuff inside and out. You should be able to sing it, play it, or rap it with your eyes closed. This kind of preparation will give you confidence. But don't forget to mix your confidence with humility. Knowing your craft doesn't mean being arrogant. The preparation comes first, and then the confidence.

It's that unknown part, that X factor (or should I say E factor?), that you can't always prepare for. So sometimes there's unexpected feedback from the sound system that might throw you off, or a band member might step on another person's solo, or I might try some rhythms that don't quite blend. It's those unknowns that keep the butterflies fluttering onstage. But that's also what keeps me interested. I am a perfectionist when it comes to my music, but if I knew each show would be perfect, and I knew exactly how it would go, I'd be ready to retire now.

Live music is live for a reason. There's excitement in the unknown and beauty in the mistakes.

Whenever aspiring musicians ask me for advice, I ask them if they get the butterflies, since that feeling of nervous excitement and passion, that overwhelming drive to create music, is such a crucial component to what keeps me going in this industry. And so to a musician who is challenged by his or her career, who wonders if it's the right one to continue with, I say, if the butterflies feeling goes away, or if it was never there to begin with, then don't quit your day job.

When I'm onstage, the butterflies I felt backstage are still there, but in a different way. I call it "stage flight." It's like they remain *with* me, but they're not *in* me the whole time. The excitement is always there, and sometimes the excitement feels like nervousness, but that comes and goes. It might even come and go several times within one song. Every song, every show, and every situation is different. I guess it's related to that good old fear of the unknown.

I also tell struggling musicians that this industry is a lot about timing. No matter how talented you are, success or exposure is often about placement, and such placement is often random. If you happen to be in the right place at the right time, then you just may meet that one person or have that lucky break that will make all the difference. And it's often about who you know—having the right connections or the right resources that can support you in the pursuit of your dream. It's a shame that there are so many gifted and talented musicians, performers, vocalists, and songwriters out there whose work may never see the light of day. Then there are some who manage to make it, despite a lack of any natural talent, because of their drive, connections, or luck.

Sometimes you have to reroute your path and face the music, as it were. Being a musician isn't everyone's calling. And being onstage isn't everyone's calling, either. Maybe you want to be in the spotlight but you're really meant to be a songwriter—giving the singer the words with which he or she can reach millions. Maybe you want to be a recording artist but you're really meant to run a recording studio—offering artists a supportive environment that allows them to fully express their creativity. The songwriters, engineers, and producers all provide an essential role because the artists can't do it all themselves. Behind every great artist is a network of important people, without whom the artist would be lost.

There's no precise career formula for artists, not the way there is for some professions. If you get through law school, you become a lawyer. If you get through medical school, you become a doctor. For artists, however, there's no clear path, which you can view as a blessing or a curse. It can be so frustrating, because it's natural to want to know when and how your career will play out. It would be so nice to have a guaranteed formula for success: if I can accomplish X, then I will get Y, and eventually I will be Z. And yet the very lack of an exact formula, the inherent unknown, is what makes the artist's career so exciting. There's a variety of options and opportunities for artists, which allows for an infinite number of ways one's career can unfold.

The other thing I warn any wannabe stars out there is that there are millions of musicians and artists all wanting the same thing. If you're not 100 percent committed or 100 percent passionate, I suggest you have a plan B.

I've always loved the quotation, credited to Mikhail Baryshnikov, who when asked what advice he would give a young dancer, reportedly said: "If you must." His suggestion was that his was such a hard career that others should only pursue it if they have no other choice—if it is what they *must* do.

If you have a plan B or something else in mind that you know you might also enjoy or be good at, then music might not be the best career choice for you; you should probably be doing that instead.

Baryshnikov was also quoted as saying something else that resonates: "Working is living to me." Making music is living to me as well. It not only gives me life, it *is* my life. For me, there was no other choice. There was never a plan B. There must be success stories out there about people who make it even though they lack passion, but I would discourage aspiring musicians from hanging their hats on that kind of exception.

Of course I was blessed to have a brilliant musician father who eventually put me in his band. And having the loving support and encouragement of my mother made a huge difference. Where I was born and raised was another huge contributing factor to my becoming established in the industry, because the Bay Area music scene is so diverse and extensive. But I still needed the passion and verve to drive my musical career, despite those connections and such a supportive environment.

If you are really passionate about what you do and what you want, here's my advice: continue to work hard at it. Practice, practice, practice. Play and perform any chance you get, with any kind of musical genre you can. While I believe playing from your heart and soul is most important, learning to read music will also help. I recently visited a school's music department and overheard the teacher telling his students, "Practice makes progress." I love this message. Becoming "perfect" shouldn't be the goal. Just keep trying to do your best. Growth, in and of itself, is the real goal.

Oh, and one last word of advice, via Pete Escovedo: always be well dressed. Pops dresses clean and sharp. We tease him that he probably wears a suit to bed, or at least irons his silk pajamas before retiring for the night. He has instilled in me the belief that dressing up is a sign of respect for yourself and for those whom you're performing with. Your appearance reflects how seriously you regard your job. Pops taught me to dress well even for a studio recording session.

I'm not saying you need to wear a tux or an evening gown in the sound booth. You can be comfortable, but do give consideration to your public appearance. It's part of the ritual that reinforces your respect for your work and your respect for those who are paying you for it.

Being in the music industry probably has more challenges for women than for men, and for me it's certainly been a fight. Before

I realized that the outside world had something to say about my gender, I saw myself as someone who just loved to make beats. Playing drums was simply part of everyday life. I thought it was the norm, just what all families did. I figured all little girls did what I did.

Over time, I realized something was a little different about me. Even when I was being bused to school in junior high I sat in the back and practiced drumbeats on the windows and on the back of the seat in front of me. All the kids around me would smile, clap, and tell me to keep going. They loved the James Brown funk beats the most.

"Come on! Join in!" I'd tell them, but they'd just stare at me.

"We don't know how to do that," they'd say.

I didn't get how they didn't know. All my life, the people around me had joined in. It was just what we did when we were bored or sitting at the dinner table, or . . . well . . . whenever!

Back then, the feedback wasn't about the fact that I was a girl who knew how to drum. It was the fact that I even knew how to drum—period—that intrigued people. I didn't really realize that there was a gender attached to playing drums until I became a professional musician. I'd walk into a studio session, rehearsal, or live show and the men would look at me as if to say, "How dare you encroach on my territory!" Or they'd be openly confused, asking, "*You* are here to play? *You're* a percussionist?"

Thanks to the confidence instilled in me by Moms and Pops, the negative reception I got didn't really bother me. When I heard things like "You're not going to last in this business" or "You were only hired because you're cute" or "If you sleep with me, I'll get you a record contract," I tried to brush it off.

Pops always told me, "They might be threatened by you. Just shake it off and don't let them bring you down." For the most part, I was able to dismiss their negativity and not take it personally. I felt like I had some kind of invisible armor on. My love for drumming and percussion was my greatest protector: nobody and nothing could get to me. *You can't hurt me with your comments or your eye rolling*, I thought. *I love playing and I'm here because I can play.*

This profound love for playing kept me focused and strong, and my increasing professional experience gave me more and more belief in myself. Eventually, the fact that I was being hired by people like George Duke, Marvin Gaye, Herbie Hancock, and Billy Cobham added to my confidence. My armor was getting thicker. If they wanted to make a big deal about the fact that I was a woman, then that was their prerogative.

At first I did feel the pressure to prove that I was hired for the right reasons, but eventually my need to prove myself lessened. I wasn't competing with men—I was competing with myself. I fought to do my best rather than fighting to be seen as good enough to hang with the guys. It was the love of the music that kept me fighting. And it still does.

To me, true musicianship comes from within. I tell all aspiring musicians that while technical skills are certainly important, it's equally if not more important to bring your spirit to your playing. So while young women may have to face particular challenges in the music industry, they can embrace their womanhood and continue to focus on playing from the heart. Playing with spirit, with heart, and with soul is not attached to any gender.

And now my purpose is much higher. I'm no longer looking for acceptance, applause, or accolades the way I once was. Once God made it clear to me that my music was a gift for me to share purposefully, I was freed from any need for external validation. When He showed me that through my music I could uplift others—that I was blessed with a career that provided me a public forum in which I could share my testimony and make a difference for other abuse survivors like myself, any need to prove myself disappeared.

Once I gave my heart to the Lord, I understood my greater purpose. My innocent love of playing was instantly restored. I have come full circle, back to that purest of places. And I count my blessings every day.

29. Reprise

A repeated passage in music

Reflecting like a mirror
Racing in my mind
These photographs remind me
Of what's not far behind

"FADED PHOTOGRAPHS"

SHEILA E

The last twenty years have been cram-packed full of so much music, love, pain, sorrow, and laughter that some of what I've done will have to wait for another day or my next book.

Outstanding highlights for me, though, included performing a song from the movie *The Mambo Kings* at the sixty-fifth Academy Awards with Placido Domingo and featuring in the house band for the 2012 Oscars. I've played with Jennifer Lopez and Marc Anthony on the 2011 *American Idol* finale and on *The Late Show* as part of Drum Solo Week with David Letterman.

I met (and hugged) Sidney Poitier while playing with Lionel

Richie and was able to thank him for one of my all-time favorite movies, *Guess Who's Coming to Dinner?*

I sat in on drums with Elton John for an Andre Agassi fundraiser in Las Vegas, and I've helped promote musicians' rights in Washington, DC, as part of the Fight for the Right campaign. I have starred and played music in two films for 20th Century Fox and became Dr. Escovedo after being awarded an honorary doctorate in music from the Musicians Institute. I set up my own record company, Stiletto Flats, and cut a new record—*Now & Forever*—with Pops and my brothers. We were blessed to be joined by Earth, Wind & Fire, Joss Stone, Gloria Estefan, George Duke, Raphael Saadiq, and Israel Houghton.

I also had the honor of performing at the Summer Olympics in 1996 with Gloria Estefan. When I arrived for a sound check, I realized I was a few meters from the Olympic track where I'd once dreamed of winning gold. Thinking of my younger self running at dusk on the high school track, I dashed toward the starting lines, got into the starting position, and took a moment to imagine what fulfilling that dream might have been like.

I told my family gleefully later, "See, I made it to the Olympics after all!"

Two years later I became the first female and first person of color to be appointed musical director and leader of the house band for the popular late-night television show *Magic Hour*, fronted by basketball player Magic Johnson.

A few years later I had another chance of a lifetime—to meet one of the Fab Four, who'd so impressed us Escovedo kids when they came to the US back in the sixties. It was 2001 when Lynn received a call from Ringo Starr's management to ask if I would like to be a part of his All-Starr Band.

My response was, "Heck, yeah. Playing with one of the Beatles? I always knew it would happen one day!" I was super excited, but then a tad overwhelmed when I heard that Ringo didn't just want me to play percussion—he wanted me to be his drummer.

I mean, man, me drumming for the drummer from the Beatles! How cool is that?

Ringo's All-Starr Tour has been going since 1989 and changes its lineup all the time, depending on who's available. All the greats have played with him, including Clapton, Joe Walsh, Todd Rundgren, and Edgar Winter. Sometimes Ringo sings and sometimes he plays the drums, depending on the song and the set.

I was nervous to meet him at a production studio in LA and even more anxious when he walked toward me looking stern. He crossed his arms and said in that droll Liverpool way of his, "So, you're going to be the drummer of my band, huh?"

I was shaking.

Then his face broke into a smile and he added, "I want you to know that *you* are the drummer, not me!"

I laughed and said, "Okay, well, what do I have to do?"

Our fellow band members on that first tour included Carl Palmer from Emerson, Lake & Palmer, Roger Hodgson from Supertramp, and Ian Hunter from Mott the Hoople. I was so anxious not to let Ringo down that I prepared for weeks. I still didn't read music very well, so I wrote everything out in my shorthand to know where I needed to be. I listened carefully to all twenty-six songs on the set list and started to break them down.

Analyzing Ringo's drumming really gave me a feel for the way he used his swing to communicate, and the way he put a break here or there. Dissecting it like that made me realize how truly different he was. He had such a feel for the drums that he'd have a conversation with John Lennon or Paul McCartney and virtually sing back to them with a drum fill. I had never played that way in my life before, and he taught me so much. The more I listened to him, the more impressed I was.

Playing with a Beatle was like going to Ringo Starr School. Even the way he played a hi-hat was different—it was just how he walks. No one walks like Ringo, and no one plays like him. I was filled with renewed respect.

As part of my ministry, I also went on a gospel tour called Sisters in the Spirit. I have performed at the 2007 Latin Grammys and on *Idol Gives Back* with Gloria Estefan. I created an all-woman band called C.O.E.D. (Chronicles of Every Diva) and toured in Europe with them. I taught Ellen DeGeneres and Orlando Bloom how to play bongos on live TV and did session work with Stevie Wonder as well as performing with him on and off. I was drummer and musical director for Beyoncé for a song called "Work It Out," which was featured in an Austin Powers movie and which we performed on *The Tonight Show* with Jay Leno.

In the years since we split, Prince and I reconnected and formed a stronger friendship than ever before. He's my musical soul mate.

There was a moment, before a sound check for his *Welcome 2 America* show in San Jose, California, in 2010, when I had a brief glimpse of the man I'd once fallen madly in love with. In a moment of childlike excitement, Prince and I hopped on bikes and rode them around the park area, across the street from the HP Pavilion.

There we were—just a boy and a girl, playfully riding our bikes, soaking in the late-afternoon sunshine, enjoying a rare moment of unstructured time. He was a superstar, preparing to play to another sold-out stadium in just a few hours. And I would be joining him as a special guest. But for a few moments, we got to let go of any concerns about our image or any serious adult thoughts. We were free from our pasts. We were just two kids, riding our bikes through the park.

When someone snapped a picture of us from his car, we were suddenly jarred back to reality. But nobody could rob us of those precious moments of whimsical play—those few minutes when we got to be kids again, reckless and free-spirited, riding our bikes, just because.

Another major highlight for me was being nominated for an Emmy for Outstanding Musical Direction for my role in organizing *Fiesta Latina: In Performance at the White House* in 2009, which aired on PBS. The program celebrated Hispanic musical heritage and featured performances by me and Pops, Gloria Estefan, José Feliciano, Jimmy Smits, George Lopez, Thalia, Tito "El Bambino" Aventura, and Los Lobos.

Eva Longoria cohosted with George Lopez and Jimmy Smits. Jennifer Lopez introduced her husband, Marc Anthony, and we musicians played in a tent on the White House lawn in front of President Obama, his wife, Michelle, their children, and illustrious guests. At the end of the show, the president and his family came up onto the stage, and I led his daughters, Sasha and Malia, to the timbales to play. The president joined us, and I have a great photo of us all together. That was truly a night to remember!

The year 2009 was also when we lost dear Michael Jackson, a friend I hadn't seen in four years. Like Marvin Gaye and Whitney Houston, he seemed to have people around him all the time who protected him too closely. In the good old days we'd go out for dinner with Michael, Lionel, and some friends, but that all stopped toward the end. I was invited to the Jackson house to give Randy percussion lessons, but it didn't happen because their dad didn't want me to come in. It was crazy. I heard the news of his death when I was on the telephone talking to my bass player. It flashed up simultaneously on the TV news. None of us could believe it. I was in total shock.

I was invited to his funeral at the Staples Center, a place I'd played a gazillion times. It was so surreal being driven past thousands of Michael's fans respectfully lining the route. When we walked into that vast entertainment space, filled with ten thousand people, you could hear a pin drop. The silence was overwhelming as we collectively mourned a life taken far too soon.

I had watched Michael onstage as a five-year-old when I was five. I had hung out with him in Germany in the seventies. We'd worked together on *Off the Wall* and "We Are the World." We'd laughed and played and horsed around together. He was like one of my brothers, and as I sat in that auditorium staring at his flower-decked coffin, I vowed that in his memory I would make the most of my life and of every new opportunity that came my way.

My parents had always done just that—filling their lives, and ours, with love and music—and they continued to be my inspiration.

One of the most remarkable things that happened to me was when they were planning the celebrations for their fiftieth wedding anniversary. They decided to renew their marriage vows, which was something they'd also done to celebrate twenty-five years of being together.

They needed a facility in Oakland large enough for all their friends and family to help them celebrate afterward. We went to look at a few places together, but decided none of them were good enough.

Moms told me of one last place they wanted me to see downtown, the name of which I didn't recognize. "Okay," I said somewhat wearily, tired of all the searching.

Lynn and I drove to this venue. It looked okay from the outside, which was a good start, and then we went inside. I wandered through the double doors into the lobby and then started walking up the red-carpeted stairs toward the main auditorium.

All of a sudden, it hit me.

"Oh, my God!"

Lynn stopped, too, and asked, "What?"

"This is the place!" I cried.

"What place?"

"The place where I played with Pops as a five-year-old kid!"

She looked blankly at me.

"This is Sweet's!"

It felt as if I had been there only yesterday.

The art deco building was still much the same inside. As I slowly climbed the stairs, breathless with memory, I could almost feel my arm reaching up to hold my mother's hand.

I hadn't been back in forty-four years. The venue had a new name and had been remodeled, but it was definitely the same. Suddenly, I was looking around at everything through the eyes of a five-year-old.

I was, quite literally, beside myself.

It was as if I could see my young self walking in next to me—the adult Sheila in tight pants and high heels holding the hand of little Sheila in her brand-new frilly white dress and patent leather shoes, eyes and mouth open as she looked around at all the grown-ups.

I remembered the way the ballroom opened out at the top of the stairs. I could see the polished dance floor, the high ceiling, and the banquette seating.

I could almost smell the cigarette smoke and feel the heat of all the people dancing. My father's timbale beat echoed in my ears, and I could see the forest of legs parting to make way for Moms and me as she led me to the stage.

Once I'd been lifted high into his arms and settled behind the congas with my uncles on either side of me, I lost all my nerves, closed my eyes, and played. And, according to Pops, I'd played real good. That had been the start of it all—my first public performance, and the night that would shape the rest of my life. I couldn't believe it.

The place was still there.

I was still there.

My parents were still alive, and still happily married.

Pops and I were about to play on that same stage again together—this time with Juan, Peter Michael, Zina, and Moms.

There had been so many years and oh, so many memories in between.

I found myself grinning so hard that my cheeks hurt.

Tears of joy filled my eyes and spilled down my face. As Lynn held back respectfully, I walked into that vast ballroom, the little girl within me full of gratitude and awe.

I had survived.

Postlude

A concluding piece of music

All around, all around
Everywhere I look
Your love is all around

"ALL AROUND"
THE E FAMILY

I can't believe that my time in this business—what seems like just the blink of an eye—has actually been over forty years. Yet in many ways I feel like I'm new to this career still.

Every time I perform, it feels like the first time I played. It's still that exciting, that magical; and I'm still surrounded by butterflies. There is so much music in me, and it never gets old. Before every show I can't wait to get out there and share the gift that God has given me.

The music industry continues to change, even to transform. And, thankfully, so do I. While I have overcome significant personal hardship and accomplished many goals, I have much more work to do on myself, and many, many more professional dreams to realize. It feels like I'm just beginning my career—again. What a blessing.

It's hard to find adequate words to express my gratitude to the fans who have supported me through the years and made my musical journey possible. I suppose certain emotional experiences, even certain thoughts, do defy language—perhaps this is why, in many ways, for most of my life, I've let my music do my talking and have always been humbled by how many have listened. Even now, the sound of applause brings fresh tears of gratitude to my eyes. Each morning I wake up, I thank God for giving me another day to continue my growth and healing and to help others with theirs. I'm in awe of the privilege.

There are no limits. No boundaries. No rules. I love what I do, and there is so much music out there still to hear, to play, and to give.

My journey so far has been a transition from pain to purpose, and it's been my family that has provided the foundation for this healing transformation. Our cohesive little group of Escovedos remains a family band—my brothers and me with Pops onstage and Moms yelling her encouragement from the audience. These days, whenever we play in the Bay Area there are always a few Escovedos and Garderes with her too. Sometimes they're on the guest list and other times they show up unannounced, having bought tickets in advance, as a surprise. In fact, a lot of our shows feel more like family reunions than gigs: these are the same relatives who cheered when we launched into our Jackson 5 routines as kids.

The difference now is that we're paid for it, we're on a real stage instead of the patio, and there's a marquee with our name on it outside. Strangers part with good money to watch us sing, play, and—yes—even dance a little. We may be in our fifties, but we're still holding it down as we yell "Here's our latest routine!" We played to eleven thousand people in San Francisco at the Stern

Grove Festival, where I recorded my father's latest CD, *Pete Esco-vedo Live*. Pops, "the Mexican Frank Sinatra," sang "Fly Me to the Moon" that day. And as I looked out into the crowd and then up to the sky, I thought about my journey so far and all the support I've had along the way. I haven't made it to the moon yet, but I'm just getting started.

We are never more relaxed than when we're playing Latin jazz with Pops. Those songs are in our DNA. Pops hasn't passed the baton; he shares it with us proudly. Even if he changes the set list midshow, we're fine. We know that music like we know each other. Being up onstage together, we don't just feel at home; we *are* home.

And whenever my brothers and I join my father's orchestra to perform, or when the four of us perform together as the E Family, I find my mind floating right back to those early days of singing and dancing to Motown in our various homes in Oakland. Once my brothers and I start an impromptu dance routine, Pops grins and moves aside—although sometimes he might join in on a fancy two-step.

Approaching his eighties, my father has that same wry shake of the head and shy smile of an esteemed bandleader and proud daddy. And while we might have to squint through the lights these days to see Moms, we know she's out there somewhere, dressed to the nines, cheering and hollering alongside Zina, always the first to start a standing ovation.

There has never been a generation gap in our family when it comes to music. The next generation of Escovedos is growing up fast, and my parents are equally encouraging to their ten grandchildren and eleven great-grandchildren—always eager to promote their musicality and their unique creative self-expression. Pops now invites all of his grandkids and great-grandkids to come up onstage, even in the middle of a Latin jazz set. All are creative and talented, whether they lean toward careers in entertainment or not.

Seeing them performing with us onstage reminds me of how my parents gave me permission from the earliest age to explore my intuitive love of music to its fullest.

And whether it's onstage in front of thousands or in the back-yard at a barbecue, the grandchildren and great-grandchildren are holding their own, teaching us the latest raps, the hottest songs, and the best new dance moves. We're all trying to learn it faster and better. And it's usually Moms who, without bothering to take a vote, declares (herself) the winner. Pops is still a prolific painter, and the color is back in his work big-time. The man who used to sketch on pieces of wood or old drum skins now shows his work in galleries and was recently commissioned to complete an exclusive series for a Bay Area hotel.

Moms keeps him alive with love, laughter, walking, and lots of dancing. She's still trying to compete in any game she can, and she'll still shoot you that Gardere face if you even think about beat-ing her. Pops hits balls at the driving range while Moms marches around the entire golf course, making new friends and feeding birds. She's always faithfully out in the audience when we play, singing along, tapping her feet, and sometimes working the guiro with that perfect timing. She prays on her knees each night before bed—asking God to watch over her family and to heal anyone in need. For her, not much has changed through the years. She's got God, Pops, and her children, and for her this is heaven on earth.

Juan, Peter Michael, Zina, and I have come full circle, each of us inspired by our parents' faith and their celebration of music, art, and life. Beneath our middle-aged facades, my brothers and I are still those same goofy kids, each fighting for the solo, each know-ing which part comes where and how it should be performed. And we're still the same joyful family who share a passion for music, who thank our parents for encouraging our talent, and who love each other madly.

That's why playing with my family means everything. The strength of our family empowers our music. And our music allows us to extend our love to others. Music is a divine gift.

It heals the hurt. It soothes the soul. It transforms pain to purpose.

I'm no longer trapped in the cocoon that held me captive for so many years. Thanks to God, family, friends, and the rhythms of my drums, I learned how to experience joy and trust. I am convinced again of my own innocence. I'm soaring free.

Now, when darkness overwhelms me, disquieting my mind by summoning painful memories, I don't have to keep the light on or wait for daylight before going to sleep. I seek solace still in God, in family, in prayer, and in the rhythms of my drums, pounding out beats that emphatically convey a message to that little girl of my past. Telling her she's beautiful after all. Encouraging her—me—to keep flying.

Tell Someone

If you have been affected by any of the stories in this book, there are places you can go to seek help, and I strongly encourage you to do so. If you are a minor who was or is currently being abused, find an adult you can trust. This might be a family member, a teacher, a counselor, or even your family physician.

You might prefer to speak to a person in a position of authority whom you have a sense of respect for—like a police officer or a teacher, or even a school crossing guard. Whoever it is, please confide in this person. I know it's scary to do this, and your abuser may have threatened to hurt you or your loved ones if you do tell, but don't stand for it! They are only trying to protect themselves.

The *best* thing you can ever do is to expose them as soon as it happens. It is important that you know that what happened to you is not your fault and you don't have to live with it anymore.

I also encourage adults who have suffered some kind of abuse in their recent or distant past—whether emotional, verbal, sexual, or physical—to begin seeking help. Start talking about it. As you reveal your secret, you can begin to free yourself from all of those painful feelings that stem from the abuse.

I used to think that by not talking, the feelings would go away.

But it turns out that the opposite is true. In my experience, when you keep abuse a secret, you are still in bed with the abuser, your actions are still being controlled, and, consequently, you're protecting that person and denying yourself the healing you most definitely deserve.

God bless.

Acknowledgments

Thank you first and foremost to my Heavenly Father, my Lord and Savior, Jesus Christ. I thank you for my life, my breath, and for waking me up this morning. Thank you for your sacrifice and for the countless blessings you've bestowed upon me. I am your eternal servant, and I know that with you, all things are possible. Thank you for family, for music, and for shining your light when the darkness overcame me. When the pain was too much to bear, and I wasn't yet ready to find the words, you gave me the language of music. And I thank Lynn and Pastor Bam for leading me to you when I needed you most. God has blessed me with such an extraordinary journey so far, and I'm thankful in advance for all of the blessings, lessons, unexpected twists and turns, and each and every precious breath to come.

Thank you to my family: Moms and Pops, my wings; my brother Juan, my hero and my heart; my brother Peter Michael, an inspiring man of God who makes me so very proud; and my beloved sister, Zina—it's an honor to watch you soar. Thank you to all my family—my sisters-in-law Patrice, Angie, and Sarah; my aunts and uncles whose support paved the way; my nephews, nieces, cousins, and my godchildren. All of you are God's greatest gifts in my life.

To those relatives and friends who've passed—I miss you dearly and feel you watching over me. I carry you in my heart.

To my dear friends Lynn, Ms. Portia, Carol, Connie, Sandra B, Twinkie, Anna Maria, Ia, Kat, Rhonda, and Courtney, thank you for your unconditional love and for always having my back. To Ruth Arzate, for introducing me to Judith Curr, EVP of Simon & Schuster. What a blessing.

The E team, Gilbert Davison, Anita First and Joel Gotler, for your legal expertise. Now let's make the movie!

To my fans, who are dear to my heart: It's challenging to find the right words to express my gratitude for your support through the years. I guess some emotions do defy language—maybe this is why, in many ways, for most of my life, I've let my music do my talking. As I reflect on this book—what once felt like an almost impossible endeavor—I'm humbled that it has made its way into your hands (or if someone's reading this to you, or you're hearing an audio version—my preferred medium, of course!, into your listening). I hope that in my story you find something for yourself—validation, inspiration, acceptance, and hope. From the very bottom of my heart, I thank you for letting me share my story.

To my *Elevate Hope, 510 Oakland* & *Elevate Oakland* Kids: Thank you for bringing meaning to my life and allowing me to live my life's purpose. Thank you for your trust, your creativity, and your unstoppable spirit. Keep realizing your dreams and pursuing your passion for life.

And to anyone who's been through it, or is still in it, keep your light shining. Know that you can heal, you can come out of the darkness, and that you can take your greatest pain and transform it into your most divine purpose.

To Oakland, California, and the Bay Area: I'm grateful that your landscape was my canvas. Your sidewalks, garages, front rooms, and backyards were my first stage. Thank you for your people, your unique rhythms and melodies, and your incomparable soul—the backdrop of my life.

If I could go back to my five-year-old self, I would tell her:

You are loved beyond words, you are safe again and pure. It was not your fault and you did not deserve it. You will learn to trust again. You are not bad, you are good. You are light. You are God's child and He loves you and so do I. It's okay to cry; this is part of our healing. Know that the physical pain will soon be gone and the emotional pain we have experienced will heal in time. Just wait and see how our spiritual walk will bring us to our purpose. One day, we will tell our story and in our telling, somebody else will be inspired to tell theirs. Your light won't be dimmed for long. In time, the true light will shine.